geog.2

NEW edition

geography for key stage 3

< rosemarie gallagher > < richard parish >

UNIVERSITY PRESS

Great Clarendon Street, Oxford OX2 6DP

Oxford University Press is a department of the University of Oxford.
It furthers the University's objective of excellence in research,
scholarship, and education by publishing worldwide in

Oxford   New York

Auckland Cape Town Dar es Salaam Hong Kong Karachi
Kuala Lumpur Madrid Melbourne Mexico City Nairobi
New Delhi Shanghai Taipei Toronto

With offices in

Argentina Austria Brazil Chile Czech Republic France Greece
Guatemala Hungary Italy Japan Poland Portugal Singapore
South Korea Switzerland Thailand Turkey Ukraine Vietnam

Oxford is a registered trade mark of Oxford University Press
in the UK and in certain other countries

© RoseMarie Gallagher, Richard Parish 2005

The moral rights of the author have been asserted

Database right Oxford University Press (maker)

First published 2001
Second Edition 2005

British Library Cataloguing in Publication Data

Data available

ISBN-13: 978-0-19-913450-2
ISBN-10: 0-19-913450-2

10 9 8 7 6 5 4 3 2

Printed in Singapore by KHL Printing Co Pte Ltd

Acknowledgements

The publisher and authors would like to thank the following for permission to use
photographs and other copyright material:

P4tl, bl & br Alamy Images; p4tr Geoff Morgan/National Trust Photographic Library;
p7l&r Owen Franken/Corbis UK Ltd.; p8 John MacPherson/Corbis UK Ltd; p9 Simmons
Aerofilms; p11t Martin Bond/Environmental Images/Photofusion Picture Library, p11b
Simmons Aerofilms; p13t Neil Rainey/National Trust Photographic Library, p13c&b
Tony Lees/Oxford University Press; p15 Simmons Aerofilms; p16t Norfolk Museums &
Archaeology Service, p16b Mike Page; p17l&r Mike Page; p19l John Giles/PA Photos,
p19r Sealand Aerial Photography; p20tr Ingram Image Library; p20tl Mike Page, p20bl
James Hughes/Alamy, p20tc David Moore/Alamy, p20bc&br Andrew Stacey; p21
happisburgh.org.uk/Jim Whiteside; p22 Alamy Images; p24 Corel/Oxford University
Press; p26(all) Corel/Oxford University Press; p28t Corel/Oxford University Press, p28b
Century Litho Limited; p29(all) Corel/Oxford University Press; p23t European Space
Agency; p32b Eurosat; p33(all) Eurosat; p34t Stone/Getty Images, p34b Oxford
University Press; p35 Cordaiy Photo Library Ltd/Corbis UK Ltd.; p36r Digital
Stock/Corbis UK Ltd; p36l Fotografia/Corbis UK Ltd.; p40t Paul Almassy/Corbis UK
Ltd., p40b Richard Bickle/Corbis UK Ltd., p41cl&l&r Corel/Oxford University Press,
p41cr Richard Hamilton Smith/Corbis UK Ltd.; p42 Michael Busselle/Corbis UK Ltd.;
p44 RoseMarie Gallagher; p46tl Andrew Park/Oxford Scientific Films/photolibrary.com,
p46bl Corel/Oxford University Press, p46tr Kathie Atkinson/Oxford Scientific
Films/photolibrary.com; p46br Terry Heathcote/Oxford Scientific
Films/photolibrary.com; p49t Sealand Aerial Photography, p49b Keren Su/Corbis UK
Ltd.; p51l FLPA/Pam Gardner/Corbis UK Ltd., p51r Buddy Mays/Corbis UK Ltd.; p52bl
Corel Professional Photos; p52cl&tc&cr Sue Cunningham/Worldwide Picture
Library/Alamy, p52bc&c Still Pictures, p52tr Stephanie Maze/Corbis UK Ltd., p52tr
Edward Parker/Alamy; p 53t USGS Landsat Project; p53b Earthshots/U.S. Geological
Survey; p54l Mark Edwards/Still Pictures, p54tr Homero Sergio/Agencia
Folhas/TopFoto, p54br Luiz C. Marigo/Still Pictures; p55t Julia Waterlow/Corbis UK
Ltd.; p55b Corel Professional Photos; p56 Buddy Mays/Corbis UK Ltd.; p57l O
Alamany & E Vicens/Corbis UK Ltd., p57tr Mathieu Laboureur/Still Pictures, p57cr
Wolfgang Kaehler/Corbis UK Ltd., p57br Muriel Nicolotti/Still Pictures; p59l Jorgen
Scatte/Still Pictures, p59r Mark Edwards/Still Pictures; p60l R O Barnes/Kenya National
Archives & Documentation Service, p60r Michael Mortimore; p62 Wolfgang
Kaehler/Corbis UK Ltd.; p66l Corel/Oxford University Press, p66c&r Yann Arthus-
Bertrand/Corbis UK Ltd.; p68tl Peter Hulme/Ecoscene/Corbis UK Ltd., p68bl Peter
Turnley/Corbis UK Ltd., p68bc Laurance B. Aiuppy/Stock Connection/Alamy, p68tr Stan
Kujawa/Alamy, p68tr Ron Giling/Still Pictures, p68br Still Pictures; p70 Corbis Royalty
Free Images; p74 Illustrated London News; p76t Corel/Oxford University Press, p76b
Mark Edwards/Still Pictures; p78tl Hulton-Deutsch Collection/Corbis UK Ltd., p78tr
Hans Georg Roth/Corbis UK Ltd., p78b David Copeman/Alamy; p79l Image
Solutions/Alamy, p79c Dubai Internet City, p79r Charles Knight/Rex Features; p81t
EPA/PA Photos, p81b Hulton/Corbis UK Ltd.; p82t Jochen Tack/Das Fotoarchiv/Still
Pictures, p82b Beltra/Greenpeace Pictures; p83l Still Pictures, p83m Shropshire Star;
p83r Lynsey Addario/Corbis UK Ltd.; p84t Cath Mullen/Frank Lane Picture
Agency/Corbis UK Ltd., p84b © Anthony Upton 2003/npower renewables; p86cl&bc
National Renewable Energy Laboratory, p86bl David R. Frazier Photolibrary, Inc./Alamy,
p86cr Lineair/Still Pictures, p86br Simon Grosse/Alamy, p86t Ecoscene, p86c Still
Pictures; p87 N. Francis/Robert Harding Picture Library Ltd/Alamy; p88l&r National
Renewable Energy Laboratory; p89tl&tr&b National Renewable Energy Laboratory; p90
Alamy Imagees; p92t Jackie Chapman/Format Photographers/Photofusion Picture
Library, p92b Joanne O'Brian/Format Photographers/Photofusion Picture Library; p93
CR World; p94 London Aerial Photo Library; p97tl Michael Yamashita/Corbis UK Ltd.,
p97cl Inge Yspeert/Corbis UK Ltd., p97bl Purcell Team/Corbis UK Ltd., p97tc&cr
London Aerial Photo Library, p97bc Mark Edwards/Still Pictures, p97tr Barnaby's
Picture Library, p97br Art on File/Corbis UK Ltd., p97c Martin Sookias/Oxford
University Press; p99t Martin Sookias/Oxford University Press, p99b CR World; p100tl
Gallo Images/Paul Velasco/Corbis UK Ltd., p100tr Martin Sookias/Oxford University
Press, p100b Oxford University Press; p101t Martin Sookias/Oxford University Press,
p101c Barnaby's Picture Library, p101b Bill Varie/Corbis UK Ltd.; p102tl Francis de
Mulder/Corbis UK Ltd., p102bl Michael Yamashita/Corbis UK Ltd., p102tc EPA/PA
Photos, p102bc Rik Ergenbright/Corbis UK Ltd., p102tr Eye Ubiquitous/Patrick
Field/Corbis UK Ltd., p102br Ute Klaphake/Photofusion Picture Library; p103t
Popperfoto, p103b Martin Sookias/Oxford University Press; p104tr&br Corel/Oxford
University Press, p104tc Jonathan Blair/Corbis UK Ltd., p104tl Tom Brakefield/Corbis
UK Ltd., p104tcr Stone/Getty Images, p104bcr Massimo Listri/Corbis UK Ltd., p104c&bl
Robert Harding Picture Library; p106l Yann Arthus-Bertrand/Corbis UK Ltd., p106tr
Ecoscene/Joel Creed/Corbis UK Ltd., p106cr Jan Butchovsky-Houser/Corbis UK Ltd.,
p106br Corel/Oxford University Press; p108tl Corel/Oxford University Press, p108bl
Yann Arthus-Bertrand/Corbis UK Ltd., p108c&r Tony Morrison/South American
Pictures; p110 Daniel Laire/Corbis UK Ltd.; p111 Stephanie Maze/Corbis UK Ltd.; p112
Tony Morrison/South American Pictures; p113t Robert Harding Picture Library, p113b
Corel/Oxford University Press; p114tl Holt Studios International, p114bl Israel
Teixeira/Coperphoto/Reuters/Corbis UK Ltd., p114tc Claus Meyer/Still Pictures, p114bc
Owen Franken/Corbis UK Ltd., p114tr Viviane Moos/Corbis UK Ltd., p114br Jon
Spaull/Corbis UK Ltd.; p116t Daniel Laire/Corbis UK Ltd., p116b Richard List/Corbis
UK Ltd.; p118t The Image Bank/Getty Images, p118b Purcell Team/Corbis UK Ltd.;
p119 Corel/Oxford University Press; p121l The Image Bank/Getty Images, p121r Tony
Morrison/South American Pictures; p123 Frederic Pitcha/;/Sygma/Corbis UK Ltd.; p124
Sue Cunningham/Worldwide Picture Library/Alamy.

The map of coastal erosion on p 18 is provided courtesy of Catherine Poulton, British
Geological Survey.

The Ordnance Survey map extracts on pp. 13, 17, and 126 are reproduced with the
permission of the Controller of Her Majesty's Stationery Office © Crown Copyright.

Illustrations are by James Alexander, Alan Baker, Barking Dog Art, Jeff Bowles, Stefan
Chabluk, William Donohoe, Michael Eaton, Antonia Enthoven, Hardlines, John Hallett,
Roger Kent, Erin Kirke, David Mostyn, Richard Morris, Colin Salmon and Martin
Sanders.

The publisher and authors would like to thank all the individuals and organizations
who have helped during research for this book. In particular, and following the topic
order: Medea Gravelle, Coastal Strategy Officer for Dorset Coastal Forum; Malcolm
Kerby of Coastal Concern Action Group (Happisburgh); Catherine Poulton of British
Geological Survey; Eileen Anne Millar, Professor of Italian, University of Glasgow;
James Lovelock; Michael Mortimore; the Energy Policy and Analysis Unit at the DTI;
Ross Hayman of National Grid Transco; Robin Cleverly of the United Kingdom
Hydrographic Office; Jack Stone of the National Renewable Energy Laboratory, USA;
Akanksha Chaurey of the Tata Energy Research Institute, New Delhi; Dr Nick Fyfe of
the Department of Geography, University of Dundee; Chris Morris, GIS Analyst at Brent
Council; Phil Spivey and Martin Garrad of the Community Safety Department, Sussex
Police; Jane Oakland of Wembley Police; Nelson Lafraia of the Brazilian Embassy,
London; Silvia and Penny Aldersley; William F Laurance, Smithsonian Tropical Research
Institute, Balboa, Panama.

We would like to thank our excellent reviewers who have provided thoughtful and
constructive criticism at various stages: Phyl Gallagher, John Edwards, Anna King,
Katherine James, Roger Fetherston, Philip Amor, and Michael Gallagher.

We would particularly like to thank Janet Williamson for her contribution to this book
and her overall contribution to the geog.123 course.

Thanks also to Ann Hayes, Pauline Jones and Omar Farooque for their invaluable help
and support.

Cover photo: Getty Images and Hemera.

Contents

A ▲ Stoer, Scotland.

B ▲ Morston Marshes, Norfolk.

C ▲ Sennen Beach, Cornwall.

D ▲ The Seven Sisters, Sussex.

SCOTLAND

NORTHERN
IRELAND

REPUBLIC OF
IRELAND

WALES

ENGLAND

The big picture

This chapter is all about the **coast**, where the land meets the sea.
These are the big ideas behind the chapter:

◆ The coast is shaped and changed by the waves – and by humans !

◆ The waves shape it by eroding, transporting and depositing material.
The result is special landforms.

◆ We humans also change it, through the way we use the land.

◆ There is a limited amount of coast, and many conflicting demands on
it. So we need to manage and use it in a sustainable way.

◆ In some places around the coast, people's homes and land are
threatened by erosion. We need to respond in a sustainable way.

Did you know?
◆ Part of our south coast is called the Jurassic coast ...
◆ ... because lots of dinosaur remains are found there.

Your goals for this chapter

By the end of this chapter you should be able to answer these questions:

◆ What causes waves ?

◆ How do waves shape the coast – and how does weathering help ?

◆ What do these terms mean ?
  erode   transport   deposit   longshore drift

◆ What are these, and how were they formed ?
  beach   bay   headland   cave   arch   stack   stump
  wavecut platform   spit   salt marsh

◆ How do we use the land along the coast, and what kinds of
conflict arise ?

◆ What causes cliffs to collapse ?

◆ What kinds of things can we do, to protect people's lands and homes
from erosion by the waves ?

◆ Why can't we protect all the places that are at risk from erosion ?

◆ How can we fight erosion in a sustainable way ?

Did you know?
◆ The UK's coastline is 12 430 km long.
◆ The straight-line distance from London to New York is 5530 km !

And then …

When you finish the chapter, come back to this page and see if you have
met your goals !

Did you know?
◆ 8 of the world's 10 largest cities are on a coast.
◆ Over half the people in the world live within 200 km of a coast.

Your chapter starter

Page 4 shows places on our coast.

What's the coast ?

What can you do there ?

How far do *you* live from the coast ?

Why does it look so different in different places ?

Has anyone seen my flippers?

Waves and tides

In this unit you'll learn what causes waves and tides, and begin to find out how waves affect the coast.

What causes waves?

Waves are caused by the **wind** dragging on the surface of the water. The length of water the wind blows over is called its **fetch**.

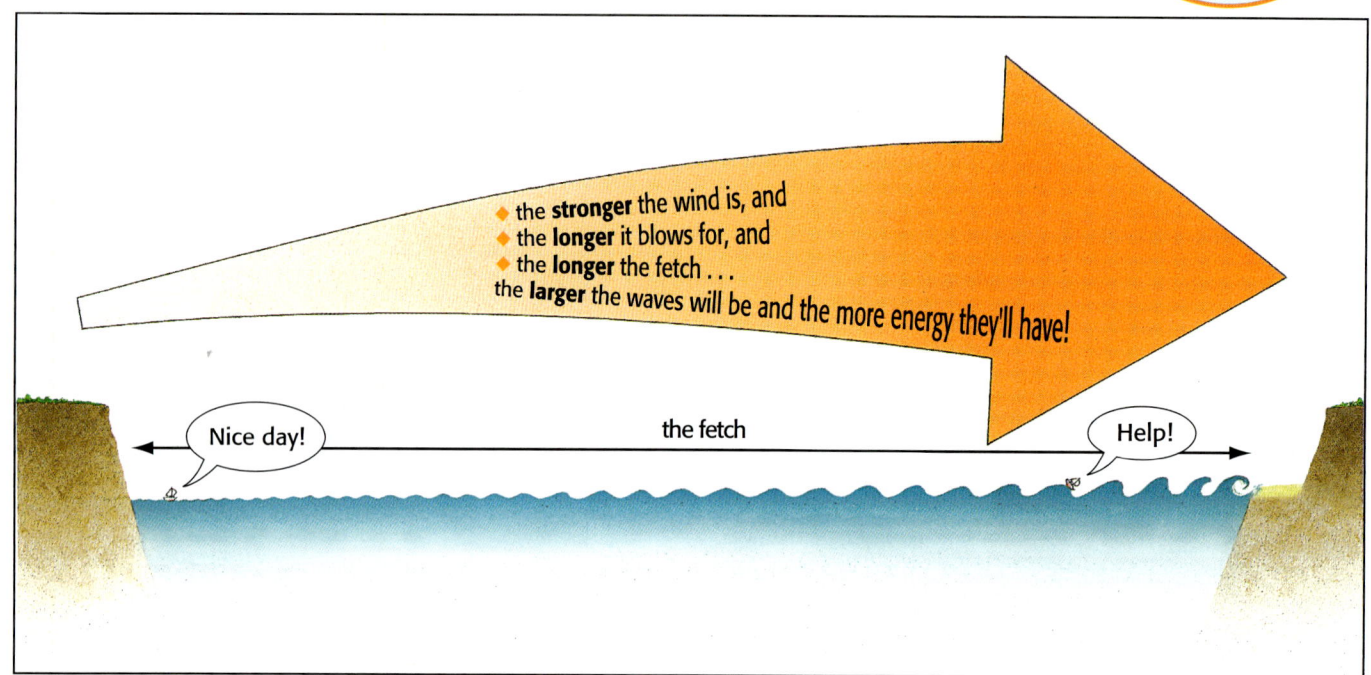

◆ the **stronger** the wind is, and
◆ the **longer** it blows for, and
◆ the **longer** the fetch . . .
the **larger** the waves will be and the more energy they'll have!

Nice day!

the fetch

Help!

When waves reach the coast

Swash this then?

Backwash!

Out at sea, the waves roll like this. In a gale they can be over 30 metres high!

They break in shallow water, like this. The water that rushes up the sand is called the **swash**.

The water rolling back into the sea, like this, is called the **backwash**.

If the backwash has more energy than the swash the waves eat at the land, dragging pebbles and sand away. (This happens with high steep waves.) But if the swash has more energy than the backwash, material is carried on to the land and left there. (This happens with low flat waves.)

Tides

Even when the sea is calm and flat, the water level is always changing. That's mainly because of the moon. As the moon travels around the Earth it attracts the sea and pulls it upwards. (The sun helps too, but it is much further away so its pull is not so strong.)

The rise and fall of the sea gives us the **tides**. Look at these photos:

Tuesday 9.00 am. The tide is **in** at this coastal town. In fact the sea has reached its highest level for today. This is called **high tide**.

Same day, 3.20 pm. Now the tide is **out**, leaving the boats resting on the mud. The sea has fallen to its lowest level for the day. This is called **low tide**.

High tides occur about every twelve and a half hours, with low tides in between. The drop in sea level from high to low tide is called the **tidal range**. It keeps changing, because the pull of the moon and sun changes as the moon moves around the Earth, and the Earth moves around the sun.

Your turn

1 Which three factors determine how high the waves in a place will be?

2 The arrows are winds blowing onto island X.

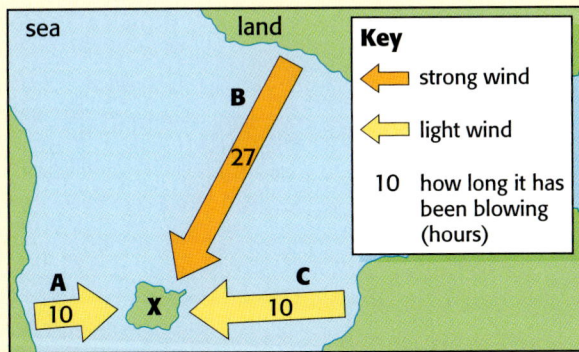

Key
- ← strong wind
- ← light wind
- 10 how long it has been blowing (hours)

Which wind will produce:
a the largest waves   **b** the smallest waves
at the coast of X? Explain your answers.

3 Now think about the waves around your own island.
a The *prevailing wind* in the UK is a *south west wind*. What do the terms in italics mean? (Glossary?)
b Explain why the south west tip of England gets some really high waves. (Check pages 128–129.)

c Most of the UK's surfing schools are in south west England, and Wales. Suggest a reason.

4 Using a full sentence, explain what these terms mean:
a swash
b backwash

5 Look at the photos on page 4.
a Which beach do you think has stronger backwash, C or D? What is your evidence?
b Which of the four places probably gets hardly any waves? Explain how you decided.

6 a What are *tides*, and why do they occur?
b Photo B on page 4 was taken at low tide. How would the scene look different, at high tide?
c Now repeat **b** for photo C.
d Look at photo D. Was this taken at high tide? How can you tell?

7 Now look at photo A on page 4. You are on holiday in Scotland. Two days ago you were scrambling around on the rocks – and got trapped at **X** by high tide! Write a really exciting entry for your diary saying how you felt, and how you were saved.

The waves at work

In thus unit you'll learn how waves shape the coastline.

What do the waves do?

Waves work non-stop, night and day, year after year, shaping the coastline. This shows what they do.

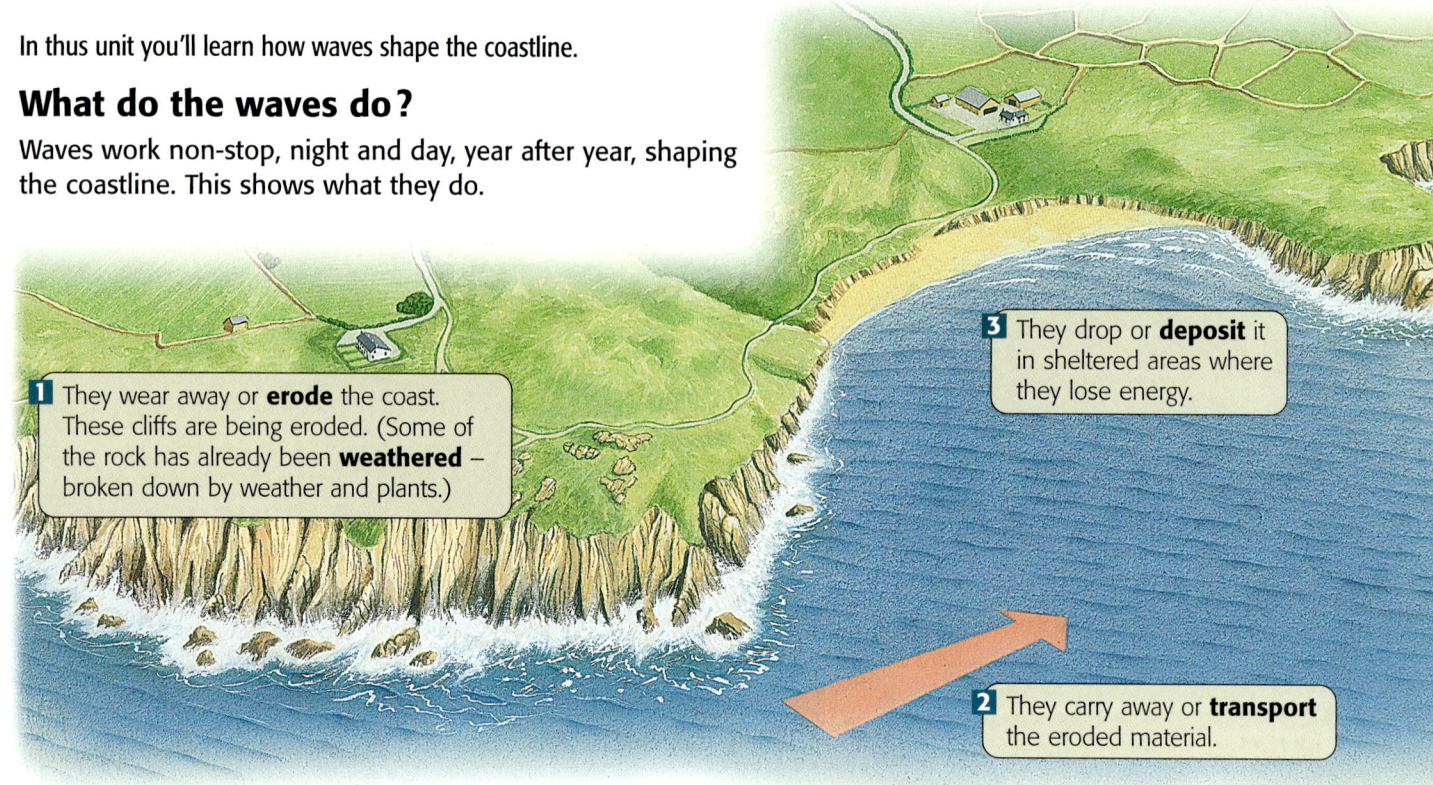

1 They wear away or **erode** the coast. These cliffs are being eroded. (Some of the rock has already been **weathered** – broken down by weather and plants.)

2 They carry away or **transport** the eroded material.

3 They drop or **deposit** it in sheltered areas where they lose energy.

Now we will look at each of these in more detail.

Erosion

This is how waves wear away the coast:

They pound at the rock like a hammer. Over time, this breaks the rock up.

They force water into cracks in the rock. That helps to break it up. It's called **hydraulic action**.

They dissolve soluble material from the rock. This is called **solution**.

They fling sand and pebbles against the rock. These wear it away like sandpaper. This is called **abrasion**.

Chunks of rock get knocked together and worn into smaller and smaller bits. This is called **attrition**. They end up as **shingle** (pebbles) and **sand**.

The more energy the waves have, and the softer the rock, the faster erosion will be.

Transport

The waves carry the eroded material away. Some is carried right out to sea. But a lot is carried *along* the coastline. Like this …

1 This pebble is carried straight down here …

2 … by the backwash (and gravity) …

wave direction

3 … then up again by the swash of the next wave …

4 … down again …

5 … up again …

6 … and so on. Look how far it has moved from A.

direction of longshore drift

In this way, hundreds of thousands of tonnes of pebbles and sand get moved along our coastline every year. This movement is called **longshore drift**.

Many seaside towns build **groynes** to stop their beaches being carried away by longshore drift. Look at this photo.

Deposition

Waves continually carry material on and off the land. If they carry more *on* than *off* – a beach forms!

Beaches form in sheltered areas. Low flat waves carry material up the beach and leave it there. Some beaches are made of sand, and some are **shingle** (small pebbles).

a groyne

N

▲ *The groynes stop the beach being carried away.*

Your turn

1 Waves do three jobs that shape the coastline. Name them.

2 Describe three ways in which waves erode rock.

3 These two pebbles are made of the same rock.
  a Which one has been in the water for longer? Explain.
  b Name the process that made Y so smooth.

4 Look at the groynes in the photo above.
  a Why were they built?
  b Are they working? How can you tell?
  c From which direction do the waves usually arrive at this beach?
    i from the south west
    ii from the south east
    Give a reason for your choice.

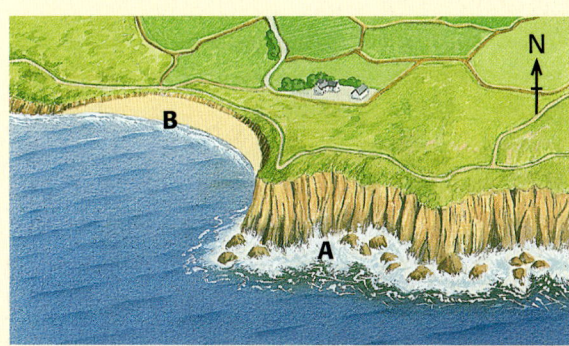

5 This drawing shows part of an island (not Britain).
  a The *prevailing wind* for the island is blowing. From where does it blow? (Look at the waves!)
  b There is no beach at A. Suggest a reason.
  c There is a good beach at B. Give a reason.
  d Where might the sand at B have come from?

6 Do you think the rock around our coast all erodes at the same rate? Give your reasons.

Landforms created by the waves

In this unit you will learn about the landforms that the waves create along the coast, by eroding and depositing material.

Sculptor at work !

This coast is made of different rocks, some hard, some soft. Once upon a time it was straight. Just look at it now !

1 Hard rock erodes more slowly than soft rock. So now, cliffs of hard rock jut out, forming a **headland**.

3 Here the softer rock has been eroded away, leaving a **bay**.

4 Another headland. Here you can see a **cave**, an **arch** and a **stack**.

cave
arch
stack

2 At the base of these cliffs is a **wave-cut platform**.

How a wave-cut platform forms

wave-cut notch

wave-cut platform

1 The waves carve **wave-cut notches** into cliffs at a headland. These get deeper and deeper …

2 … until, one day, the rock above them collapses. The sea carries the debris away.

3 The process continues non-stop. Slowly the cliffs retreat, leaving a **wave-cut platform** behind.

How caves, arches and stacks form

cave

arch

stack
stump

1 The sea attacks cracks in the cliff at a headland. The cracks grow larger – and form a **cave**.

2 The cave gets eroded all the way through. It turns into an **arch**. Then one day …

3 … the arch collapses, leaving a **stack**. In time, the waves erode the stack to a **stump**.

6 Some is deposited in sheltered areas like this one, forming a **beach**.

7 Here the coast bends to form a bay with calmer water, which interrupts the longshore drift …

10 Silt and mud may build up in this sheltered area. It becomes a **salt marsh**.

salt marsh

9 The end of the spit is curved by the waves.

5 Eroded material is carried along the coast by longshore drift.

spit

8 … so sand and shingle are deposited here, in the sea. They build up a **spit**.

Your turn

1

Landform	Created by ...	
	erosion	deposition
headland	✓	

Make a table like the one started here. Write in the names of all the landforms you met in this unit. Then put a ✓ to show how each was formed.

2 Make a larger sketch of the landforms in photo A.

  a On your sketch, label:
  a wave-cut notch   an arch   a stump

  b Explain how the arch was formed.

  c Draw a dotted line to show where there was once another arch.

  d What will happen to the stump over time?

3 Photo B shows the spit at Dawlish Warren in Devon.

  a Make a sketch of the spit. Don't forget to show and label the groynes, and salt marsh areas.

  b From which direction does the prevailing wind blow? How did you decide? Mark the direction on your sketch.

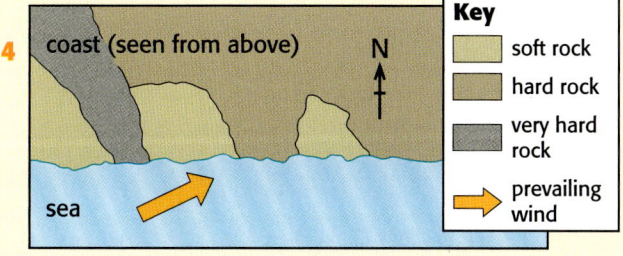

4

	Key
coast (seen from above) N↑	☐ soft rock
	☐ hard rock
	☐ very hard rock
sea ➡	➡ prevailing wind

This shows some coast before erosion. Make a larger drawing to show how it may look 10 000 years from now. Label any landforms, and annotate (add notes to) your drawing to explain what has happened.

A

B

Along the Dorset coast

In this unit you'll find out a lot about one stretch of coast, using an OS map.

Be a Dorset detective!

The OS map opposite shows part of the south coast of England, in Dorset.
Study the map. Then try these questions. (The key on page 126 will help.)

Your turn

1 Photos A–C were taken at sites on the map.
   a Write two sentences for each photo, to describe what it shows.
   b Now match each photo to one of these grid references: 028862   054825   042787
      008788   031835   036788

2 Find three clues on the map, to show that:
   a this is a historic area
   b Swanage is now a seaside resort.
   For each clue, give a four-figure grid reference.

3 Longshore drift is a problem at Swanage.
   How can you tell this from the map?

4 The map below shows the **geology** of the area –
   what kind of rocks it is made of.
   a What kind of rock is Old Harry (055825) made of?
   b What kind of rock is Furzey Island made of?
   c Give a six-figure grid reference for a farm where the soil is clay.
   d Of these rocks, which two types seem hardest to erode? Explain your choice.
   e What clue is there that clay is easy to erode?

5 **a** Pick out the rectangle on the OS map with corners at 020830, 020870, 050870 and 050830.
   b Now draw a sketch map of that area, showing the *main* features – such as the dunes, sea, and woodland, but not the phone box!

6

1600 — Studland Bay

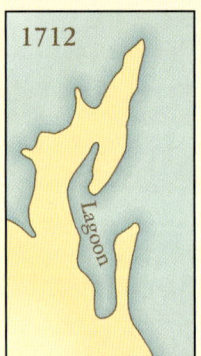
1712 — Lagoon

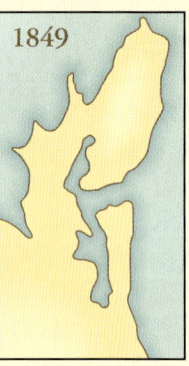
1849

Above are old maps of the area you sketched in **5**.
   a As you can see, the shape has changed a lot over the years. Suggest reasons. (Hint: any sign of spits?)
   b Now explain how Little Sea (on your sketch map) has been formed over the years since 1849.

7 You are staying with a group at the camp site at Ulwell. It's summer. The weather is fine. You have to plan a long walk for the group. These are the rules:

> ◆ If possible, use footpaths rather than roads.
> ◆ You may join the South West Coast Path.
> ◆ Include a visit to a nature reserve.
> ◆ Include a walk along the beach.
> ◆ Give the group a good view of arches and stacks.
> ◆ Let them look over a steep cliff.
> ◆ Return to the camp site by a different route.

   a Draw a sketch map for your planned route, showing:
   i the coastline
   ii your route – and say roughly how long it is
   iii the coastal landforms you'll see on the walk
   iv any ancient sites you will pass
   v any other points of interest
   b Mark any places where the walk may be extra difficult or dangerous. Add a note to say why.
   c And finally, make a list of what to take with you.

Rocks of the Dorset coast

Poole Harbour
South Haven Point
Studland Bay
The Foreland
Swanage Bay
Peveril Point
Durlston Bay
Durlston Head

N

0   1   2km

Key
- sand and clay
- chalk
- clay
- limestone

Did you know?
◆ In 878, King Alfred defeated the Danes in a fierce sea battle off Swanage.

A

B

C

THE NATIONAL TRUST

STUDLAND HEATH

Map labels

88 | 88
Brownsea Island
Fire Twr
Stone
Branksea Castle
North Haven Point
Sandbanks
P
Ferry P (summer only)
Hotel
Ferry V
South Haven Point
87 | 87
Oil Wells
Furzey Island
Green Island
South Deep
Jerry's Point
Toll
P
Shell Bay
Dunes
86
Cleavel Point
Goathorn Plantation
Brand's Bay
Oil Well
Newton Bay
South West Coast Path
85
Newton
Drove Island
Goathorn Fm
Greenlands Fm
Dunes
Little Sea
84
Newton Heath
Studland Heath
Studland Bay
83 | 83
Godlingston Heath
Knoll House Hotel
Puckstone
Tumuli
PC
Redend Point
Hotel
Studland
Old Harry
The Foreland
Tumulus
Agglestone
Black Down
PH
22
The Pinnacles
82
gswood
Tumuli
CH
Tumulus
fishing Barrow
67
King Barrow
81
116
Currendon Fm
Dean Hill
Godlingston Hill
Tumuli
Obelisk
Tumulus
Ballard Down
Tumuli
Ballard Cliff
Ballard Point
he Barrow Down
Strip Lynchets
Ulwell
Whitecliff Fm
80 | 80
New Barn
Godlington Manor
Cemy
25
New Swanage
Groynes
Swanage Bay
01 | 02 | 04 | 05 | 06
79
Sch
A 351
Herston
Mus
TH
SWANAGE
Pier
V
LB Sta
Peveril Point
CG Sta
78
on ravers
outh Barn
California Fm
Hospl
Durlston Bay
125
Durlston Country Park
DURLSTON HEAD
77 | 77
123
Round Down
Globe
South West Coast Path
Tilly Whim Caves
Blackers Hole
Anvil Point

Scale 1 : 50 000
0   0.5   1 km

01 | 02 | 03 | 04 | 05 | 06

Managing land use in coastal areas

In this unit you will learn why land use in coastal areas needs to be managed.

We do love to be beside the seaside!

People love the coast. But there's only a limited amount of it, and if we all did as we pleased there, it would be chaos.

So the coast has to be **managed**. That means people have to agree on a plan for the best way to use it, and then put the plan into action.

Who manages land use in our coastal areas?

The coast, like the rest of the UK, is managed mostly by **local councils**. These are made up of local people. (When you are 18 you can vote for your local council.)

Suppose you want to build a new golf course or hotel along the coast. This is what to do:

Did you know?

- You can own land along the coast – but not under the sea.
- The sea bed, and land below high tide, belong to the Crown.

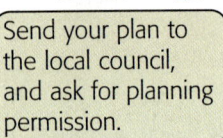
Send your plan to the local council, and ask for planning permission.

The council may like the plan. But it still has to send out notices to ask if anyone objects.

A **public inquiry** may be held, where people come to state their objections.

An inspector will study the objections, and decide if the plan can go ahead.

Sometimes, for big projects, the government gets involved.
It can over-rule the council and turn down a plan, or agree to it.

Your turn

1

Work	Leisure
farming	walking

Make a table like this to show how the coast is used. Write in all the activities from the drawing on page 14.

2 A **conflict grid** is started below, for the drawing on page 14. It's a way to show where conflicts arise.

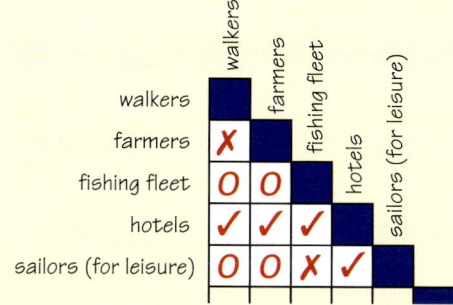

	walkers	farmers	fishing fleet	hotels	sailors (for leisure)
walkers					
farmers	X				
fishing fleet	O	O			
hotels	✓	✓	✓		
sailors (for leisure)	O	O	X	✓	

a The ✗ shows that farmers and walkers may come into conflict with each other. Suggest a reason why.

b The ✓ shows that the hotels and fishing fleet may benefit each other. Explain why.

c The *O* shows that sailors and walkers do not affect each other. Why not?

3 a Draw your own grid for the people in the drawing. (Your table for question **1** will help.)

b Fill in a ✓, ✗ or *O* in each empty square.

c For each conflict (✗), suggest a way to solve the problem.

4 Now turn to the OS map on page 13. What activities take place in this coastal area? Look for clues, and give four-figure grid references.

5 Dream Developments wants to build a leisure complex on the Dorset coast. See the photos of the site and the drawing of the complex, below.

a Identify their chosen site on the map on page 13, and try to give a six-figure grid reference for it.

b What is the site used for at the moment?

6 You are the head of Dream Developments. Write a letter to the council to say how your plan will help the area. For example you could mention:
- how good the complex will look
- how you can provide work for local people.

7 List any bad points about the leisure complex. For example think about how it might affect:
wildlife   the scenery   traffic in the area

8 Do *you* think the leisure complex should go ahead? Write a speech for the public enquiry, stating your opinion. Give your main reasons (no more than three).

How long can Happisburgh hang on?

In this unit you'll see how erosion by the waves is causing big problems in one coastal village.

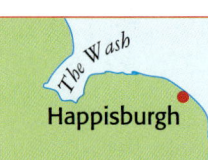

North Sea

The Wash

Happisburgh

Life on the brink

George and Jeanne Scott had planned to enjoy their retirement in their home by the sea, in Happisburgh in Norfolk. (Pronounce it *Haisbro* !)

But their plans have changed. On Monday the waves claimed their garden. Now their porch is teetering on the edge of the cliff. They have moved into the back bedroom, just in case. But they know it won't be long before the whole house falls into the sea.

They won't sleep much tonight. Outside, the storm is still raging. Waves crash over the roof, and slam against the windows, and make the whole house shake.

'We don't like to make a fuss,' said Mrs Scott, 'but we are upset about losing our home. We can't afford another, because we won't get compensation for this one. But the council has found us a bungalow to rent.'

Meanwhile their neighbours watch the storm nervously. If nobody helps Happisburgh to fight erosion, how long can it hang on?

Adapted from a newspaper article, 22 February 1996

▲ *The Scotts' home (●). Going, going …*

Why is erosion so severe at Happisburgh?

1 The main problem is that the cliffs are soft – sand on top and clay below.

2 Rain soaks into the cliffs and helps to weaken them. (This is one form of **weathering**.) The more rain they hold, the weaker they get.

3 Meanwhile, the waves erode the cliffs from below. In calm weather erosion will be slower …

4 … but when there's a storm, big waves batter the cliffs, and big chunks of them collapse.

5 These wooden barriers (or **revetments**) were meant to slow down erosion, by making the waves break early. But they were destroyed in a past storm.

groyne

Your turn

1 What part did each play in the loss of the Scotts' home to the sea?
  a the material the cliffs were made of
  b rain
  c strong north winds blowing down the North Sea

2 Now look at the aerial photos below. They show Happisburgh in 1996 and 2004.
  a What are all the white objects near the top of each photo? (The OS map will help.)
  b In which compass direction was the camera pointing?
  c Look at the wooden barriers on both photos.
    i What are the ones at right angles to the cliffs called? What is their job?
    ii What are the ones parallel to the cliffs called? What is their job?
    iii The second photo shows another type of barrier. What is it called? Find out from page 18.

3 a Now list all changes you notice for that stretch of coast, between 1996 and 2004.
  b From the photos, do you think the barriers:
    i prevented erosion? **ii** slowed it down?

4 Even where there are barriers, the cliffs at Happisburgh are eroding at a rate of about 2 m a year. Where there are no barriers, the rate is about 8 m a year.

Suppose the barriers remain as they are in the second photo below. Based on this OS map, about how long will it be before the sea reaches:
  a the church?
  b the lighthouse?
    (The lighthouse is not shown in the photos below.)

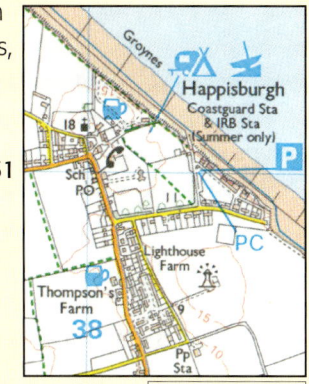

Scale 1cm : 250m

▲ Happisburgh in 1996, over eight months after the Scotts lost their home. (It was around ● .)

▲ Happisburgh in 2004. Homes are still disappearing, at a rate of about one a year.

The war against erosion

In this unit you'll find out where erosion is a problem on the UK coast, and what we can do about it.

It's not just Happisburgh!

In the last unit you saw that erosion is a big problem in Happisburgh (say *Haisbro*). But it's not the only place.

This map shows the main stretches of coast where erosion is a problem. In these places the sea is nibbling away at land and homes, causing many people a great deal of worry.

Key

Rock types

🟥	very hard	igneous and metamorphic
🟧	hard	limestone
🟨	medium	sandstone and mudstone
🟡	fairly soft	chalk
⬜	soft	soft sediments

〜 where coastal erosion is a problem

• places mentioned on pages 18–20

So how can we stop coastal erosion?

Coastal erosion is caused by the waves, and helped by weathering. So here are ways to stop or at least reduce it.

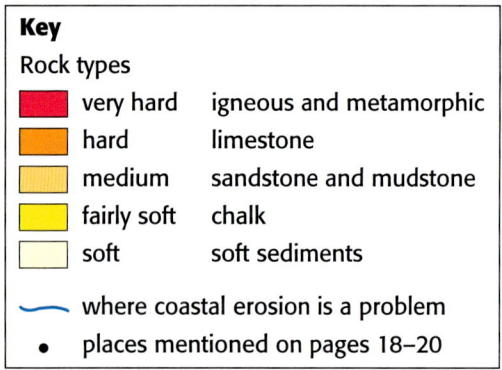

Rock types in the UK

Mappleton

Happisburgh

Highcliffe

Courtesy of Catherine Poulton, British Geological Survey

You could build **sea walls** like this one, to stop the waves reaching valuable land ...

... or a barrier of large rocks (**rock armour**) to soak up their energy. Less energy means less erosion.

You could even build the barrier out at sea, to make the waves break earlier, away from the beach.

You could build **groynes** to stop sand being carried away. The sand in turn protects the land behind.

So you could build up a beach by adding more sand or shingle. This is called **beach replenishment**.

pipes

And where cliffs soak up the rain, you could put pipes in to drain them. That means less weathering.

How Mappleton was saved

The first photo below shows the village of Mappleton, on the north east coast of England, in 1990. (Look on the map on page 18.) It's about to slide into the sea.

But the people fought hard for a grant to build coastal defences. The second photo shows the defences in place. They cost over £2 million.

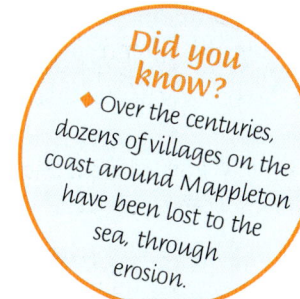
Did you know?
◆ Over the centuries, dozens of villages on the coast around Mappleton have been lost to the sea, through erosion.

▲ Mappleton in 1990 – just hanging on.

▲ Mappleton in 1992, after its new coastal defences were built.

Your turn

1 Look at the map on page 18.
  a Where is most of:
    i the very hard rock? ii the soft rock?
  b Does the map show a link between rock type and erosion? Describe what you notice.
  c You need to tell someone (who can't see the map) where on the coast erosion is a problem. Write down what you will say.

2 Look at the photo of Mappleton above, after its coastal defences were built.
  a What was done: at A? at B? at C? Explain how each will help to prevent erosion.
  b Look again at C. Has the structure here helped to prevent erosion? Explain your answer.
  c They could have continued the defences from C to D, or even further. But they stopped at C.
    i Why do you think they stopped? (Hint: land use.)
    ii What's likely to happen, as a result?

3 Now look back at the second photo of Happisburgh, on page 17. You live in one of the houses with the red roofs, near the sea. And you are getting very worried about erosion.
  a Write a letter to the local newspaper saying why you are worried, and what you think the local council should do.
  b Say how much you think the council might have to spend. The list below *might* help, depending on your suggestions.

Cost of coastal defences	
Defence	Costs about
Sea wall	£5000 per metre
Rock armour	£2500 per metre
Wooden revetment	£1500 per metre
Typical rock groyne	£125 000
Typical wooden groyne	£100 000
Beach nourishment	£10 per cubic metre

Managing the defence of the coast

In this unit you'll find out what the problems are in defending the coast against erosion – and who makes the decisions, and what the strategy is.

The problems with fighting erosion

In many places around the coast, erosion is threatening land and homes. So why don't they just build defences everywhere? It's not that simple!

First, coastal defences cost a lot. Rock armour like this costs about £2500 per metre. Sea walls cost about £5000 per metre.

And they don't last forever. Look at these revetments at Happisburgh, destroyed in a storm. So you just have to keep on spending.

There's another big problem: global warming. It is causing sea levels to rise – and causing more storms too.

That means we'll get bigger and stronger waves – so we'll need bigger and stronger defences to cope with them.

Finally, preventing erosion in one place can make it worse in others. These groynes at Highcliffe (see the map on page 18) may have …

… speeded up erosion at Naish Farm, nearby. (But you'd need to measure erosion before and after building groynes, to prove it.)

So who decides?

There are many towns and cities on or near near the UK coast. Over 15% of the population live within a few km of it. So erosion is a big headache for the government.

What happens is this:
◆ The government sets out a strategy for coastal defence.
◆ Along the coast, local councils make decisions based on the strategy.
◆ Some of the money for defences comes from the government. The local councils come up with the rest.

Did you know?
◆ Millions of tonnes of sand and gravel are dredged from the sea bed each year, for new buildings and roads.
◆ Some people think this is making coastal erosion worse.

What's the strategy ?

The strategy is to defend the coast in a **sustainable** way. That means build defences only where it makes sense, and where they won't do harm. These are the key ideas:

◆ If land and houses are worth less than the defences will cost, do not defend them.

◆ Think about the effect of defences on other places, and on wildlife.

◆ When planning land use along the coast in future, always keep erosion in mind.

So where does this leave Happisburgh ?

As you saw on page 16, more of Happisburgh (say *Haisbro*) will slip into the sea. So far, plans for new defences have been rejected, because they will cost more than the land and houses are worth. But the local people say it's not fair. They are still fighting their case.

▲ *Raising money to save Happisburgh.*

Your turn

1 Make a list of the problems we face, in defending the coast against erosion. Give them in order, with what you think is the most serious one first.

2 Do you agree with this person ? Explain.

PROTECT US NOW!
GIVE US SEA WALLS
ALL ALONG THE
COAST NOW !

3 The map on the right shows the local council's plans for fighting erosion on the north coast of Norfolk (where Happisburgh is).

a Some of the coastline will not be defended. What do you think is the main reason?

b Name two villages that won't be defended, at least for the present.

4 a The council plans to keep on defending Cromer. Using clues from the map, suggest a reason. Say which clues you used.

b It plans to protect Sea Palling, which has fewer than 600 people. See if you can find a reason for this, from the map.

c It does not plan to protect Winterton for now. What questions would you ask about Winterton, to understand why ?

5 You live in Happisburgh, near the cliffs. (See the photos on page 17.) You want to sell your house and move away. But no one will buy it, because of the council's plans. So what will you do? Come up with a plan of action.

Key

▬ defend the coastline	▬ main road
▬ let the coastline retreat for now	▬ secondary road
	— railway
⦾ town	National Park (protected area)
○ village	

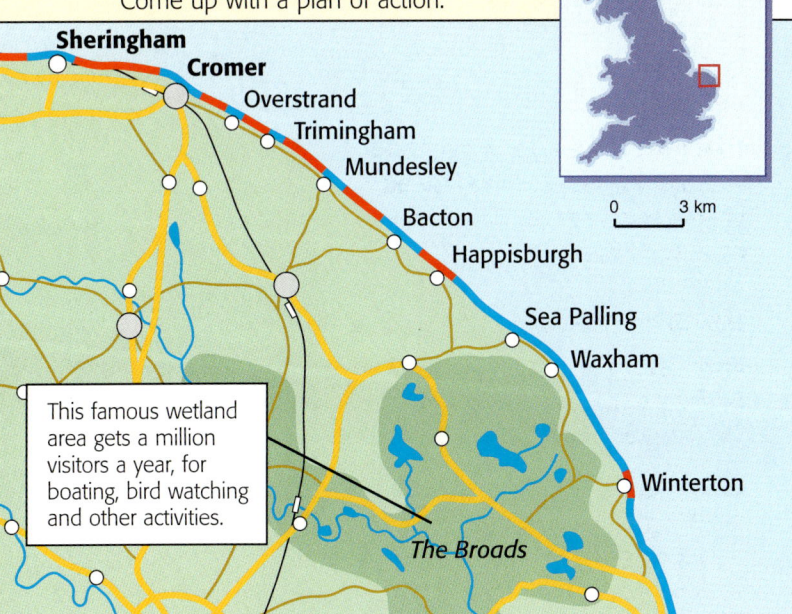

Sheringham
Cromer
Overstrand
Trimingham
Mundesley
Bacton
Happisburgh
Sea Palling
Waxham
Winterton

This famous wetland area gets a million visitors a year, for boating, bird watching and other activities.

The Broads

0   3 km

2 Weather and climate

The big picture

This chapter is all about **weather** and **climate**. These are the big ideas behind the chapter:

◆ Weather is the state of the atmosphere around us at any given time. (Warm? wet? windy?) It can change from day to day.

◆ Climate is different. It's the 'average' weather in a place – what the weather is usually like there.

◆ Climate depends on several factors, such as how far a place is from the equator, or the sea. So it can be very different in different places.

◆ Climate affects our lives in many different ways.

Your goals for this chapter

By the end of this chapter you should be able to answer these questions:

◆ What does this weather term mean?

temperature   precipitation   air pressure   wind speed
wind direction   cloud cover   visibility

◆ How is each item above measured – and what units are used?

◆ What are the three different kinds of rainfall, and how does each form?

◆ What kind of weather is linked with:

low pressure?   high pressure in summer?   high pressure in winter?

◆ Why can the weather in the UK change very quickly?

◆ What are these, and how would you show them on a weather map?

warm front   cold front   depression

◆ What kind of things can satellite images tell us about the weather?

◆ What's the difference between weather and climate?

◆ What's a climate graph, and how do I draw one?

◆ What factors influence climate, and which is the main one?

◆ What different climate zones are there in Europe, and where?

◆ In what ways does climate affect our lives?

And then …

When you finish the chapter, come back to this page and see if you have met your goals!

Did you know?
◆ The wettest place in the world is Cherrapunji in India (1270 cm of rain/year).

Did you know?
◆ Weather exists only in the lowest 10 km of the atmosphere.

Did you know?
◆ During the last Ice Age a third of the Earth was covered in ice – over 240 m thick.
◆ It ended 10 000 years ago. (Lucky for us!)

Did you know?
◆ The lowest ever recorded temperature was −89.2 °C, in Antarctica, on 21 July 1983.

Your chapter starter ◀

Look at the photo on page 22.

What's the white stuff?

What caused it?

How would it feel to be there? What kinds of things could you do?

What might this place look like in six months' time?

Out, penguin.

Measuring and mapping the weather

In this unit you will find out how the weather is measured – and how to read simple weather maps.

Measuring the weather

Weather is the state of the atmosphere at a given time. You can tell a lot about it just by looking.

But to describe it fully, you need to ask questions like these. And answer them by measuring!

All around the world, night and day, the weather is continually monitored and measured. At weather stations on land, and by special equipment on planes, ships, weather balloons, and in satellites.

Then **meteorologists** or weather scientists use the data to write weather reports, and draw weather maps, and make weather forecasts.

Your turn

1 First, look at the weather map on the right. It's the kind of map you see on TV and in the newspapers.
Below are symbols it uses. Say what you think each means:

2 The photo above shows Seaburn on the day this weather map was drawn. Find it on the weather map.
What can you say about the weather there?
Describe it as fully as you can, giving some figures.

3 Now say what you think the weather was like at:
a X on the weather map   b Y on the weather map

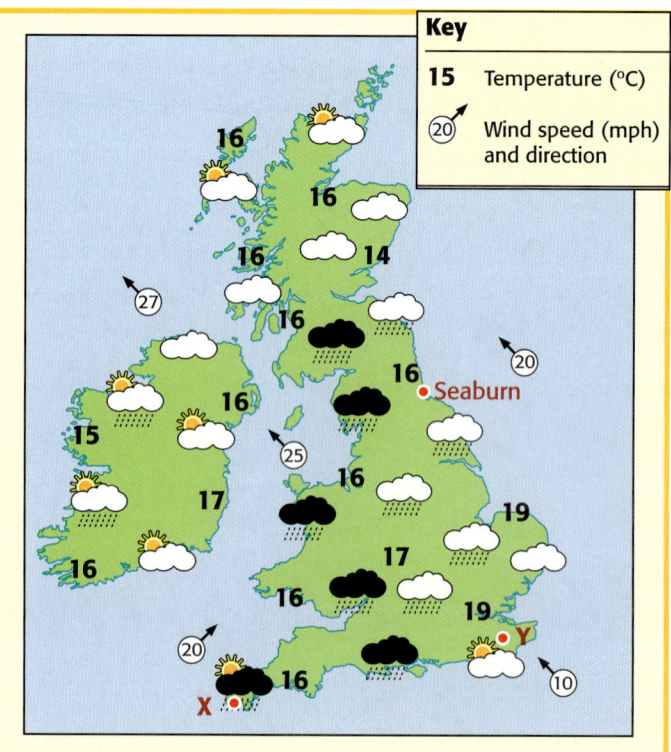

Key

15	Temperature (°C)
(20) ↗	Wind speed (mph) and direction

Weather term	Means ...	Usually given ...	Measured using ...
temperature	exactly how hot or cold it is		
	how 'heavy' the air is	in millibars (mb)	
	how much of the sky is hidden by clouds		your eyes; satellite image
	how fast the wind is blowing		
	where the wind is blowing from (a south west wind blows from the south west)	as a compass bearing (N, NW, SW and so on)	
	water falling from the sky in any form (rain, hail, sleet, snow)		
	how far ahead we can see, for example on a foggy day	in metres or kilometres	

4 This question is all about measuring the weather. You have to work out the answers for yourself, just like a detective. (The glossary will help.)

  a First, make a copy of the table above.

  b Write the words from list **A** below in the first column of your table, in the correct places.

  c Complete the third column using list **B**. Start with the easiest units.

A Weather terms	**B** Units
wind direction	kilometres or miles
visibility	per hour (like a car)
air pressure	millilitres
precipitation	oktas
wind speed	degrees Centigrade (°C)
cloud cover	

5 Now look at box **C**. It shows equipment for measuring the weather. Look at each item in turn. What do you think it measures? Write its name in the correct place in the fourth column of your table.

6 **Cloud cover** means how much of the sky is covered in cloud. It is one thing you can measure just by looking. Cloud cover is measured in eighths or oktas, like this:

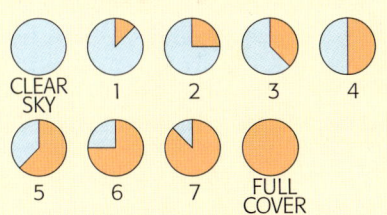

CLEAR SKY 1 2 3 4
5 6 7 FULL COVER

Note!
They use more complex symbols for oktas on weather charts.

  a Now look at the photo on page 24. As far as one can tell from a photo, what do you think the cloud cover was at Seaburn that day? Answer in oktas.

  b Do the same for the photo on page 22.

7 a Look back at your table. Which of those aspects of the weather could you measure at home?

  b Choose one. Say *how* you would measure it, and *when*. Draw a diagram to show any equipment you'd use, and where you would place it.

C **Equipment for measuring the weather**

The wind turns the cups ...

30 °C (hot)
0 °C (freezing)

... which turn a counter.

thermometer   anemometer

RAIN   FINE

barometer   wind vane

A beam of light is sent out ...

... and a sensor measures how much arrives.

rain gauge   visibility meter

Clouds and rain

In this unit you'll learn how clouds form, and about three types of rainfall.

Where do clouds come from?

Look at this photo. It's 3 pm. Warm day. Blue sky. Fluffy clouds.
But there were no clouds a few hours ago. Where did they come from?

3 The warm air is rising. (You just can't see it!)

4 As warm air rises it cools. So the water vapour in it condenses to form **clouds** of tiny water droplets.

5 If the water droplets join to make larger drops, they'll fall as rain.

2 The ground is warming the air.

1 The sun has been warming the ground all morning.

Different kinds of clouds

All clouds are formed from water vapour. But they appear in many different shapes and sizes. Here are three important types:

cumulus clouds

Fluffy clouds. They form low in the sky and can bring short, heavy showers. (Some grow into tall dark clouds that bring very heavy rain.)

stratus clouds

Big blankets of dull cloud. They hang low in the sky, and can cover it all. They can give a light drizzle, but no real showers.

cirrus clouds

Thin wispy high clouds (over 6 km up). It's freezing up there, so they are made of ice crystals! They can mean bad weather is on the way.

Three types of rainfall

All rain is just water. All rain is caused by air rising.
But it rises for different reasons – so we give rain different names.

Convectional rainfall

Here the air rises because the ground heats it.
It rises in warm currents.
We call these **convection currents**.
So we call the rain **convectional rainfall**.

In the UK we get convectional rainfall inland in summer, where the ground gets hottest, far from the cooling effects of the sea.

3 The rising air cools.
The water vapour condenses.
Clouds form. It rains.

2 Currents of warm air rise.

1 The sun warms the ground … which then warms the air above it.

Relief rainfall

Wind is moving air.

When the wind meets a line of high hills or mountains, there's only one way to go – up !
So the air rises and cools – and we get rain.
We call it **relief rainfall**.

In the UK the prevailing wind is from the south west. So we get relief rainfall on the high land along the west coast.

3 The rising air cools. The water vapour condenses. Clouds form. It rains.

2 The air is forced to rise.

1 Warm moist air arrives from the Atlantic Ocean.

leeward (sheltered)

4 The rain falls on the **windward** side of the mountain. The **leeward** side stays dry.

windward (facing the wind)

Frontal rainfall

As you'll see in Unit 2.4, huge blocks of air called **air masses** move around the Earth.

When a warm air mass meets a cold one the warm air is forced to rise. So we get rain.
This is **frontal rainfall**.

Frontal rain can fall anywhere, since air masses can travel anywhere. But in the UK, they often arrive in from the Atlantic Ocean. So the west of the UK gets a lot of frontal rain.

warm

2 The warm air mass slides up over the cold one, or gets driven up by it.

3 The rising air cools. The water vapour condenses. Clouds form. It rains.

1 A warm air mass meets a cold air mass.

cold

Your turn

1 Look at the clouds in the main photo on page 26.
   a Which type of clouds are they?
   b Why did they form?
   c If it rains, which kind of rainfall will this be?

2 To form clouds, two things are always needed.
   Which are they? Choose from this list:
   wind   rising air   mountains   hot sun
   warm ground   water vapour

3 Can clouds form in the dark? Explain.

4 Name a type of cloud which:
   a is made of ice crystals
   b forms a dull blanket and gives drizzle.

5 Which type of rainfall is caused by:
   a mountains in the way?
   b a mass of warm air meeting a mass of cold air?

6 Write a letter to your friend Gelop on Mars.
   Tell him what rain is, and why we humans just can't live without it.

Air pressure and weather

Here you'll learn about the weather you get with high and low air pressure.

What's air pressure?
Although we can't feel it, all the air above us is pressing down on us, giving **air pressure**. If air pressure is **low**, it means air is rising. If it is **high** it means air is sinking. And each brings different weather.

Low pressure weather
Look what happens when warm air rises …

▲ *Low pressure weather!*

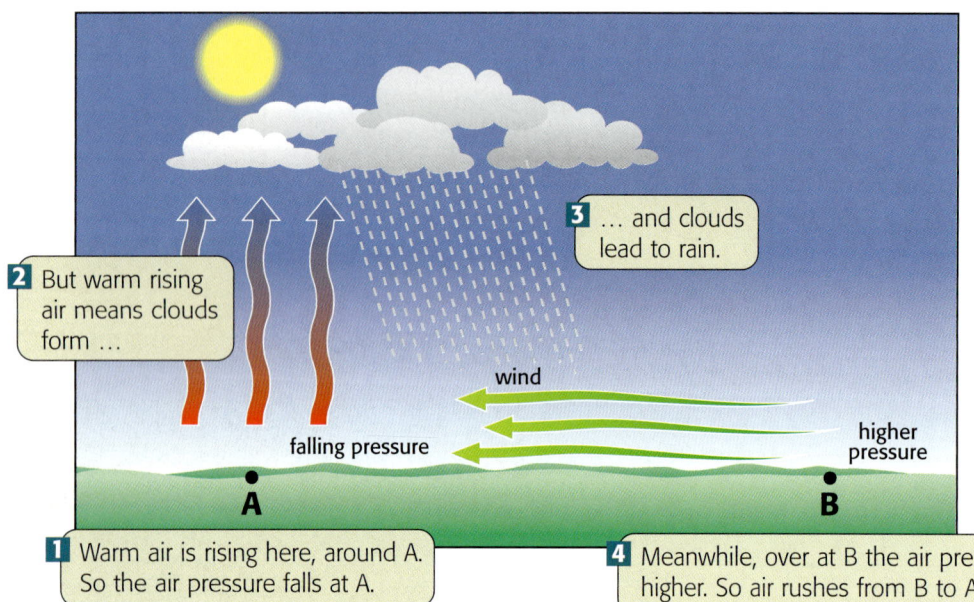

3 … and clouds lead to rain.

2 But warm rising air means clouds form …

wind

falling pressure

higher pressure

A   B

1 Warm air is rising here, around A. So the air pressure falls at A.

4 Meanwhile, over at B the air pressure is higher. So air rushes from B to A as **wind**.

So a fall in air pressure is a sign of rain and wind.
The lower the pressure the worse the weather will be.

High pressure weather
When warm air rises in one place, cool air sinks somewhere else.

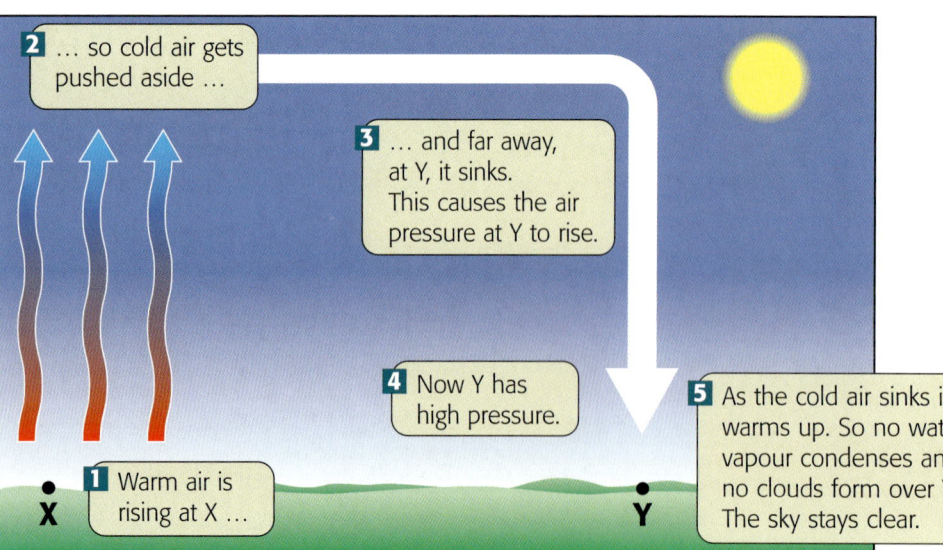

2 … so cold air gets pushed aside …

3 … and far away, at Y, it sinks. This causes the air pressure at Y to rise.

4 Now Y has high pressure.

5 As the cold air sinks it warms up. So no water vapour condenses and no clouds form over Y. The sky stays clear.

1 Warm air is rising at X …

X   Y

So high pressure means no clouds. Which means it gives us our hottest summer weather and coldest winter weather, as you'll see next.

▲ *To see if the air pressure is rising or falling, check a barometer.*

When there's high pressure in summer ...

There are no clouds in the way so the sun is strong. Take care you don't get burned!

Since there is no cloud to trap the heat in, the evenings can be cool.

No cloud means no rain. So there may be **drought** in some places.

No cloud also means the ground gets cold at night. Water vapour condenses on grass to form **dew**.

But inland, on very hot days, the hot air may rise rapidly, cool, and form huge black clouds.

Inside these clouds, strong currents of air whip around, causing **thunderstorms** ...

... and thunderstorms can lead to heavy rain and even **flooding**.

When there's high pressure in winter ...

There is no cloud to act as a blanket. So the days are clear, cold and bright.

With no cloud, the ground cools fast at night and cools the air above it. Water vapour condenses and freezes on cold surfaces, giving **frost**.

It also condenses on dust and other particles in the air, giving **fog**. This makes driving dangerous.

Pipes may burst and homes may get flooded.

Water on roads freezes into ice as the sun goes down.

Ice and frost mean animals have trouble finding food.

Your turn

1 Write this out, using the correct word from each pair.

Low pressure is a sign of fine/unsettled weather. The lower the pressure the calmer/stormier the weather will be. High pressure brings clear/cloudy skies, which means very hot/cold weather in summer and very warm/cold weather in winter.

2 For some jobs, long spells of high pressure weather can bring problems. Try to give three examples.

3 For some jobs, long spells of low pressure weather can bring problems. Write down three examples.

4 It's August, and high pressure. You're going camping. List four items you'll pack, to cope with the weather.

5 a What do fog, dew and frost have in common?
  b Explain how each forms.

6 Which type of weather do you prefer – high or low pressure? And in which season? Give your reasons.

Sudden changes in the weather

In this unit you will learn why our weather in the UK can change so quickly.

Air masses

Some parts of the world are hot. Some are cold. The result is that the air moves around – like the air in a cold room when you turn on a heater.

The air moves around the world in huge blocks called **air masses**. An air mass can be thousands of km across. It can be warm or cold, damp or dry, depending on where it came from.

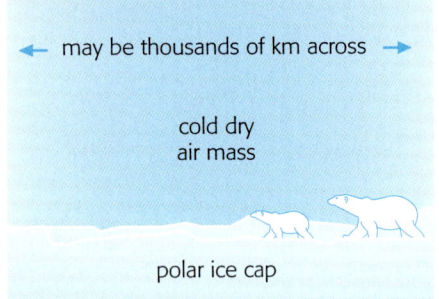

An air mass coming from the North Pole will be cold and dry …

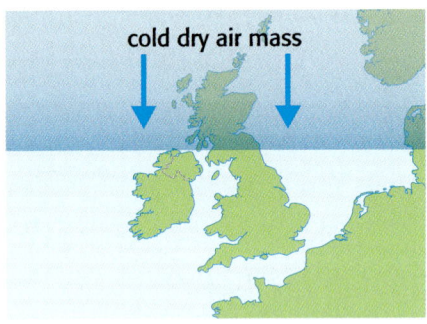

… so if it moves over the UK you'll get cold dry weather.

An air mass coming from a warm ocean will be warm and damp …

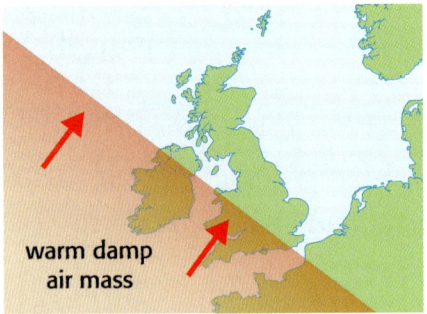

… and if it moves over the UK you get warm dampish weather.

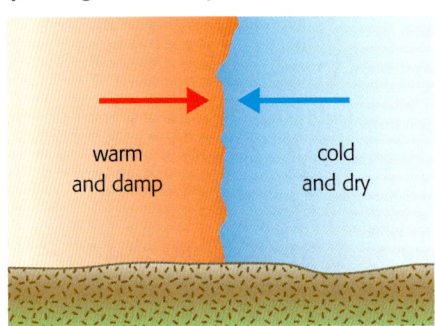

Often, two different air masses will meet and clash over the UK …

… and the result is sudden changes in the weather!

Many different air masses cross Britain. That's why our weather can change so fast. But when an air mass moves very slowly, or sits still for a while, we get the same weather for days.

Fronts

The leading edge of an air mass is called a **front**.

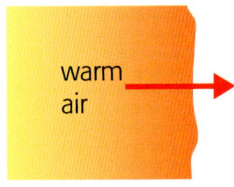

A **warm front** means a warm air mass is arriving.

That is shown on a weather map by red frills.

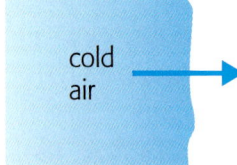

A **cold front** means a cold air mass is arriving.

That is shown on a weather map by blue teeth.

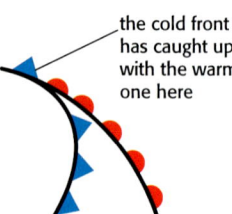

Here a cold front is chasing a warm one. (We call this a **depression**.)

When a new front reaches the UK, it always brings a change in the weather.

When a warm front arrives

8 am

It's cool and dry. The sky is clear.

There's a cold air mass over your area. But a warm front is on the way.

How will it affect the weather?

midday

warm front

warm air sliding up

1 Warm air is lighter. So it slides up over the cold air.
2 As it rises, the pressure falls. So the weather gets a bit windy.
3 The rising air cools. The water vapour condenses to form a sloping bank of cloud.
4 It starts to rain. It may rain for hours.

4 pm

Time to put away the brolly!

Now the front has passed. The warm air mass has taken over.

So the temperature has risen. The rain has eased off. The wind has dropped.

When a cold front arrives

8 am

Nice and warm – but a bit cloudy!

There's a warm air mass over your area. But a cold front is on the way.

How will it affect the weather?

midday

cold front

cold air pushing under

1 The heavy cold air advances fast. It pushes sharply under the warm air.
2 So the pressure rises sharply, causing strong gusty winds.
3 As the warm air is driven upwards, its water vapour condenses. A steep bank of thick cloud forms.
4 It rains heavily. You may even get thunderstorms.

1 pm

I wish I'd brought my coat!

Now the front has passed. (Cold fronts travel much faster than warm ones!)

The cold air mass has taken over. So it is cooler. The rain has stopped. The sky is clearing.

Your turn

1 What is an air mass?

2 Five main types of air mass cross Britain. This map shows where they come from. (See page 129 too.) Answer these questions using the labels A – E:
   a Which air mass is coldest, and dry? Why?
   b Which two are dampest? Why?
   c Which one is very cold and dry in winter, but warmer in summer? Try to explain why.
   d Which one is warm even in winter?

3 What is: **a** a warm front?   **b** a cold front?
   Draw symbols for them. Beside each symbol write *warmer* and *colder* where you think they should go.

4 It is 7 am on 16 March. There is a cold air mass in your area. A warm front will arrive about 4 pm. Write a weather forecast for your local radio.

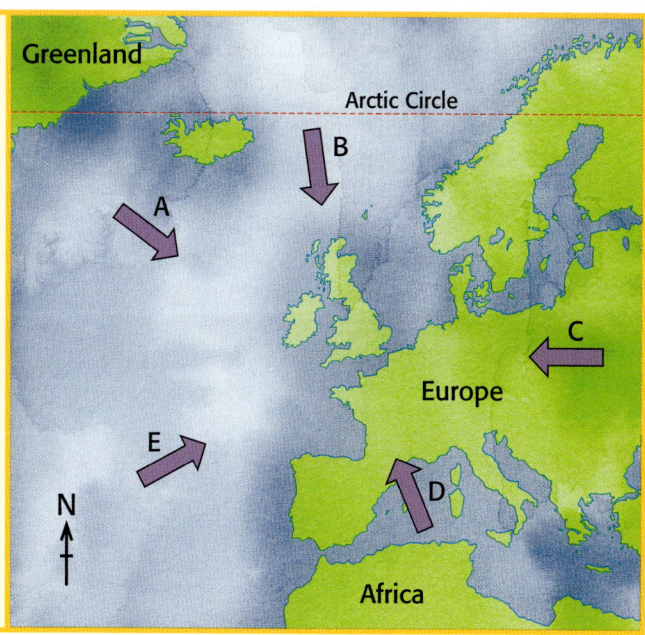

Greenland

Arctic Circle

A

B

C

Europe

E

D

N

Africa

Getting the weather picture

In this unit you'll see how satellite images give us clues about the weather.

Making satellite images

Several times an hour, high above the Earth, satellites take pictures to help us track the weather. This is what happens:

1 Satellite cameras detect light and heat from the Earth.

2 They send signals to a computer on the Earth.

3 The computer converts the signals into images.

4 It adds country outlines. It may also add colours to make the images clearer.

5 Then we use the images to help us forecast the weather.

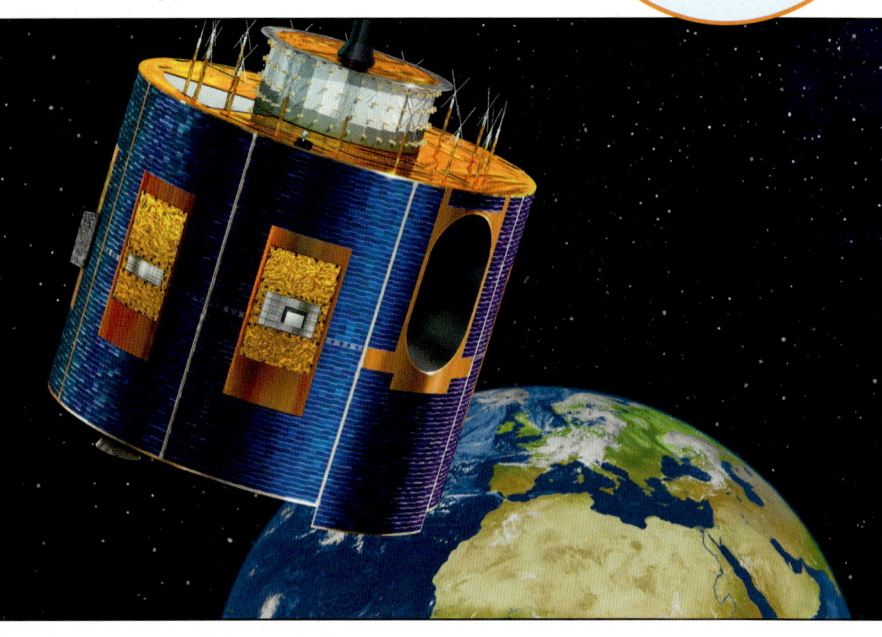

▲ *Taking pictures of the Earth from space.*

Satellites can detect heat even in the dark. So we can have infrared images 24 hours a day. But they can only detect light in the daytime!

Example of a satellite image

This is a heat or **infrared** image showing Europe and part of Africa. On an infrared image the *coldest* things show up *whitest*.

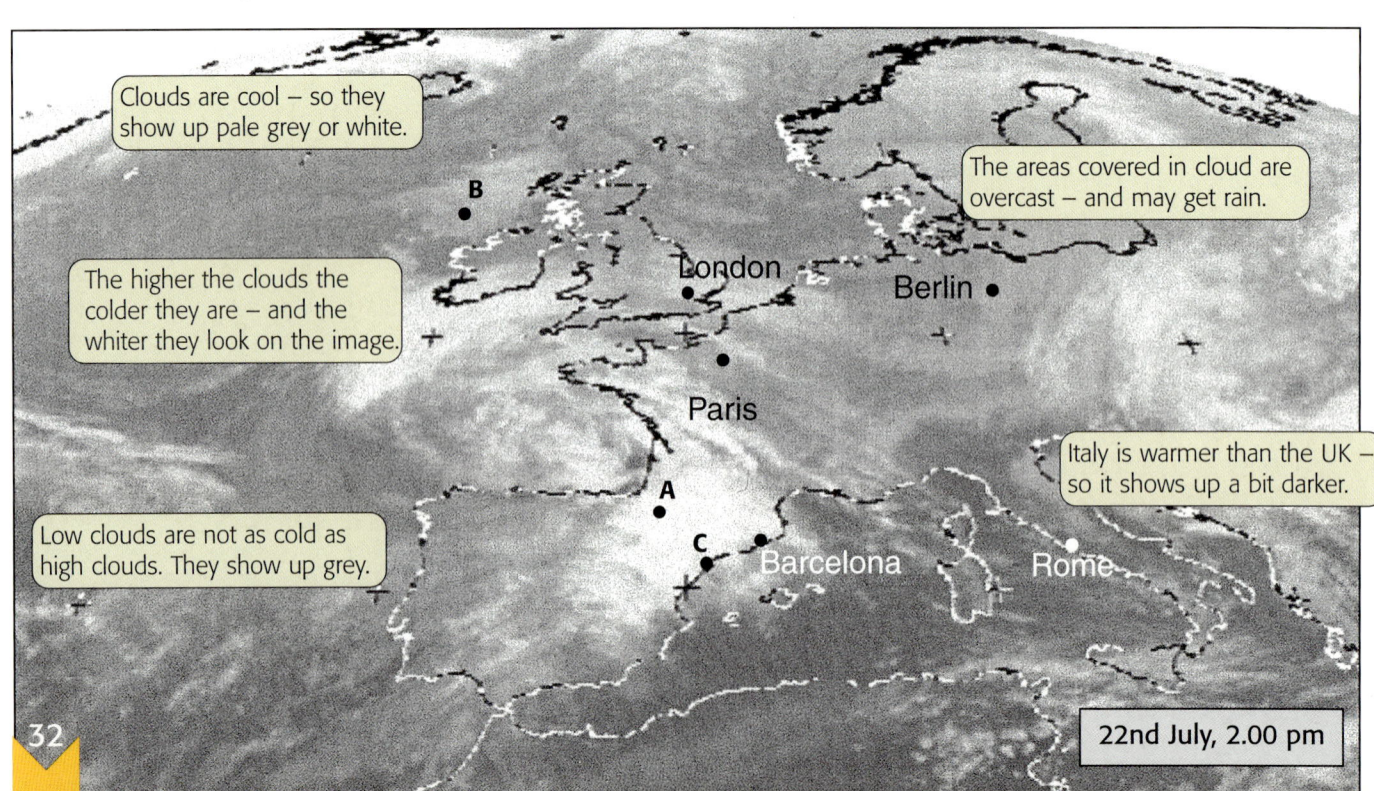

Clouds are cool – so they show up pale grey or white.

The areas covered in cloud are overcast – and may get rain.

The higher the clouds the colder they are – and the whiter they look on the image.

Italy is warmer than the UK – so it shows up a bit darker.

Low clouds are not as cold as high clouds. They show up grey.

22nd July, 2.00 pm

Using satellite images to forecast the weather

Look at the satellite images below. (This time colour has been added.)
They show a big swirl of cloud passing over the British Isles. It's the sign
of a **depression** – a weather system where a cold front is chasing a warm
one. We get lots of depressions coming in from the Atlantic Ocean.

Did you know?
◆ A depression is Nature's way of mixing warm and cold air masses.

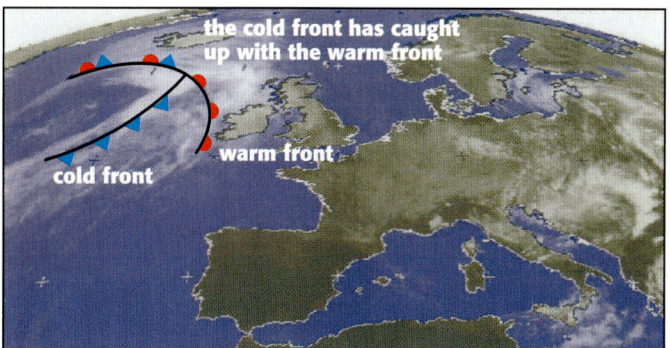

17 November, 6.30 am
The swirl of cloud shows where the cold front is
pushing under the warm air mass, forcing it to rise.

the cold front has caught up with the warm front
cold front
warm front

17 November, 1.30 pm
Down on the Earth, below the thick cloud, there will
be lots of rain, and strong gusty winds.

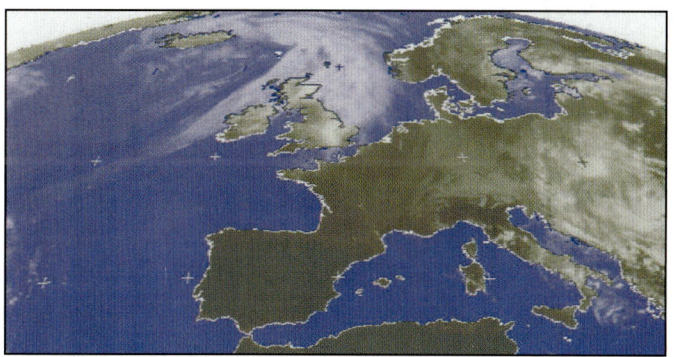

18 November, 7.00 am
The depression is moving across the UK.
So the forecast warns of heavy rain and blustery
showers – especially in the south and east.

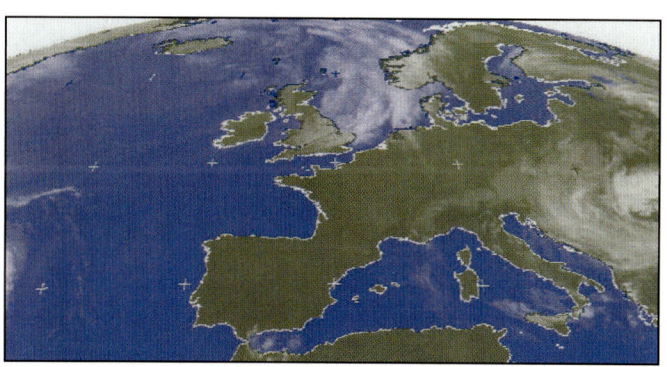

18 November, 2.30 pm
It is moving off towards Europe, where it will die
away. The forecast predicts drier weather for most
of the UK this afternoon, except the south east.

Your turn

1 Copy and complete, using words from the list below:
  An _____ satellite image is made by detecting _____.
  A _____ satellite image is made by detecting _____.
  light   heat   infrared   visible
  Questions 2–5 are about the image on page 32.

2 Where is the cloud higher, at A or at B?

3 Imagine you were on the beach at C at the time.
  a Which country is C in? (Check on page 129.)
  b Was it sunny at C, or cloudy? How much can you
    tell about the weather at C, from this image?

4 Which was warmer that day, the Mediterranean
  Sea or the Atlantic Ocean? How can you tell?

5 Which of the five marked cities had little or no cloud
  cover, when the image was taken?

Answer these questions using the four images above.

6 What is a *depression*?

7 Describe the cloud shape that indicates a depression.

8 It is 17 November.
  Write a weather forecast for Radio Bristol giving
  tomorrow's weather. (Pages 127 and 31 may help.)

9 It is 1.30 pm on 17 November.
  Which of these three places do you think is having
  the worst weather?
  a London   **b** Bristol   **c** Aberdeen
  Give reasons for your answer.

10 It is 18 November, 2.30 pm.
  Name one other European country that is already
  being affected by the depression.

From weather to climate

In this unit you will learn what climate is, and how to draw a climate graph.

Weather: a reminder

Weather is the state of the atmosphere at any given time.

The weather was good when this photo was taken. But an hour later it may have been raining … because weather can change from hour to hour and day to day. Not like climate.

So what is climate?

Climate is the *average* weather in a place. It's what the weather is *usually* like.

It is worked out by taking measurements over a long period (like 30 years) and then calculating the average. Look at this table:

▲ *A nice day in Plymouth – but what's the climate like there?*

Plymouth

Climate data for Plymouth												
Average values	Jan	Feb	Mar	Apr	May	Jun	Jul	Aug	Sep	Oct	Nov	Dec
Temperature (°C)	8	8	10	12	15	18	20	19	18	15	11	10
Rainfall (mm)	99	74	69	53	63	53	70	77	78	91	113	110
Hours of sunshine/day	1.8	2.9	4.0	6.0	7.0	7.3	6.7	6.5	5.2	3.4	2.7	1.6
Number of days with gales	3.4	1.9	1.5	0.5	0.3	0.1	0	0.3	0.9	1.3	2.2	3

The table shows that Plymouth is usually mild and quite wet in winter, and warm with less rain in summer. It also gets a lot more gales in winter.

Climate across the UK

Climate varies across the UK. (See why in the next unit.) But we can divide the country into four climate regions.

The map on the right show the four regions. Note that:

◆ it gets colder and drier towards the east in winter
◆ the south of the UK is the warmest part.

▲ *A meteorologist working on climate data.*

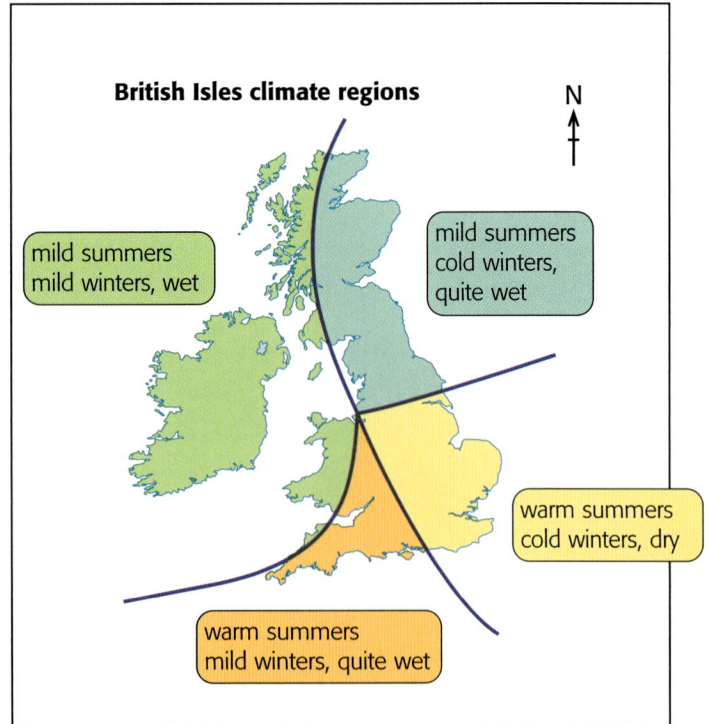

British Isles climate regions

N

mild summers mild winters, wet

mild summers cold winters, quite wet

warm summers cold winters, dry

warm summers mild winters, quite wet

Your turn

1 What is: **a** weather?   **b** climate?

2 Look at each statement A–H below and say whether it describes weather or climate.

  A It was a hot day in Boscombe when the photo on the right was taken.

  B November is usually the wettest month in Plymouth.

  C Egypt is usually very hot in August.

  D It rained heavily all afternoon.

  E May to September is the monsoon season, in South East Asia.

  F In September a terrible storm carried Richard's garden shed away.

  G A heavy fog on the motorway reduced visibility to less than a metre last night.

  H January is a good time to head for Florida, to catch some winter sun.

3 Look at the table for Plymouth, on page 34.

  a Which month usually has least sunshine?

  b Which month usually gets most gales?

  c Which month is usually warmest?

  d Which month do *you* think would be best for a camping holiday around Plymouth? Why?

  e Which do you think would be worst? Why?

4 Now look at this graph. It is a **climate graph** for London. It shows a bar chart and line graph together.

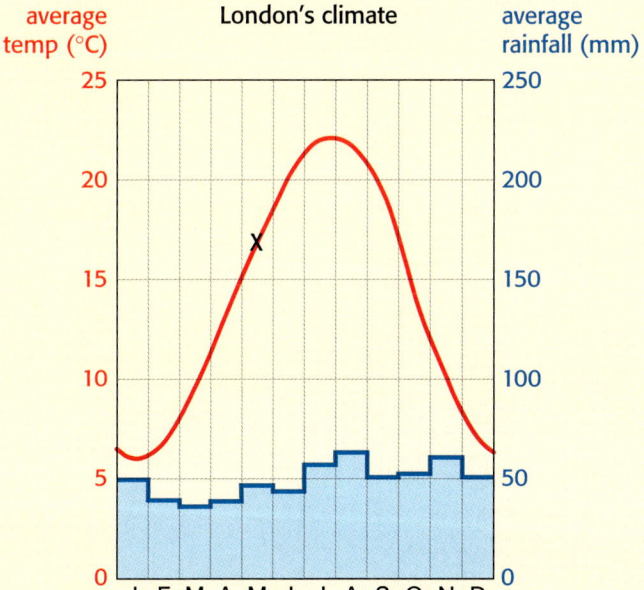

▲ *Boscombe in Dorset, basking in the sun.*

  a What does the bar chart show? (Look on the blue axis.)

  b What does the line graph show? (The red axis.)

  c Which two months are usually hottest in London?

  d Which month is usually driest?

  e Which gets most rain? Can you explain why?

5 It's your turn to draw a climate graph – for Plymouth. You will use the data from the table on page 34.

  a Make a larger copy of the axes shown below, and complete the labels. (Use graph paper if you can, and label each axis in a different colour.)

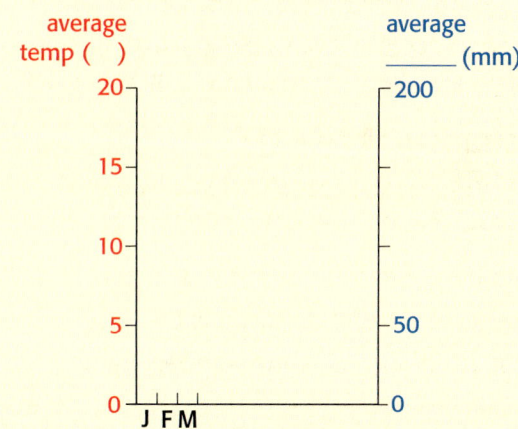

  b Now draw in a bar chart showing rainfall for Plymouth. Check the bar chart for London, to see how to do it.

  c Next draw in a line graph for the temperature. Mark each point at the centre of the month (like the X for May, for London). Join the points with a smooth curve.

  d Give your graph a title.

6 Compare the climate graphs for London and Plymouth. Which of the two places:

  a gets more rain?   **b** is hotter in summer?

  c is colder in winter?

See if you can come up with a reason for each answer.

The factors that influence climate

In this unit you will learn why climate can be so different in different places.

Climate: a reminder

Climate is the average weather in a place. It's what the weather is *usually* like there. It can be very different in different places. For example …

… in London the average maximum temperature for August is 21 °C, and the average rainfall is 59 mm.

But at Giza near Cairo in Egypt, the average maximum temperature for August is 35 °C. And rainfall is zero!

The factors that influence climate

Climate depends on many factors. We'll start with the main one.

1 Latitude – the main factor

The further you go from the equator the cooler it gets. That's because the Earth is curved.

Look at A. These rays heat the area around the equator. The Earth gets hottest here.

Now look at B. Because the Earth is curved, these rays are spread over a larger area – which means it gets less hot.

C covers an even larger area – so this hardly even gets warm!

So that is why:

◆ the UK is always cooler than Egypt.

◆ the north of the UK is usually cooler than the south.

◆ it is very cold at the North and South Poles.

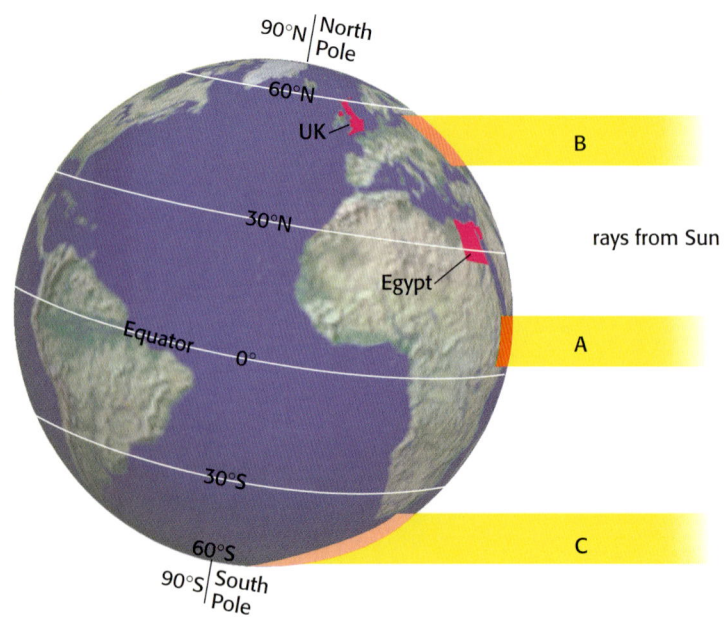

2 Other general factors

Distance from the coast
The sea is cooler than land in summer, and warmer in winter. So a sea breeze keeps the coast cool in summer – and warm in winter!

Prevailing wind direction
For example in the UK the prevailing wind is from the south west. It brings water vapour from the ocean – and that means rain!

Ocean currents
For example a warm ocean current called the **North Atlantic Drift** warms the west coast of the UK in winter, by warming the wind.

3 Local factors

Even places close together can have different climates, due to these factors:

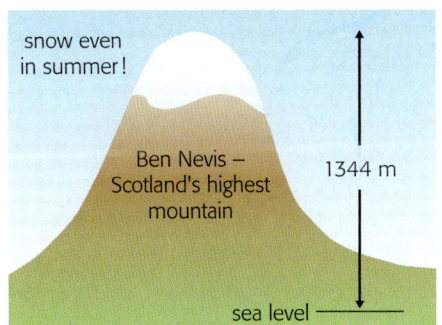

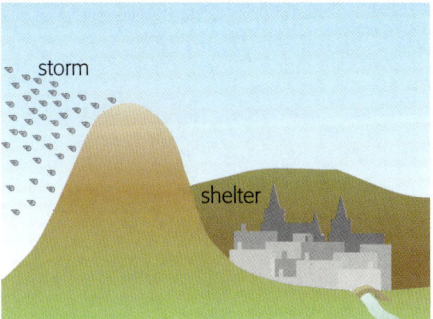

Height above sea level
Or **altitude**. The higher you are above sea level, the cooler it is. The temperature falls by about 1 °C for every 100 metres.

Shelter
One place may be warm and dry because it is sheltered by hills. Another may be exposed to the wind and rain.

How built up a place is
Roofs and streets store up heat. Cars and central heating give out heat. So the city tends to be warmer than the countryside.

Your turn

1 Draw a spider map to show the factors that influence climate. Make it look interesting!
You could use a symbol for each factor, and a different colour for each group of factors.

2 Using the map on page 127, give *two* reasons why:
  a Aberdeen is colder than Plymouth in winter
  b It's colder up Ben Nevis than in Plymouth
  c London is warmer than Belfast in summer.

3 In the UK, the *prevailing wind* is a south west wind.
  a What does this mean? (Glossary!)
  b Explain how this wind affects the climate.

4 Suppose the prevailing wind in the UK was a north wind. How do you think this would affect the climate?

5 This is about the effect of distance from the coast.

In an oven, soil heats up faster than water. When you take them out of the oven, the soil cools faster too. Using this idea, and the map on page 129, explain why:
  a Tehran is hotter than Lisbon in summer
  b Lisbon is warmer than Tehran in winter.

6 Now design and draw a diagram to explain why it is warmer in winter by the coast than inland.

7 Here's a challenge! Try to explain why it gets colder as you go up a mountain.

Climate across Europe

In this unit you will learn about the main physical features of Europe, and explore its climate zones.

Europe's main physical features

This map shows Europe, the continent you live on. 10 million square km !

Look at all those mountain ranges and seas.
And look at the British Isles. They form only one thirtieth of Europe's area.

Did you know?
◆ Europe is only about a third the size of Africa.
◆ It is the world's second smallest continent. (Oceania is smallest.)

Arctic Ocean

Norwegian Sea

ICELAND

Atlantic Ocean

Ural Mountains

North Sea

BRITISH ISLES

Baltic Sea

NORTH EUROPEAN PLAIN

Volga

English Channel

Rhine

Loire

Danube

Rhône

△ A l p s
Mt Blanc (4807m)

Pyrenees

Appennines

Caucasus
△ Elbrus (5642)m

Black Sea

Mediterranean Sea

AFRICA

Europe's climate zones

This map shows Europe's **climate zones**.
Note the general pattern:

◆ Europe gets warmer towards the south.

◆ It gets drier towards the east.

◆ The **prevailing wind** blows in from the Atlantic Ocean. (But other winds blow in too – for example from the North Pole and from Africa.)

◆ The change from hot summer to cold winter is greatest in eastern Europe.

Key

🟩	mild winters, quite cool summers, rain all year (west coast maritime)
🟨	mild wet winters, hot dry summers (Mediterranean)
🟦	cold winters with snow, warm summers with showers (Alpine mountain)
🟧	cold dry winters, hot damp summers (continental)
🟪	cold all year, little rain (tundra)

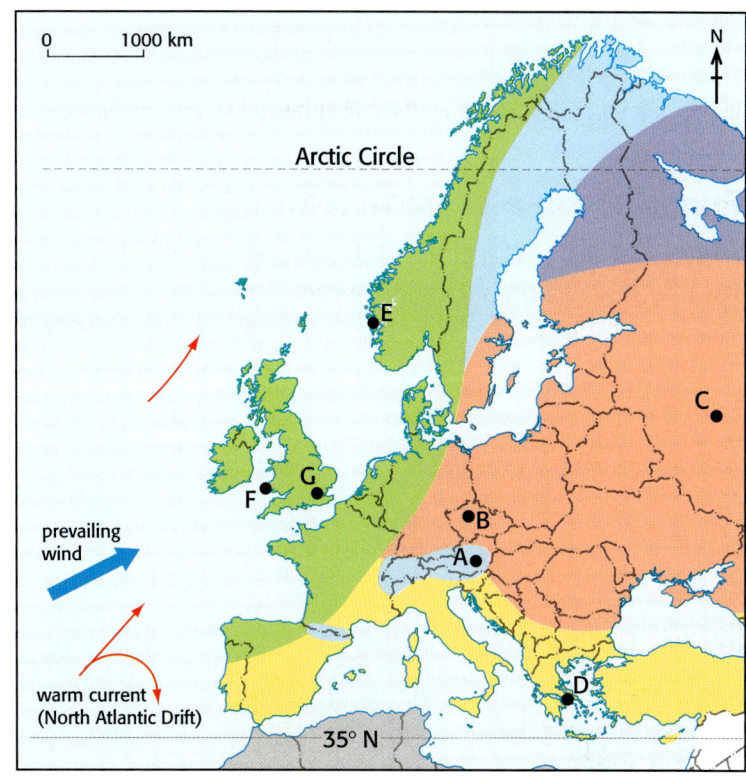

Your turn

Now you are about to become a detective, and work out *why* Europe's climate varies the way it does. You will use what you learned in Unit 2.7.

1 The map opposite is a *physical* map of Europe. The one on page 129 is a *political* map. Explain what the difference is.

2 Use both maps to help you answer these.
   a Name the mountain range on the borders of France and Spain.
   b Name the mountain range that shelters Italy from cold north winds, and four countries it goes through.
   c Which country has Europe's highest mountain?
   d What is a plain? Name the largest plain in Europe.

3 Now look at the map of climate zones above.
   a To which climate zone does the UK belong?
   b Explain why this climate zone has mild winters.
   c Give a reason why it has quite a lot of rain.
   d Name four other countries with a climate like ours.

4 a Name Europe's most southern climate zone.
   b Why is it called this?
   c Give one reason why it is hotter than the west coast maritime zone in summer.
   d In summer this area often has high pressure. What effect does that have on the climate?
   e This zone gets rain in winter, but not as much as the UK does. Suggest a reason.

5 Three areas on the map have an Alpine climate. Explain why, for each of them. (Page 38 will help.)

6 Look at the places marked on the climate map above. Using page 38 to help you, suggest reasons why:
   a A is always cooler than B even though it is further south.
   b C gets quite hot in summer and very cold in winter.
   c B gets mainly convectional rain in summer.
   d D is very hot and dry in summer.
   e E gets a lot of relief rain.
   f F gets more rain than G.

7 Now look at these climate graphs. Your job is to match them to A, B, C and D on the climate map. Give your answer like this: ① = ___.

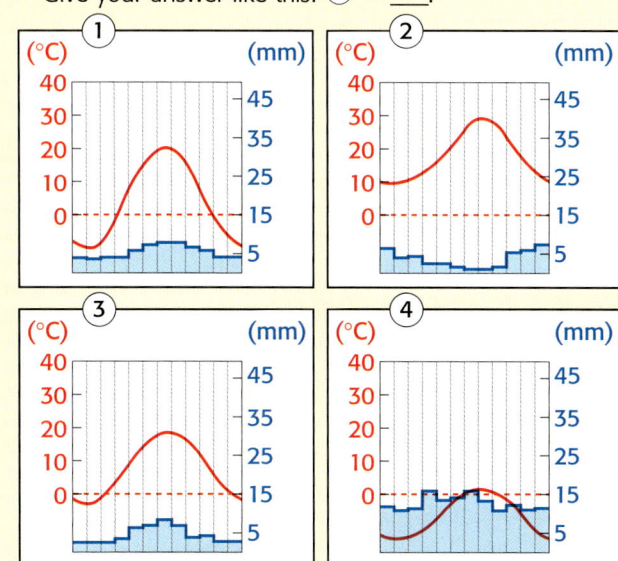

How climate affects our lives

In this unit you'll explore some of the ways in which climate affects us.

Climate control ?

Climate affects our lives in all kinds of ways.
For example when we are deciding …

◆ what clothes to buy, and wear
◆ where to go on holiday
◆ what to do in our free time
◆ what to grow, if we're farmers or gardeners !

Here again is the map of Europe's climate zones.
It will help you explore some of the ways in which climate affects our lives.

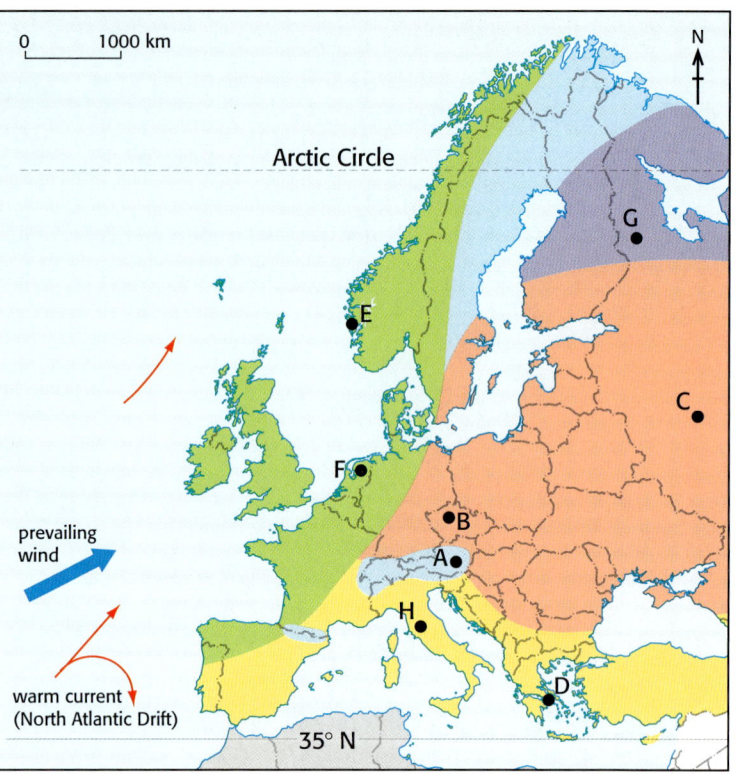

Arctic Circle

prevailing wind

warm current (North Atlantic Drift)

35° N

0   1000 km

N

Key

🟩	west coast maritime
🟨	Mediterranean
🟦	Alpine mountain
🟧	continental
🟪	tundra

Your turn

1 You want to go on holiday in Europe. But where ?
  a For each wish on the list below , choose a matching destination from A – H on the map above. (The maps on pages 38 and 129 will help.) Answer like this: ① = ___
  b For each place you choose, say what country it's in, and why that place is a good choice.

Holiday wish list

① You want to go sailing this summer – somewhere warm and sunny with lots of islands.

② It's Easter. You'd like to go skiing.

③ You'd like to go camping somewhere really hot this summer – but far from mountains and sea.

④ You like really cold winter weather. You'd like to go on a sledge drawn by huskies. And you like lakes.

⑤ You like mild summers – and this summer you just want to go cycling, and practise your Dutch.

⑥ You'd like to go hiking up mountains this summer – and you love Italian food.

i

ii

2 Now look at the two houses above.
Match each house to one of the four places A, C, D and F, marked on the map above.
Then explain how it suits the climate there.

Orange trees suit high areas with cool dry winters and warm wet summers. Frost and drought can kill them.

Wheat can grow in a wide range of climates. But it does best in hot summers with frequent light showers.

Cotton grows best in a warm climate with at least 150 frost-free days. It needs water – but not lots of rain.

Warm summers with lots of sunshine and not much rain are best for grapes. Frost in spring can ruin the harvest.

3 Look at the crops above, and the conditions they need.
a Which of these would be best for growing oranges?
UK   Poland   Spain
b Which of these climate zones would suit grapes best?
west coast maritime   tundra   Mediterranean
c One of these countries grows quite a lot of cotton. Which one do you think it is?
Norway   Greece   Ukraine
d One of these countries is among the world's top wheat producers. Which do you think it is?
Russia   Greece   Iceland

4 Look at the six events on the right. They took place in a village called Porziano in Italy. (It's at H on the map on page 40.) Each event is linked to the climate.

Climate graph for Porziano

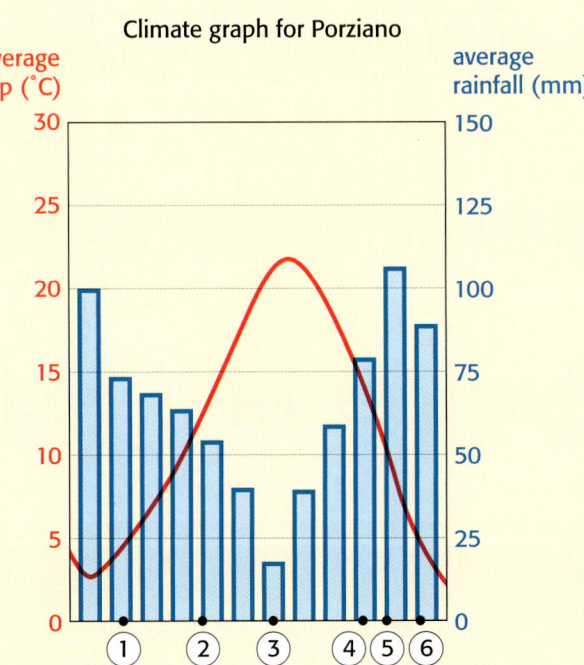

average temp (˚C)   average rainfall (mm)

Your task is to match each event to one of the numbers ① – ⑥ on the climate graph.
Answer like this: ① = ___

This one's for below 15 ˚C.

a Georgio puts on his special jumper, for the first time since spring.

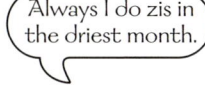
Always I do zis in the driest month.

b The mayor sends out his annual letter asking people to save water.

At 5 above freezing, stew is so pleezing.

c At Sergio's, it's time to put his winter stew on the menu again.

Mamma mia! É orribilé at this time of year.

d Maria greets last month's electricity bill with horror.

For you, carote mie bellissime!

e Uncle Paulo starts to water his carrots. They need at least 60 mm of water a month.

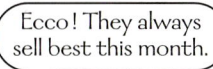
Ecco! They always sell best this month.

f At the door of her shop, Alice puts out a tub of umbrellas.

A robin snacks on a crispy spider.

A caterpillar feeds on a crunchy leaf.

Millions of leaves are busy making food from air and water – with sunlight as fuel.

A squirrel considers. Eat the nut now, or hide away for later?

A fox munches on a woodmouse – a treat! It had earthworm and caterpillar for starters.

A wood mouse chews on a caterpillar.

The mushrooms feed silently on dead wood.

A blackbird tugs at its wriggling lunch.

An earthworm drags a leaf home to its larder.

A woodlouse dines on a dead leaf.

Millions of roots are busy taking in water and minerals from the soil.

In the soil, billions of bacteria are busy feeding on dead things. Yummy!

The big picture

This chapter is about **ecosystems** – the units made up of living things and their non-living environment. These are the big ideas behind the chapter:

♦ In an ecosystem, the living things depend on each other and on their non-living environment.

♦ The Earth has some very large ecosystems, all with different climates and vegetation (plants).

♦ We humans have spread through the Earth's ecosystems, and we've done a lot of damage.

♦ Now we are learning that we must live sustainably, and protect ecosystems and the species in them.

Did you know?
♦ *There are around 6 million species of living things on the Earth.*

Your goals for this chapter

By the end of this chapter you should be able to answer these questions:

♦ What do these terms mean?
ecosystem   producer   consumer   decomposer
food chain   food web   biome   sustainable

♦ Why are plants a key part of any ecosystem?

♦ A whole ecosystem may be affected if I destroy one thing in it. Why?

♦ Where on the Earth will I find the rainforest ecosystem, and what kind of climate does it have?

♦ In what ways have plants adapted to the climate, in the rainforests?

♦ How and why are we humans destroying the rainforests?

♦ What example can I give, of humans living sustainably in the rainforest?

♦ Where on the Earth will I find the savanna ecosystem, and what kind of climate does it have?

♦ In what ways have plants adapted to the climate, in the savanna?

♦ How and why are we humans destroying the savanna?

♦ What example can I give, of humans living sustainably in the savanna?

Did you know?
♦ *There are only about 8000 tigers and 700 mountain gorillas left in the world.*

Did you know?
♦ *If we continue to destroy the rainforests at the present rate, they may all be gone by 2030.*

And then …

When you finish the chapter, come back to this page and see if you have met your goals!

Your chapter starter

Page 42 shows some animals that live in the woods, like the one in the photo. And in fields and parks and gardens.

Which of them have you seen? Where? What were they doing?

Name some animals that you won't find living wild in this country.

Why don't they live here?

Where's my dinner?

Introducing ecosystems

Here you will learn what an ecosystem is, and how the things in it are linked to each other. (You will meet these ideas in science too.)

What's an ecosystem ?

An ecosystem is a unit made up of two parts:

♦ living things (plants, animals, bacteria) and

♦ their non-living surroundings or **environment** – air, water, soil and the climate (how warm or wet it is).

On the right, and on page 42, you can see part of a woodland ecosystem.

In an ecosystem, the living things interact with the environment and each other. For example the caterpillars in a wood breathe the air. They feed on leaves. They get eaten by birds. If it gets too cold they die.

▲ *Bluebells in a woodland ecosystem.*

How big is an ecosystem?

An ecosystem is any size you choose to study. For example:

| a pond | a meadow | a forest | the Sahara desert | the whole Earth |

Each is a unit made up of living things and a non-living environment.

It all starts with plants …

In some ways, an ecosystem is like a canteen where living things eat. And it all starts with plants.

The caterpillar, wood mouse and fox are called **consumers** because they eat other living things.

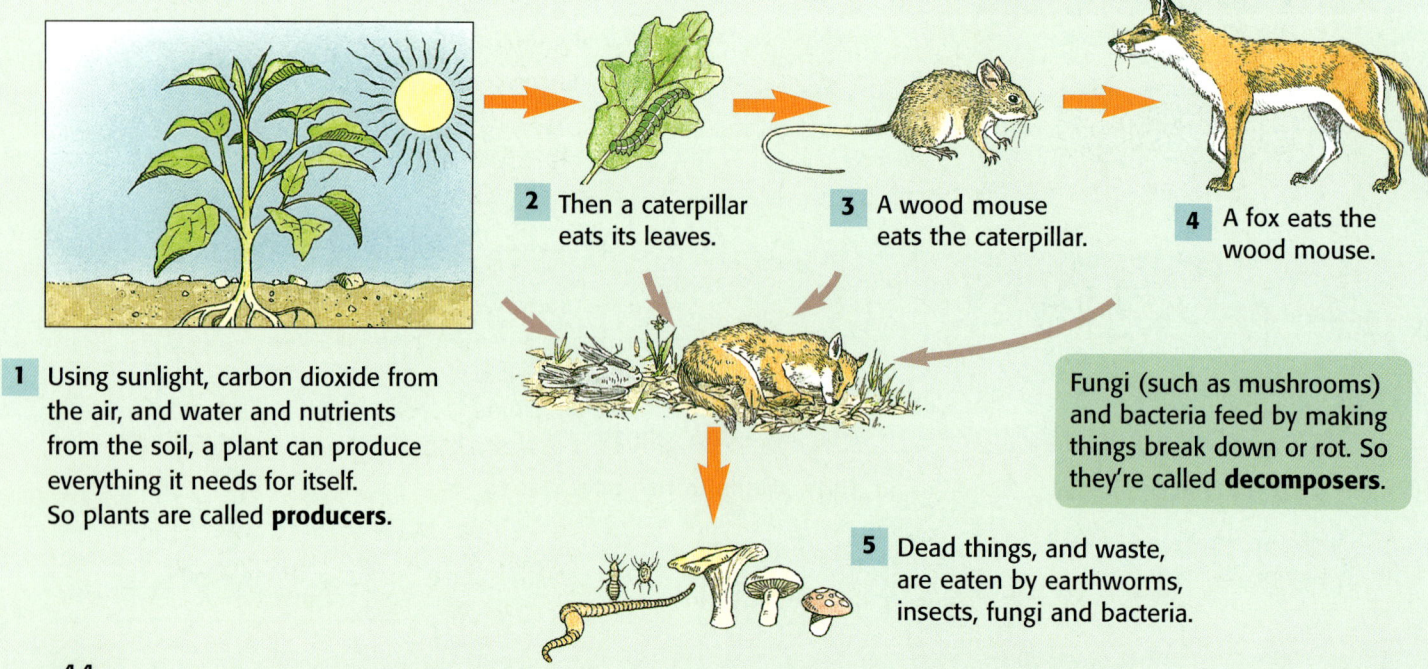

1 Using sunlight, carbon dioxide from the air, and water and nutrients from the soil, a plant can produce everything it needs for itself. So plants are called **producers**.

2 Then a caterpillar eats its leaves.

3 A wood mouse eats the caterpillar.

4 A fox eats the wood mouse.

5 Dead things, and waste, are eaten by earthworms, insects, fungi and bacteria.

Fungi (such as mushrooms) and bacteria feed by making things break down or rot. So they're called **decomposers**.

It's always the same pattern

The pattern is the same in every ecosystem, large or small.

◆ The plants make their own food. (Plants include trees!)

◆ The animals feed on plants, or each other.

◆ Decomposers feed on dead and waste material – and **recycle** nutrients that the plants can use again.

◆ Without plants, all other living things would die.

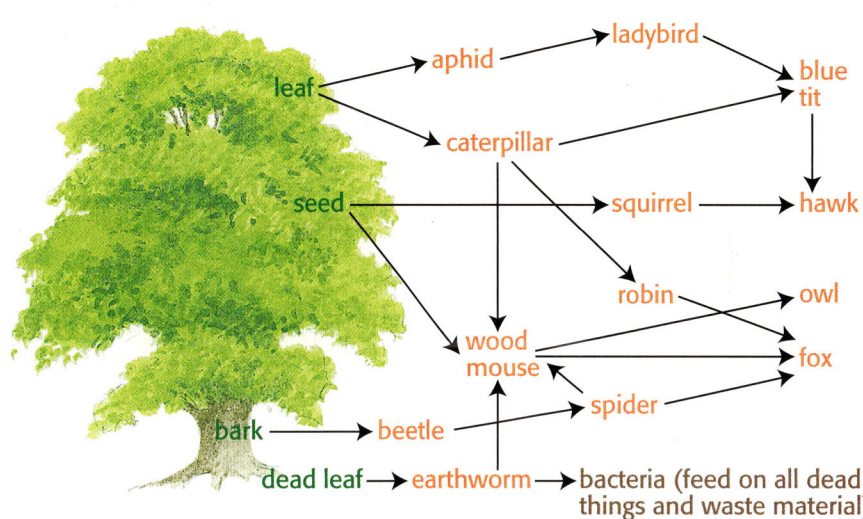

▲ *How living things are linked, in an ecosystem.*

Food chains in an ecosystem

This is a **food chain**. It shows what eats what. The arrow means *eaten by*.

plant ⟶ caterpillar ⟶ wood mouse ⟶ fox

You can draw food chains for any ecosystem. They always start with plants.

Food webs

Often several consumers eat the same food. For example in an oak wood, both caterpillars and aphids (a type of fly) feed on oak leaves.

So food chains link to form a **food web**. This diagram shows just part of the food web for an oak wood.

The complete food web for a wood (or any ecosystem) can be large and complex.

Your turn

1 Is this an ecosystem? Explain your answer.

a an ocean

b a jungle

Moi?

c a goldfish in a bowl

2 Copy and complete, choosing words from page 44. Plants are called _____ because they make their own food, using the gas _____ _____, and water. Animals are called _____ because they obtain food by eating _____ and other _____. Bacteria in the soil are called _____ because they make dead material rot away.

3 a Name a producer found in the school playing field.

b Name a consumer that is also a farm animal.

c Name a decomposer that gets put on pizzas!

4 Look at the food web above. What would suffer if:

a a disease wiped out all the aphids in a wood?

b all the trees in the wood got chopped down?

5 Look again at the food web. If all the foxes were wiped out:

a what might happen to the number of wood mice?

b what else could happen because of the change in **a**?

DOWN WITH FOXES

6 *'All ecosystems depend on the sun'.* Do you agree? Draw a diagram to help you explain your answer.

The Earth's main ecosystems

In this unit you will meet four of the Earth's main ecosystems – and learn *why* they're so different.

The big ones

You can divide the Earth into eight huge ecosystems or **biomes**. Each has its own type of plants or **vegetation**. Here are four of them …

Hot desert

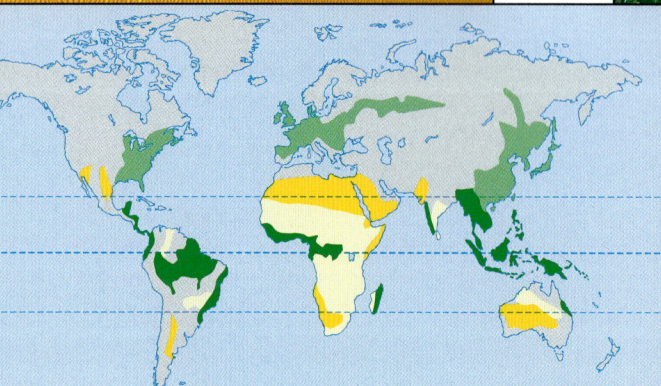

Savanna

Tropical rainforest

Deciduous forest

The UK belongs to the deciduous forest biome. **Deciduous** means the trees lose their leaves in winter. Most trees in the UK are like this.

5000 years ago, most of the UK was covered in great deciduous forests. It would still be like that if no-one lived here. But over the centuries we humans have cut down the forests for wood and fuel, and to make way for farms and villages, towns and cities. So there aren't many forests left.

The woodland on page 42 is the remains of a large forest.

Why are they so different?

The ecosystems on the last page have very different vegetation – mainly because they have very different climates!

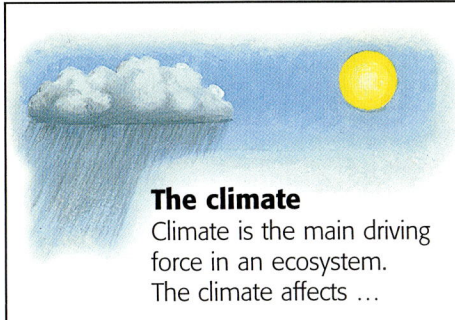

The climate
Climate is the main driving force in an ecosystem. The climate affects …

1 the soil
How thick and rich the soil is depends partly on the climate. Rock weathers fastest into soil in a hot damp climate.

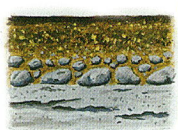

which affects …

2 the vegetation
It has developed or **adapted** to suit the climate and soil. Plants grow fastest and thickest in a hot damp sunny climate.

which affects …

3 the animals
They have adapted to feed on the plants or each other, and to cope with the climate.

Later you'll see how this works for the rainforest and savanna.

Your turn

1 a Make a table with headings like this, for the four ecosystems shown on page 46.

Ecosystem	What is the climate like?	You'll find it in…
hot desert		

b Write their names in the first column – in order of temperature. Start with the one that gets hottest. The climate graphs on the right will help.

c Write these descriptions in the correct places in the second column. (Check the climate graphs.)

> Hot. Quite a lot of rain – but has a dry season with little or no rain.

> Very hot in some months, much cooler in others. Hardly any rain.

> Hot and wet all year. The temperature does not vary much. In some months the rain is really heavy.

> Never gets very hot. Rains quite a bit all through the year.

d In the last column name two countries where you'd find that ecosystem. (Pages 128–129 will help.)

2 Now use the photos on page 46, and your table for question **1**, to help you answer these questions.

a Which ecosystem has least vegetation? Why is this?

b Which has the tallest, thickest vegetation? Why?

c The vegetation in the savanna gets all dried out for part of the year. Why is this?

d Deciduous forests lose their leaves in winter. Why?

e The rainforest stays green all year. Why?

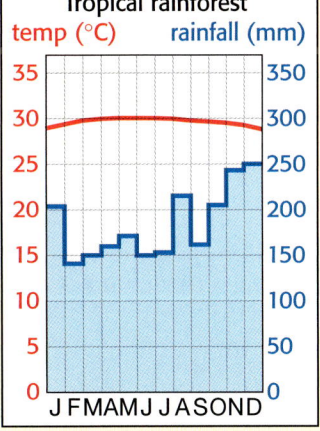

Tropical rainforest

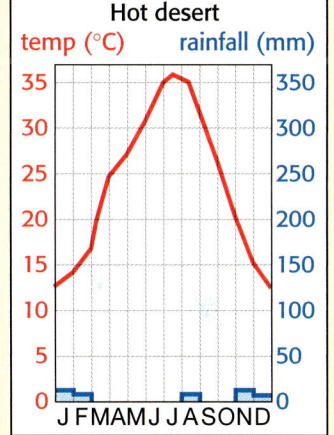

Hot desert

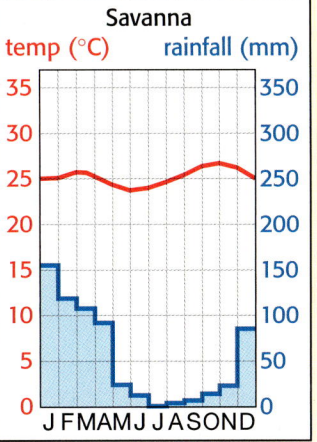

Savanna

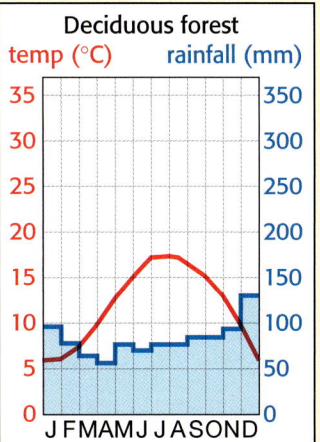

Deciduous forest

Where do humans fit in?

In this unit you'll see where we humans fit, in the Earth's ecosystems – and how we are affecting them.

How humans have spread

We think there have been human-like species (or **hominids**) on the Earth for about 6 million years.

But humans like us first appeared only about 200 000 years ago. (The other hominids died out.)

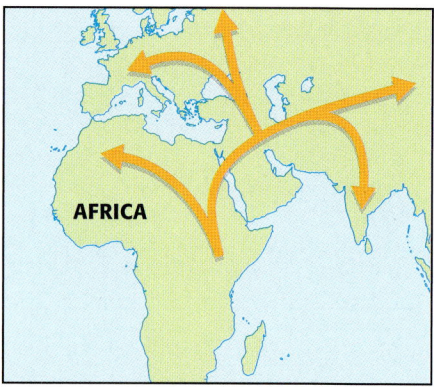

Experts think we evolved in East Africa, and spread across the Earth from there.

At first we lived like the other animals – by hunting, and eating nuts, seeds, berries and insects.

But then we began to settle down to farm our food. We cleared land, grew crops, and herded animals.

And as time went by, the shelters we built turned into villages, and towns, and cities.

So where have we got to?

Unlike most animals, we've got everywhere!

◆ We have invaded every ecosystem. (But some climates don't suit us so well.)

◆ Our numbers have grown fast. Now there are over 6.4 billion of us. There are more of us than of any other many-celled species, except perhaps termites (a type of insect) and krill (like tiny shrimp).

◆ We consume a lot. Over 40% of the plants now growing on the Earth will be consumed by us and our livestock (our hens, cows, sheep …).

◆ We use a lot of land. Not just to live on, but to grow food, and provide water and fuels, and dump waste, and so on. Experts say we each 'use' 2 hectares of land (= 1.5 football pitches) in our lifetime. That's called our **footprint**.

▲ *All this, to make my lunch.*

So is there a problem?

Is there a problem? Yes.

- The more land we use up, the less there is for the Earth's other 6 million species.
- As we spread through ecosystems we take them over, and drive many species to extinction.
- In places we have treated the soil so badly that we've ruined it.
- We burn a lot of fossil fuels, and now we think this is causing global warming. That will affect every ecosystem on the Earth.

It does not have to be this way …

We need food, and fuel, and houses, and water.

But we are learning that we must get them in a **sustainable** way. That means in a way that does not harm us, or other species, and is not wasteful.

The rest of this chapter looks at two ecosystems: tropical rainforests and savanna. You will learn how we have damaged them – and how some damage is being repaired.

▲ Taking over an ecosystem.

Did you know?
- The dodo was a big bird that couldn't fly, and lived on the island of Mauritius.
- It was hunted to extinction by European sailors, in the 17th century.

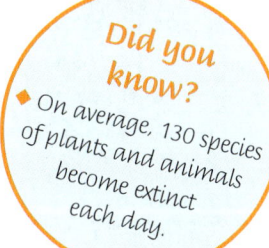
Did you know?
- On average, 130 species of plants and animals become extinct each day.

▲ Happy – but only about 1600 left on the Earth.

Your turn

1 Look at the four ecosystems on page 46. Which one do you think suits humans *least* well? Give reasons.

2 Humans belong to food chains too. Draw the food chains for someone eating a hamburger. The drawing at the bottom of page 48 might help.

3 Your *footprint* on the Earth is about 2 hectares. What does that mean? Explain as if to an 8-year-old.

4 Write down the things that we humans take over land for. You could answer using a spider map, like this.

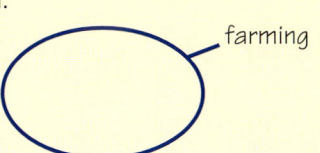 farming

What will you write in the loop?

5 These drawings show one way we kill off birds. But they're all mixed up.

a Redraw them in the correct order. (Keep your drawings very simple.)

b Now write a caption under each drawing to explain what's happening – not more that 10 words each.

6 You belong to a species that is almost extinct, thanks to humans. (For example the Siberian tiger or Chinese panda.) Write a letter of protest to the human race.

The tropical rainforests

Here you'll see how the rainforests grew and adapted to a hot wet climate.

Here we go!

The tropical rainforests are in the tropics, where it's hot and wet all year. So let's see how the vegetation has adapted to the climate.

It's about 140 million years ago. The tropical rainforests are just starting to grow.

Plants grow well in the damp heat – so well that soon they have to fight for sunlight.

One way to win is to grow tall and straight. But that's not the only way. For example …

… thick vines called **lianas** just loop around tree trunks to reach sunlight.

Air plants or **epiphytes** forget about roots, and perch up high on branches.

Species like **ferns** solve the problem by adapting to life in the shade.

On the ground, insects munch. And bacteria work fast, releasing nutrients from all waste material.

The soil is poor. So the plant roots grow close to the surface, to grab these nutrients.

The tallest trees have developed huge **buttress roots** like these, to stop them toppling over.

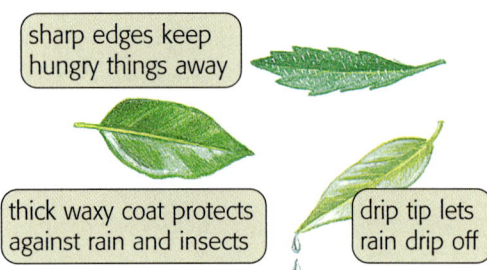

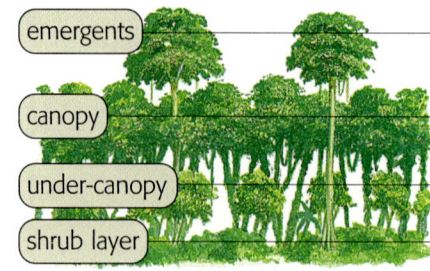

High up, the leaves have also developed ways to protect themselves.

Now, after millions of years of growth, the vegetation in the rainforest forms four layers …

The canopy is the thickest layer. So most of the animals and insects have adapted to living there.

Why the rainforests are our richest ecosystem

For millions of years the rainforests lay undisturbed. Small tribes of humans lived there, but they did no damage. So the plants and animals were able to develop and adapt in peace.

And that's why the rainforests now have *thousands* of different kinds of plants and animals. Look at these two examples:

The tree frog. The pads on its fingers and toes help it to grasp branches. It climbs high in the canopy to get all that nice rain.

The sloth. Its strong claws allow it to hang from branches. Its hair is filled with green algae (tiny plants) to help it hide among the leaves.

Some rainforest trees
mahogany
ebony
palm
rubber
banana

Some rainforest animals
apes
parrots
sloths
jaguars
pythons
alligators

Did you know?
♦ The rainforests cover 6% of the Earth's surface.
♦ But they are home to over half its species.

Your turn

1 A two-storey house is about 6 metres tall.

This table shows the heights of the layers in the rainforest.

Layer	Height (m)
1	35–60
2 canopy	20–30
3	3–5
4	less than 1

a Make a larger copy of this diagram.

b Draw in the four layers on your diagram, at the correct heights, and name them.

c Give your diagram a title.

d The tallest emergent is __ times as tall as the house. What's the missing number?

e Now look back at the photo of the rainforest on page 46. What layers can you see there?

2 Copy and complete these statements.

a Most insects and animals in the rainforest live in the canopy, because …

b Many leaves have drip tips so that …

c Roots grow close to the soil surface so that …

d The emergents have buttress roots so that …

e The plants on the forest floor have dark green leaves all year round so that …

3

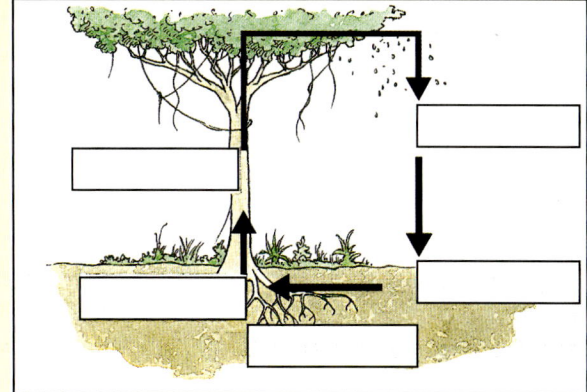

This drawing shows part of rainforest. Make a large copy of it, and add these labels in the correct boxes.

The roots quickly take up the nutrients again.

Decomposers release the nutrients from them.

The nutrients help the vegetation to grow.

Dead leaves and animal waste fall all year round.

The soil down here is poor because the nutrients don't get a chance to sink in.

What are we doing to the rainforests ?

Here you'll find out how we humans are destroying the tropical rainforests.

The destruction of an ecosystem

Today the Earth has only about half as much rainforest as 200 years ago.
Most of the destruction has taken place in the last 50 years.
And it is still happening.

Large areas are being burned, to clear land for farming. Some by poor farmers, to grow food …

… and some by big companies, to set up cattle ranches, or palm oil plantations, to make lots of money.

Logging companies are big culprits. They cut down trees, for wood for things like furniture and doors.

The rainforest is also cleared by companies searching for oil and metals …

… and by governments building roads, or dams, that they hope will help the country.

But once the trees go, the soil suffers. It soon loses any nutrients it had, and the rain erodes it away.

The animals suffer and die away when they lose their tree homes.

The rainforest tribes suffer when they lose the lands they live on.

We help to protect you against global warming, by taking in carbon dioxide.

We have given you many plants that cure diseases - and we may have many more.

If you kill off the millions of species who live here, you destroy the Earth's riches.

And we suffer, because rainforests help us in many different ways.

17 June 1975

10 July 1992

1 August 2000

▲ *Satellite images of the rainforest in Bolivia. Red shows living trees. The wavy blue line is a river. The pale lines are tracks into the forest. The pale patches show where the forest has been cleared.*

Your turn

1 Look at the three images above. They all show the same place.
  a Describe the changes between 1975 and 2000.
  b Who or what will suffer because of these changes? List them, and give your list a heading.
  c Describe the pattern of pale lines and shapes in the image for 2000. See if you can explain the pattern.

2 Much of the rainforest is destroyed by burning.

  a In A, where does the soil get its nutrients?
  b In A, the trees help to protect the soil from erosion. See if you can explain how.
  c The soil in B will soon be useless. Give at least two reasons for this.

3

Draw a strip cartoon like the one started above, to show how a hamburger may be linked to destruction of the rainforest. You can show up to 7 boxes.

4 *'People living far from the rainforest help to destroy it.'* Is that true? Explain your answer.

5 This graph shows how fast the rainforest is being lost.

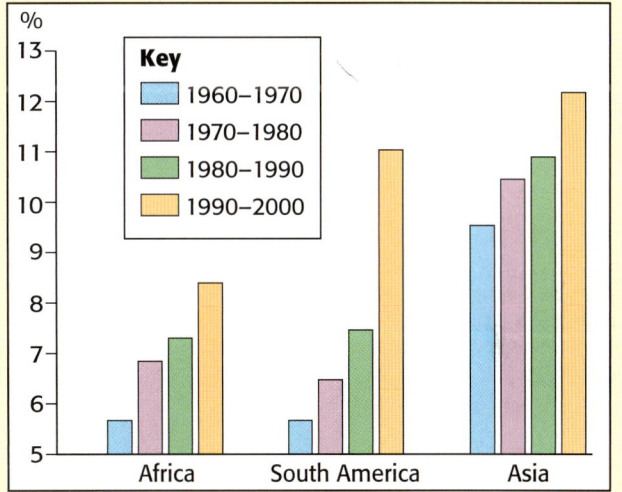

%

Key
- 1960–1970
- 1970–1980
- 1980–1990
- 1990–2000

  a Which continent is losing its rainforest fastest?
  b In which ten-year period was rainforest lost fastest, in South America?
  c Describe the overall trend the graph shows.

6 Rainforests are being destroyed all around the world. Here are three people's opinions.
Write down what you will say to each in reply.

a The rainforests belong to the whole human race, so we must look after them.

b You people in Europe have cut down most of your forests. So why shouldn't we?

c We are a poor country. We need to make as much money from our rainforest as we can.

Living sustainably in the rainforest

In this unit you will see how people are learning to earn a living from the rainforest, without destroying it.

Acre leads the way

Acre is a state in the rainforest in Brazil. About 550 000 people live there. Once it was quite well off. It has lots of rubber trees, and **rubber tappers** collected the **latex**. This was exported to make things like car tyres.

Then cattle ranchers and loggers moved in, and began to cut down the rainforest, including the rubber trees. The rubber tappers were angry and tried to have them stopped. The conflict led to the murder of the tappers' leader, Chico Mendes, by a rancher's son in 1988.

There were other problems too. Synthetic rubber (made from oil) was spoiling the sales of latex. So the people of Acre got poorer and poorer. But they had to eat! So they cut down and burned trees to plant crops. When the soil got worn out, they moved on and cut down more trees.

This type of farming is called **slash-and-burn**.

Today, things are changing. The people of Acre are learning how to use the rainforest **sustainably**. That means in a way that helps them, *and* protects the rainforest.

What the people of Acre are doing

1 Restoring the cleared areas

This is what the farmers do now, where trees have been cleared:

♦ They plant some crops that will grow quickly, to feed their families and to sell. For example corn, banana, and peanut.

♦ In spaces between the crops they plant trees that take longer to grow, but will earn money in a few years. For example apple and guava.

♦ They also plant some slow-growing trees like mahogany and cedar, to replace those that were lost. So in 10 or 20 years the area will begin to look like rainforest again.

▲ Chico Mendes and his child.

▲ A rubber tapper at work. The latex runs from the cuts in the bark.

◄ Planting new trees in the rainforest.

2 Sustainable logging

The government of Acre knows there's no point in banning *all* logging.

◆ So some logging is allowed – but only in certain areas.
◆ The loggers can't cut down all the trees in an area – only some.
◆ They must plant new trees in their place.

3 Using the rainforest in other sustainable ways

People are finding other ways to use the rainforest, without ruining it.

◆ They collect things they can sell, like Brazil nuts, and seeds from valuable trees, and fruits that can be turned into juices.
◆ Rubber tappers now collect latex to make things like bags and sandals.
◆ **Sustainable tourism** is being developed. Tourists visit the rainforest to see plants and animals, without doing them any harm.
◆ Small factories have been set up. For example to process Brazil nuts, and make things from latex, and make furniture.

4 Managing the rainforest

It's hard to check what is going on in a big rainforest. So:

◆ satellite images are being used to map and monitor it.
◆ it has been divided into zones, to make it easier to manage. There are zones for sustainable logging, tourism, farming, and cattle ranching. And for the rainforest tribes of Acre, where they can live in peace.
◆ the **infrastructure** is also being improved. For example tracks are being paved to help farmers move their goods to sell. And some places are getting **solar power**.

Acre is still poor. But now the people are hopeful. By taking care of the rainforest, they know they are taking care of themselves.

▲ A rainforest factory making … ?

▲ A Scarlet Macaw from Acre – a tourist attraction ?

Your turn

1 Find terms on these pages to match the definitions below. Then write out each term with its definition.

A Things like roads, electricity, water supply.
B It is electricity from sunlight.
C You clear land for farming by cutting down trees and burning the undergrowth away.

2 a What and where is Acre? Give your answer as a full sentence.
b How did the farmers of Acre carry out their farming in the past?
c Do you think this was *sustainable*? Explain.

3 Now the farmers are changing the way they farm.
a What kind of things are they doing?
b Do you think these things are sustainable? Explain.
c What do you think the benefits will be? Give them in order, the main one first.

4 Look at these two protestors:

STOP ALL FARMING IN THE RAINFOREST NOW!

PROTECT THE RAINFOREST- MOVE EVERYONE OUT!

Choose one of the protestors. Say whether you agree with the person or not, and give your reasons.

5 a What is *sustainable tourism*?
b Make up a conversation between two Scarlet Macaws about whether it is a good idea to allow tourists into the rainforest.

The savanna

In this unit you'll see how the vegetation, animals and humans have adapted in the savanna ecosystem.

What's the climate like in the savanna ?

You saw earlier that vegetation grows best in warm damp places.

◆ In the savanna it is warm to hot all year (20–35 °C).

◆ Some parts get quite a lot of rain. But others get only a little.

◆ And there is one big problem. Most of the rain falls in just a few months – the **wet season**. There is hardly any rain for the rest of the year. The vegetation and animals (and people) have had to adapt to this.

In the wet season

Africa has the largest area of savanna in the world. The photo below shows the savanna in Kenya, in the wet season. (Look at the map.)

Tropic of Cancer

A F R I C A

Equator

KENYA

savanna

Tropic of Capricorn

The vegetation springs to life in the wet season. It's the **growing season**.

Since there is plenty of space and plenty of vegetation to eat, there are lots of large animals.

In fact there are over 40 species of herbivore, including zebra, gazelles and wildebeest.

There are not so many trees – because trees need a lot of water.

Many have adapted to travelling long distances – to look for grass in the dry season.

The trees that do grow here have adapted to survive drought.

Other animals like lions, hyenas and cheetahs have adapted to feed on them!

Giraffes have developed long necks to feed on acacia leaves.

Bushes have thorns instead of leaves, to prevent water loss and protect them from animals.

The grass grows fast – and up to 3 m tall.

For example the **acacia tree** has small leaves covered with wax, to cut down water loss.

The soil gets soaked in the wet season – and baked in the dry season. So a brick-hard layer forms below the surface.

It has long **tap roots** to reach moisture in the dry season.

The hard layer stops roots pushing down into the soil. (So trees can only grow where there are cracks in it.)

In the dry season

This is savanna in Kenya, in the dry season.

The trees have lost their leaves, to prevent water loss.

The **baobab tree** stored water in its huge trunk in the wet season. That will help it survive now.

The grass has turned brown and died down.

The thick bark of the baobab and acacia help them to withstand fire. (There are many fires in the dry season.)

Scale for baobab tree

3m

0

Nothing left to eat – so the large animals have moved away.

▲ Burning the savanna. The ash makes the soil more fertile for next season.

▲ Wildebeest – strong shoulders and long legs help them travel long distances.

Your turn

1 Name:
   a two producers **b** six consumers
   c two carnivores **d** three herbivores
   that are found in the African savanna. (Glossary?)

2 This sketch shows an acacia tree and a baobab tree. Make a larger copy. Then add labels to show how each has adapted to the climate.

3 Give two ways in which the wild animals have adapted to the savanna ecosystem.

4 In the past, the farmers of the savanna have been **pastoralists**.
   a What are *pastoralists*?
   b Explain how this was a way of adapting to the ecosystem.
   c They often had to walk a long way. Why do you think that was?

5 Today, many farmers in the savanna grow crops as well as herd animals. Explain why:
   a they set fire to the savanna in the dry season
   b they often find it difficult to plough the soil.

6 Now look at the savanna climate graph on page 47.
   a The dry season never has more than 30 mm of rain a month, and usually much less. How long is it?
   b What problems might this cause for crop farmers?
   c What problems might it cause for their families?

How the savanna can get destroyed

In this unit you will see how human activity can destroy the savanna.

Savanna under pressure

In the past, farmers in the savanna have been **pastoralists** – herding cattle, and moving around with them to find grass. But as time went by, and the population grew, people were unable to move so freely (often prevented by the government). So more farmers settled down and grew crops …

Did you know?

◆ All these (and more) can be grown in the savanna: maize, coffee, cotton, peanuts, cocoa, tobacco.

1 A place in the African savanna. Trees, grass, wild animals. Sometimes farmers bring their herds here to graze.

2 Now your tribe starts to settle here.

- ◆ You drive the wild animals away.
- ◆ You chop trees down to build huts, and for firewood.
- ◆ You clear the land to grow crops.
- ◆ When the soil in one patch gets too hard or worn out, you move to another.

3 The population is growing fast. There are farms and cattle everywhere. And soon …

- ◆ there is no new land to move to. So you stay on the same old patch.
- ◆ the soil is getting worn out because the crops are taking all its nutrients.
- ◆ your herd is eating up all the grass, and there's nowhere to go for more.
- ◆ most of the trees are gone. You have to walk miles for firewood.

4 Now …

- ◆ Your soil has lost all its goodness. It is turning to dust.
- ◆ There are no trees or grass to protect it.
- ◆ So it gets blown away by the wind in the dry season, and washed away by the rain in the wet season.

You have a rock-hard patch of ground, and hungry cattle. Your family is starving.

Did you know?

◆ Millions of hectares of savanna have been ruined by human activity.
◆ Millions of people are suffering as a result.

▲ *Eat up all the grass, and the soil gets blown away.*

The problems in the savanna

Look at these photos. In both, soil is being ruined – no good for animals or crops. This is a problem in many parts of the savanna.

Often the rains fail too. So the 'rainy season' is dry. Then drought may kill any crops you do grow. That can mean famine.

But the good news is – it doesn't have to be that way. You can find out more in the next unit.

▲ *Heavy rain on bare worn-out soil caused this big gash or **gully**. They can't grow any crops here now.*

Your turn

1 a Make a large copy of this flowchart:

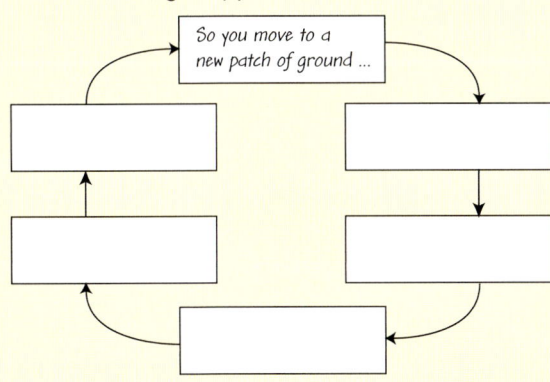

So you move to a new patch of ground ...

b Now write these statements in the correct boxes in your flowchart, to show how savanna can get ruined.

> But your family needs food or it will starve.
>
> ... and burn the scrub and plant more crops.
>
> ... and without any shelter, it dries up and gets blown away.
>
> So your crops grow poorer and poorer.
>
> But over time the soil loses all its nutrients ...

2 Look at the photo on the left above. **Desertification** is taking place here.
   a What do you think *desertification* is?
   b See if you can explain how cattle can help to cause it. (You could draw a straight flowchart.)

3 Look back at page 58.
   a Can you see any signs that these people are trying to adapt to the ecosystem, or protect it?
   b What will happen in this place if the rainy season fails, and there is no rain for a whole year?

4 Suppose the rains fail, in the village on page 58. Will it help if people have:
   a saved up some of the crops they grew last year?
   b managed to store rain water from the last rains?
   c saved up some money?
   Give reasons for your answers.

5 You are the leader of the people on page 58. You are worried about their future. Write a letter to the Prime Minister of that country, asking for help. Try to say exactly what help your people need, and why.

6 Famine is often a problem in savanna regions. Draw a spider map showing the factors that may contribute to this. Think of as many as you can.

The Machakos miracle

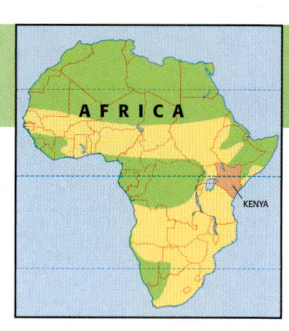

Here you will learn how farmland in the savanna was rescued from ruin.

From despair to hope

These photos show a place called Machakos in the savanna in Kenya.

In 1937

Here the soil is worn out and eroded. A soil inspector wrote: *The land is turning into a desert of rocks, stones and sand. And the people are drifting into hopeless poverty*.

In 1987

50 years later – and the soil is in far better shape. There is no sign of erosion. Now there are more trees, more crops – and more people! They call it the Machakos miracle.

The next page shows how the people of Machakos rescued their land.

Your turn

1

How the population of Machakos grew		
Year	1930	1987
Population	240 000	1 320 000

  a How many times larger was the population in 1987 than in 1930?

  b A rise in population *could* make soil worse. Explain.

2 List all the steps the Machakos farmers took, to:
  a prevent soil erosion **b** improve soil quality
  c conserve trees.

3 Look at the bar chart on the right. *Output* means the amount produced. (For example of maize.)
  a About how many times larger was the total output in 1987 than in 1930?
  b Output fell in 1961. Suggest a reason.
  c Give one cash crop grown in Machakos. (Glossary?)
  d What happened to the output of cash crops between 1961 and 1987? Give a reason.
  e Which output:
    i didn't change much over the years? Suggest why.
    ii grew fastest, between 1977 and 1987?

4 Now, time to evaluate. Write a short report saying:
  a what you think are the *three* key things the Machakos farmers did, to adapt to the ecosystem.
  b whether they were successful. (Give evidence!)

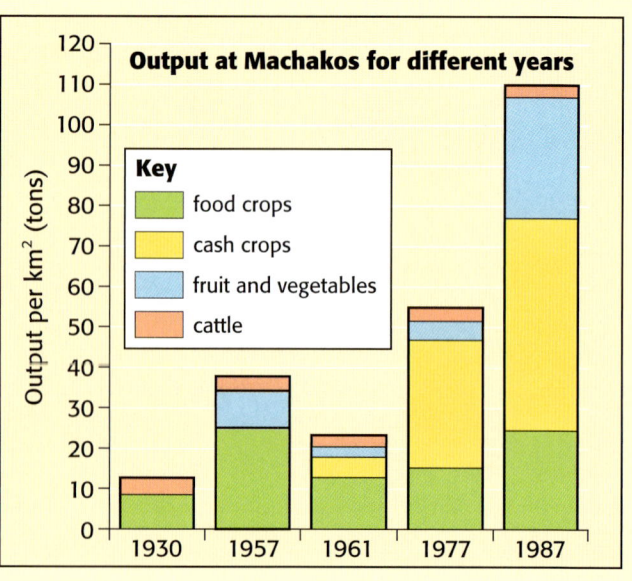

Output at Machakos for different years

Output per km² (tons)

Key
- food crops
- cash crops
- fruit and vegetables
- cattle

1930   1957   1961   1977   1987

Learning to live sustainably in Machakos

The people of Machakos are not rich. They have no electricity. They don't have enough wells. The rains are not dependable. But they have learned to live **sustainably** in the savanna, and turn disaster into success. Here's how:

The big picture

This chapter is about the Earth's population and resources.
These are the big ideas behind the chapter:

◆ The Earth's population is growing fast.

◆ It is not spread evenly around the Earth. Some places are very crowded, and some are quite empty.

◆ Resources are not shared equally among countries or people.

◆ Many of the world's problems are about resources – about not having enough of them, or misusing them, or using them unfairly!

Did you know?
◆ About 13 out of every 100 people in the world don't have enough food.
◆ Many of these are children.

Your goals for this chapter

By the end of this chapter you should be able to answer these questions:

◆ Why has the Earth's population risen so fast?

◆ What do these terms mean?

birth rate   death rate   natural increase

◆ What kinds of things affect a country's birth and death rates?

◆ Which are the most crowded parts of the world, and which are the most empty?

◆ In what ways (if any) is population distribution linked to climate?

◆ What do these terms mean, and what examples can I give?

resource   natural resource

◆ Which areas of the world have the highest % of undernourished people? And what are some of the reasons?

Did you know?
◆ Of all the countries in the world, Belgium depends the most on imported food.

And then …

When you finish this chapter you can come back to this page and see if you have met your goals!

Did you know?
◆ The world's population is expected to reach 8 billion by the year 2025.
◆ It was 6 billion in 2000.

Your chapter starter

This photo shows Jintana and her younger brother. She's cooking dinner.

What five things do you notice about her kitchen?

In what ways is it like your kitchen? In what ways is it different?

Do you think most kitchens around the world are like yours, or like Jintana's?

Is there any more?

People everywhere

Here you'll discover how quickly our numbers are rising – and explore why.

Here we go !

200 000 years ago   2000 years ago   200 years ago   Today

> **Did you know?**
> ◆ Three out of every ten people on the Earth in 2002 were under the age of 15.

How does the population rise so fast?

As you can see above, the number of humans on the Earth is rising fast. This shows what happened in one family …

> **Did you know?**
> ◆ The Earth's population is growing by about 9000 people an hour.

1750

Bo and Ella fell in love. They got married and had **4** children.

1780

All 4 of these had children of their own. **18** altogether.

1820

16 of the 18 in turn had children of their own – **76** altogether.

So Bo and Ella's family just kept on growing.
It has been like this all over the world, for centuries.
So it's easy to see how the population has risen so fast.

Birth rate and death rate

Every year, millions of humans die. But the population still keeps rising !

1000 people live in country X. If 20 babies are born there this year, the birth rate is 20 births per 1000.

If 3 people die there this year, then the **death rate** is 3 deaths per 1000. So this means …

… there's a **natural increase** in the population this year of 17 people per thousand, or 1.7%.

Your turn

1 What does *population* mean?

2

How the human race has grown	
Year	**Population (billions)**
10 000 BC	0.004 (which is 4 million)
5000 BC	0.005 (or 5 million)
1000 BC	0.05 (or 50 million)
1 AD	0.2 (or 200 million)
1000	0.3 (or 300 million)
1600	0.5 (or 500 million)
1800	1.0 (or 1000 million)
2000	6.0 (or 6000 million)

A graph for this table is started below.

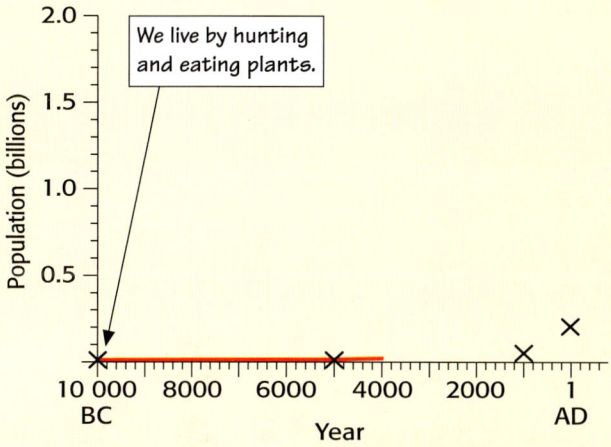

We live by hunting and eating plants.

a Each tiny division on the lower axis represents:
   i 50 years? **ii** 100 years? **iii** 200 years?
b Make a *large* copy of the axes started above.
   Continue the lower axis to **2400 AD**.
   Continue the side axis up to **8 billion**.
   (Use a full page, or even two joined together.)
c Plot the eight points from the table, and add a title.

3 Now add these notes to your graph. The first one has been written on the graph above, as an example.

At this year ...	write this ...
10 000 BC	We live by hunting and eating plants.
9000 BC	The first farms appear.
7500 BC	The first towns appear.
4500 BC	The wheel is invented.
3000 BC	The first cities appear, and the first writing.
1000 BC	The Iron Age starts. (We begin using iron for tools and weapons.)
43 AD	The Romans invade Britain.
400 AD	The Romans leave Britain.
1750 AD	The Industrial Revolution starts. (We begin using engines, and build lots of factories.)
?	I was born.

4 Look at your graph.
   a Write a sentence to describe its shape.
   b If the Earth's population keeps growing like this, about what will it be in the year 2200?

5 These helped the Earth's population to grow faster. See if you can explain why.

A the discovery of iron

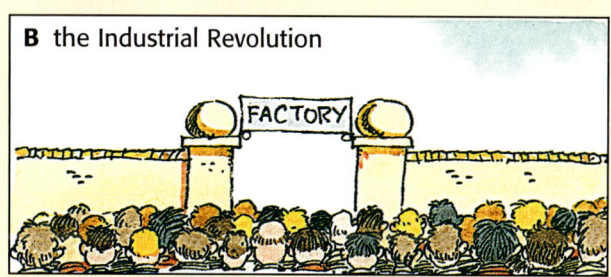

B the Industrial Revolution

6

The island of Timu, 2000	
Population at the start of the year	2000
Number of births during the year	60
Number of deaths during the year	40

Using the data in this table, work out:
a the birth rate for Timu that year
b the death rate for Timu that year
c its population at 31 December 2000
d the natural increase that year (as a %).

7 Look at these two lists:

1 Changes in a country
a Everyone gets better food to eat.
b A terrible war breaks out.
c A deadly disease spreads.
d There is a severe famine.
e More hospitals and doctors are provided.
f Birth control pills are provided.
g More and more women get good jobs.

2 Possible results
A Death rate rises.
B Death rate falls.
C Birth rate rises.
D Birth rate falls.
E No effect on birth or death rates.

For each change in list **1** choose the likely result(s) from list **2**. (You can choose more than one result.)
Write your answer as a complete sentence, like this:
If everyone gets better food to eat, then ... .

So where is everyone?

> **Did you know?**
> ◆ Around 60% of the world's poplulation lives in Asia.

In this unit you'll see how we are spread unevenly around the world – and explore some reasons.

From empty to crowded

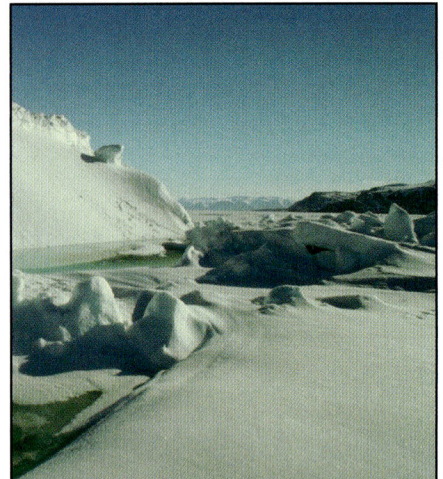

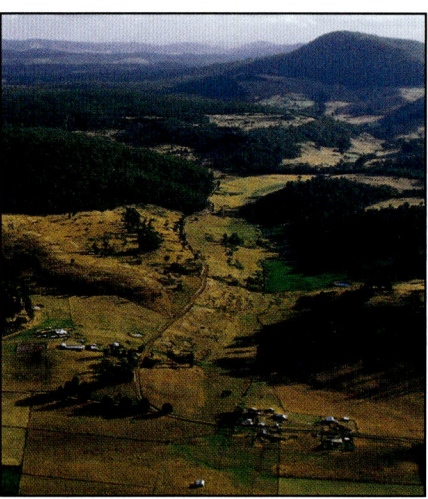

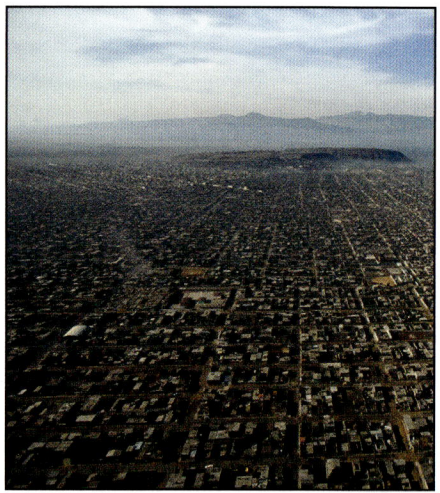

Some places, like Antarctica, are empty. Far too cold to settle here!

Some parts are lightly populated. For example much of Australia.

Some parts are very crowded. Like Mexico City.

The world's population distribution

The map below shows how we are spread or **distributed** around the world. There are many reasons why we are spread like this. The map in **Your turn** will give you some clues.

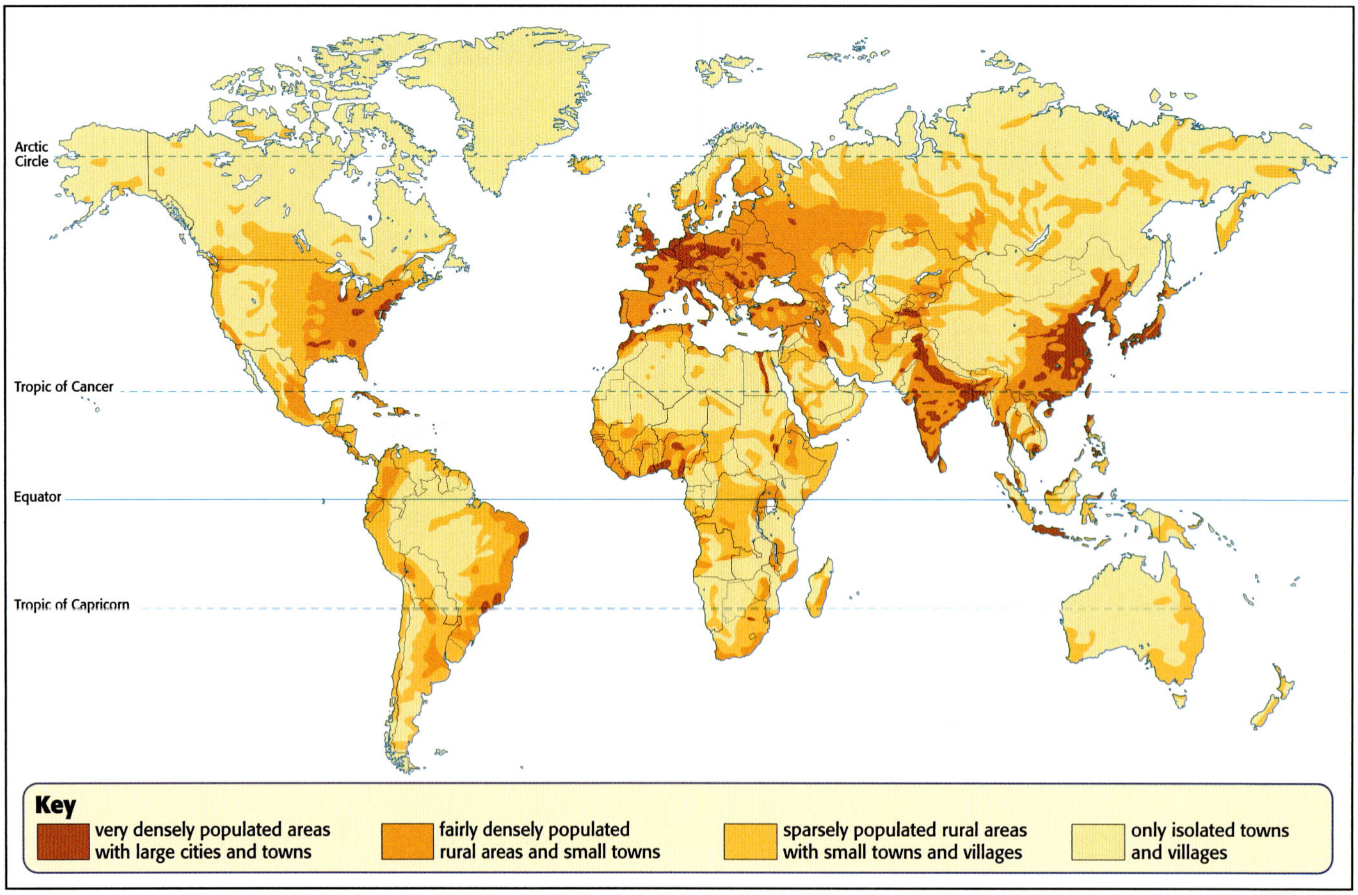
Arctic Circle
Tropic of Cancer
Equator
Tropic of Capricorn
Key
very densely populated areas with large cities and towns
fairly densely populated rural areas and small towns
sparsely populated rural areas with small towns and villages
only isolated towns and villages

Your turn

The world map on pages 128–129 will help with these.

1 Look at the key for the map on page 66.
What does this term mean?
a sparsely populated   **b** isolated
(Try to answer without looking in the glossary.)

2 Name two countries that are:
a very crowded, overall   **b** very lightly populated

3 In general, where do more people tend to live?
a in the middle of continents
b on or near the coast
See if you can come up with a reason for this.

4 Climate affects all living things. It is one reason why some regions are less crowded than others.
a What's the climate like, at A on the map below?
b This shows what crops need:

① some **warmth** to help them grow and ripen
② some **sunlight** so the leaves can make food
④ **soil** for minerals
③ **water** which the roots take in

Will crops grow well at A? Give reasons.
c Is the population density at A high, or low?
Give as many reasons as you can to explain why.

5

Place	Country	Climate	Population density	Reasons
B				

Make a table like the one started above, but much larger. Leave room to write quite a lot in the last column.
a Write the letters B, C, D and E from the map below, in the first column.
b Name the countries they're in, in the second.
c Describe the climate at each place in the third column. (Use the key, and what you know already.)
d In the fourth column describe the population density at each place, using one of these phrases:
very high   fairly high   fairly low   very low
e In the last column give as many reasons as you can to explain why the population density is like this.

Key

Hot tropical rainy climates
- rain all year
- monsoon
- dry in winter

Very dry climates
- no reliable rain
- a little rain

Cold polar climates
- no warm season and fairly dry

Warm summers, mild winters
- dry in summer (Mediterranean climate)
- dry in winter
- no dry season

Cool climates
- rain all year
- dry in winter

Mountain climates
- the higher you go, the colder it gets

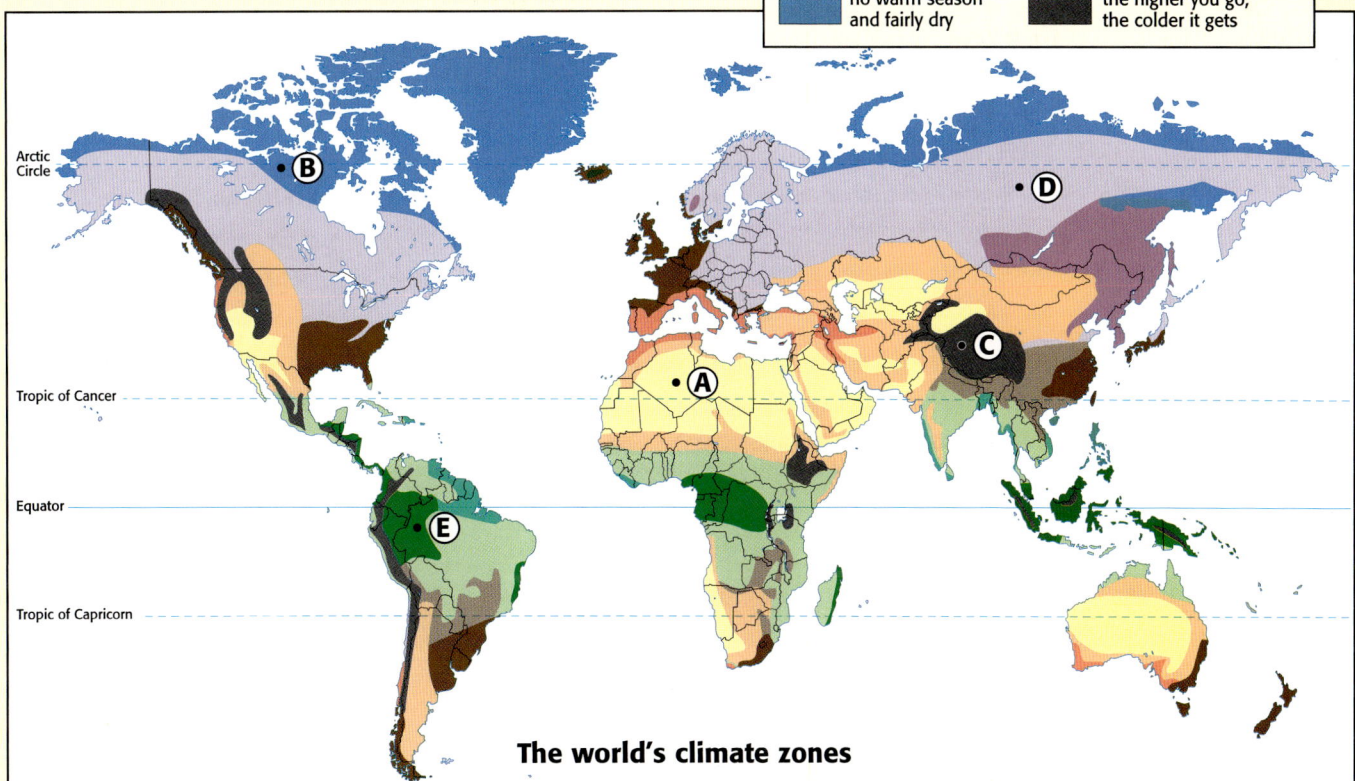

The world's climate zones

People and resources

In this unit you will learn what resources are – and how they are not shared equally around the world.

What are resources?

Resources are things you need to live, or can use to earn a living. For example food, and a fuel to cook with, and paper to write on.

A **natural resource** is one that occurs naturally in or on the Earth, that we can make use of.

Rivers are a natural resource. They provide water for drinking, and for watering crops. We even dam them to make electricity.

Soil is another natural resource. We use it to grow crops for food. We would find it really hard to live without soil.

Coal, oil, gas, metal ores – all these are natural resources. We can use them ourselves – and sell them to earn money!

Are resources shared out equally ?

As you saw in the last unit, people are not spread equally around the world. And neither are resources.

For example many people around the world consume more food than they need. Others spend their whole lives hungry. Some countries are rich in oil and gas, to use as fuels. Others have little or none of these, so have to do without, or buy them.

The problem with resources

Most of the big problems facing the world are about resources – about having too little, or misusing them, or using them unfairly. For example:

Did you know?
◆ Tonight about 100 million people will sleep outside – they have no homes or shelter.

Did you know?
◆ It is likely that there will be wars in the future, over water!

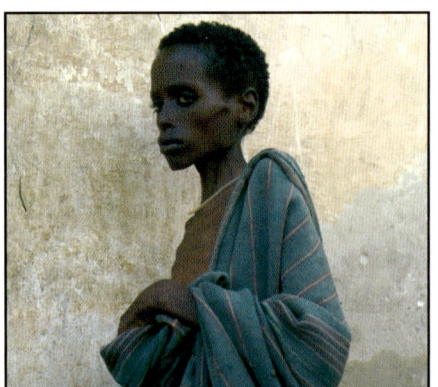

Food is something we all need. You must have a certain amount to live a normal healthy life. But some people never get enough, ever.

In some rich countries, farmers get big grants to grow crops such as sugar, that it would make more sense to buy from poorer countries.

In many poor countries, farmers get paid less and less for the crops they export to richer countries. So the farmers grow poorer and poorer.

Food – a scarce resource?

At present the world grows more food than it needs. But this does not mean that everyone gets enough to eat.

Over 820 million people around the world are **undernourished**. They do not get enough food for a normal healthy life.

This map shows the % of people who are undernourished in different countries.

Did you know?
◆ Every 3.6 seconds someone dies of hunger.

Did you know?
◆ Over 200 million children go to bed hungry, night after night.

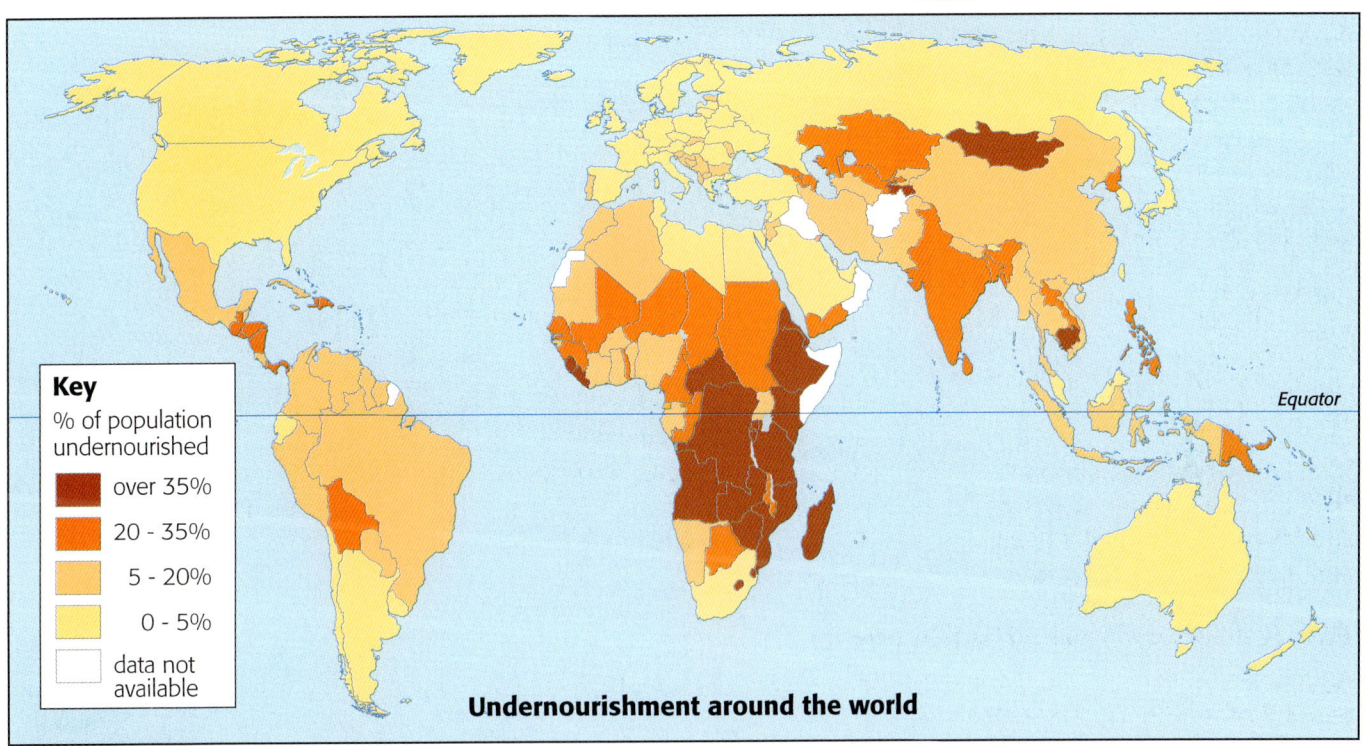

Key
% of population undernourished
- over 35%
- 20 - 35%
- 5 - 20%
- 0 - 5%
- data not available

Equator

Undernourishment around the world

Your turn

1 a First, make a table with headings like this:

I think it's a resource	Because ...

b Now go through the list below. If you think an item is a resource, write it in the first column of your table. In the second column, give your reason.
the sea   cattle   sunshine   rainfall
a computer   trees   knowledge   gold
money   rainforest   iron ore   electricity
the wind   limestone   a field of wheat   a factory

c Underline the things in your list that are *natural* resources. Add a key to explain the underlining.

2 There are some resources that we'd die without. Write a list of resources that you think are essential for life.

3 Now look at the map above.
a Name four countries where over 35 out of every 100 people are undernourished.
b Which continent has the largest number of countries with over 35% undernourished?

4 The UK is in the group of countries with 0 – 5% undernourished. Do you think the exact value for the UK is closer to 0%, or to 5%? Explain your answer.

5 *'The more crowded a country is, the higher the % of undernourished people'.* Is this true or false?
Use the map on page 66 to help you decide.
Give three examples to support your answer.

6 Now, a challenge. Think of as many reasons as you can why so many people in some countries are undernourished. Give your answers as full sentences.
At least *some* of these terms might help you.
money   drought   worn-out soil   education
move to cities   wars   population growth   roads
diseases such as AIDS   fertilisers   food factories

7 In 2000, world leaders met in New York to discuss world hunger. They promised to reduce the number of undernourished people by 400 million, by 2015.
You are a world leader. Write a plan of action to help the world meet this goal.

The big picture

As you saw on page 68, **resources** are things we need to live, or can use to earn a living. This chapter looks at one resource: energy. These are the big ideas behind the chapter:

◆ We use energy to cook, and heat and light our homes, and drive machinery and so on.

◆ The fossil fuels are stores of energy. We burn them to release it.

◆ We use a lot of energy in one convenient form: electricity. We use the fossil fuels to make this.

◆ But fossil fuels pollute the atmosphere, and speed up global warming – and they'll run out one day.

◆ So we need to switch to cleaner sources of energy, for making electricity.

Your goals for this chapter

By the end of this chapter you should be able to answer these questions:

◆ What do these terms mean, and what can I give as examples?

fossil fuel   a renewable source of energy

a non-renewable source of energy

◆ Why do we like electricity so much, as a form of energy?

◆ How is electricity made?

◆ Why are fossil fuels so important – and why is oil the most important?

◆ How can having a resource, such as oil, change a country?

◆ In what ways do the fossil fuels damage the environment?

◆ What is global warming, and how is it affecting our Earth?

◆ What's likely to be the main renewable source of energy in the coming years, in the UK? And how can we use it to make electricity?

And then …

When you finish this chapter you can come back to this page and see if you have met your goals!

Did you know?
◆ *Energy can take many different forms.*
◆ *Heat, light, sound, movement, electricity – they're all forms of energy.*

Did you know?
◆ *Around 2 billion people in the world (or 1 in 3 of us) don't have electricity.*
◆ *They depend on firewood, kerosene, or animal dung, for cooking, heating and lighting.*

Did you know?
◆ *Many young people in poorer countries spend long hours every day searching for firewood.*

Your chapter starter

Look at the photo on page 70.

What is that structure?

Why did they put it there?

Has it anything to do with you?

Don't run out on me.

Fuels – just a store of energy

In this unit you'll learn that fuels are a store of energy – and see how we release and use this energy.

Where we get our energy

Energy is a key resource. We need it for cooking, and lighting and warming our homes, and driving machinery. We get most of it from fuels that have stored it up from the sun. Like this:

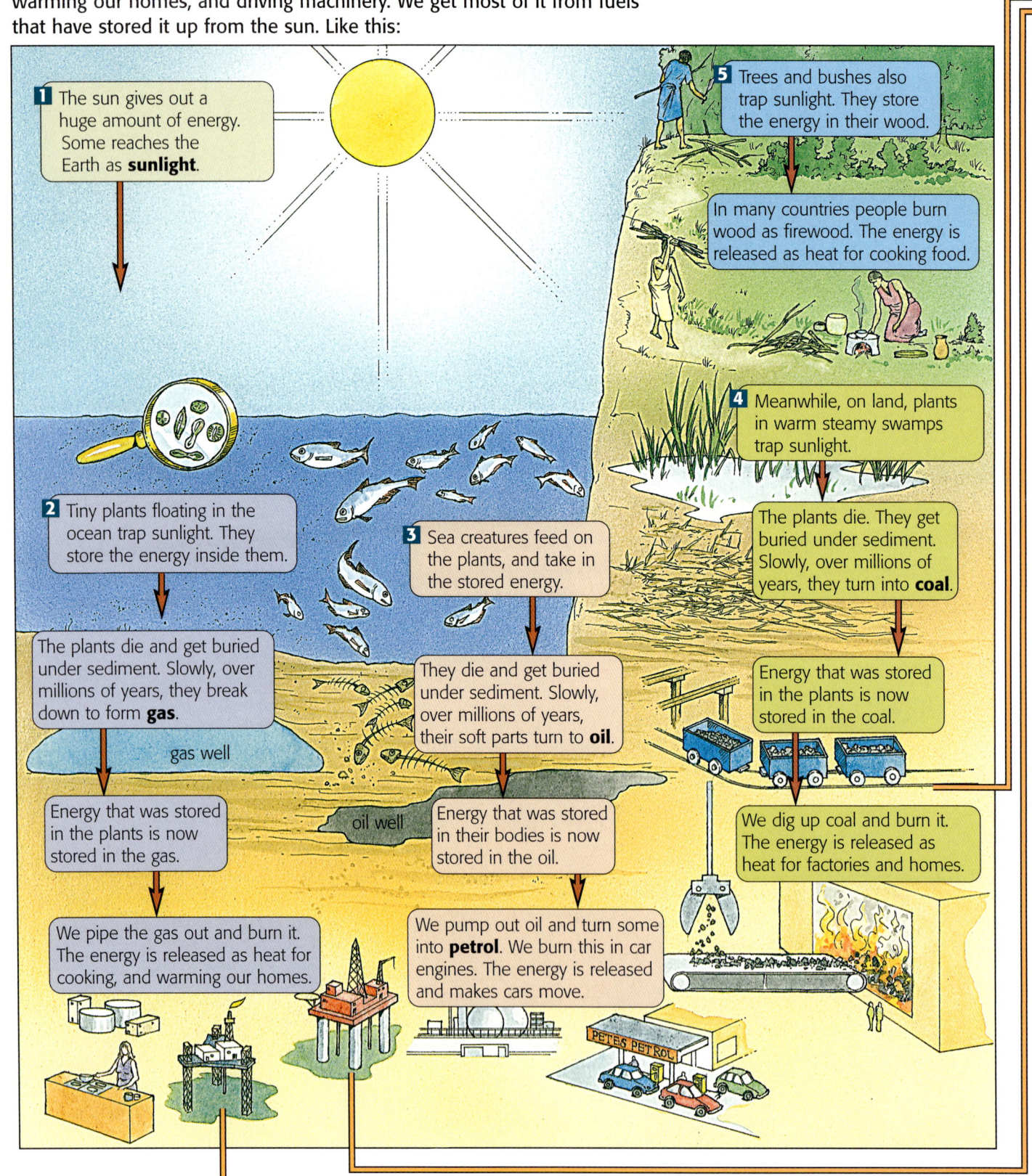

1 The sun gives out a huge amount of energy. Some reaches the Earth as **sunlight**.

2 Tiny plants floating in the ocean trap sunlight. They store the energy inside them.

The plants die and get buried under sediment. Slowly, over millions of years, they break down to form **gas**.

gas well

Energy that was stored in the plants is now stored in the gas.

We pipe the gas out and burn it. The energy is released as heat for cooking, and warming our homes.

3 Sea creatures feed on the plants, and take in the stored energy.

They die and get buried under sediment. Slowly, over millions of years, their soft parts turn to **oil**.

oil well

Energy that was stored in their bodies is now stored in the oil.

We pump out oil and turn some into **petrol**. We burn this in car engines. The energy is released and makes cars move.

5 Trees and bushes also trap sunlight. They store the energy in their wood.

In many countries people burn wood as firewood. The energy is released as heat for cooking food.

4 Meanwhile, on land, plants in warm steamy swamps trap sunlight.

The plants die. They get buried under sediment. Slowly, over millions of years, they turn into **coal**.

Energy that was stored in the plants is now stored in the coal.

We dig up coal and burn it. The energy is released as heat for factories and homes.

PETE'S PETROL

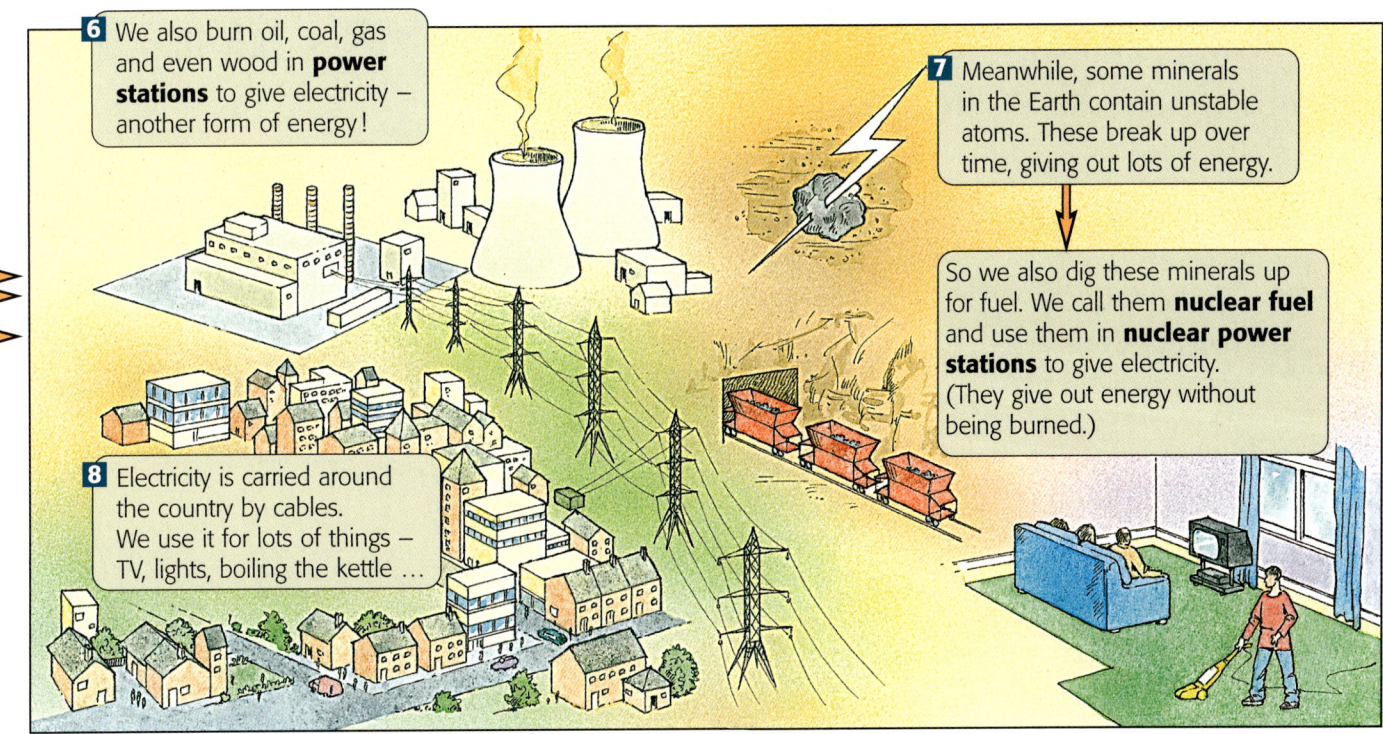

6 We also burn oil, coal, gas and even wood in **power stations** to give electricity – another form of energy!

7 Meanwhile, some minerals in the Earth contain unstable atoms. These break up over time, giving out lots of energy.

So we also dig these minerals up for fuel. We call them **nuclear fuel** and use them in **nuclear power stations** to give electricity. (They give out energy without being burned.)

8 Electricity is carried around the country by cables. We use it for lots of things – TV, lights, boiling the kettle …

Running out of fuel?

Somewhere on the Earth, coal, oil and gas are still forming. But we are using them up millions of times faster than they can form. We will run out of them one day. So we call them **non-renewable**.

It's the same with nuclear fuels. The Earth contains only a certain amount of them. Once we have dug them all up – that's it, folks!

But wood is different. We can keep growing new trees. So wood is a **renewable** resource.

When will we run out? This is what some experts think:	
At our present rate of use we could run out of …	in about …
oil	40 years
gas	60 years
coal	250 years

Your turn

1 A fuel is a store of energy.
  a Name five fuels.
  b What do we usually have to do to a fuel, to release its energy?

2 When you travel to school by bus or car, you really travel by the sun's energy. Draw a strip cartoon to explain why. You could start like this …

tiny sea plants

3 The energy stored in fuels can be changed into electricity. Give six examples of how electricity is used in your home.

4 Now make a larger copy of this table. In each box write a ✓ for yes, or a ✗ for no. One has been ticked for you. (You may need to use the glossary.)

Some different fuels				
	Stores energy from the sun	A fossil fuel	Used to generate electricity	A renewable resource
Gas	✓			
Oil				
Coal				
Wood				
Nuclear fuel				

5 Is our use of fossil fuels sustainable? Explain your answer.

Electricity: energy made easy

In this unit you will see how electricity is made, and brought to your home.

How electricity is made

There's one form of energy we use a lot: electricity! So how is it made?

In 1831, Michael Faraday made a discovery: move a magnet inside a coil of wire, and you get an electric current! And that's what we still do today.

In a power station they **generate** electricity by spinning a big magnet called an **electromagnet** inside a wire coil. They use steam to make the magnet spin, and **fuel** to make the steam.

▲ The electric Mr Faraday.

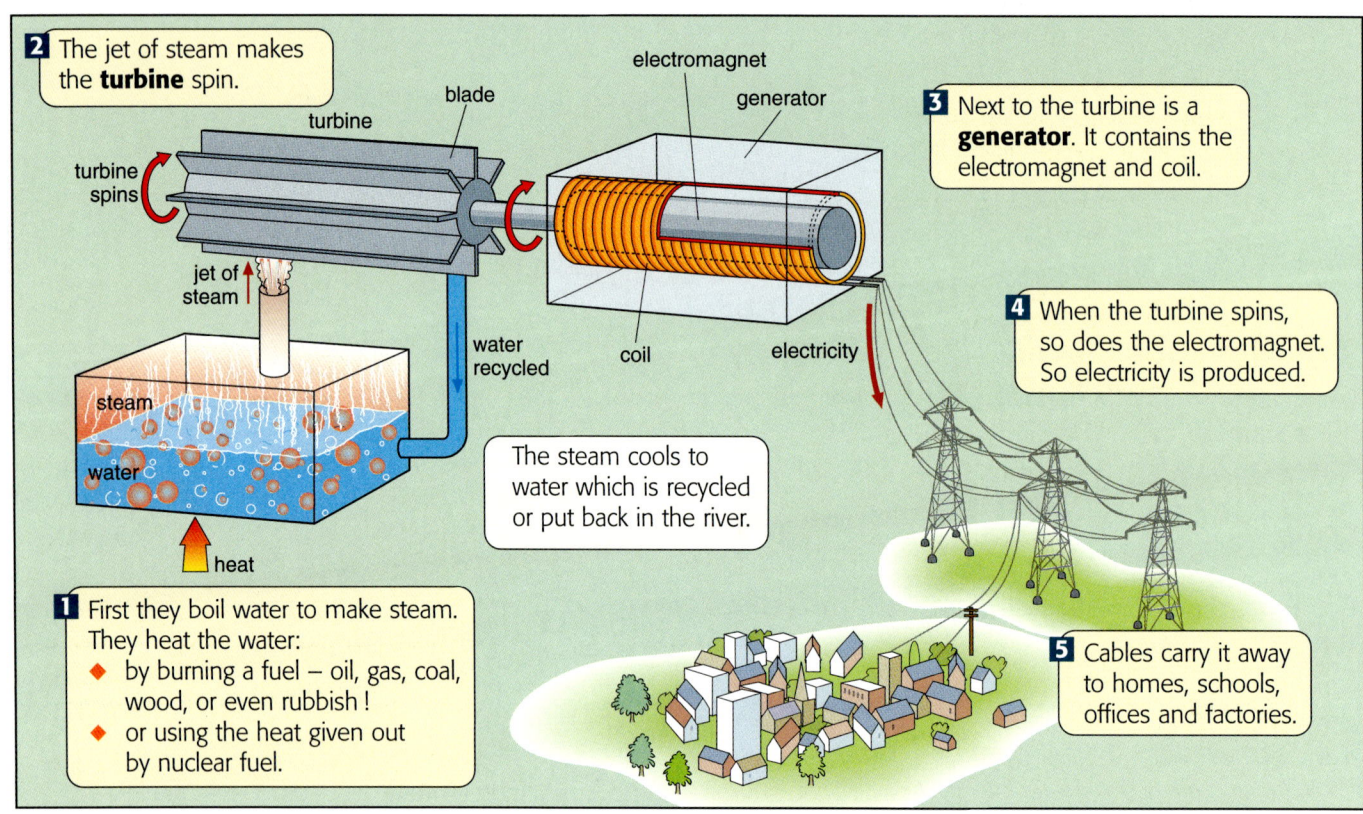

2 The jet of steam makes the **turbine** spin.

turbine spins

turbine

blade

jet of steam

steam

water

heat

electromagnet

generator

water recycled

coil

electricity

3 Next to the turbine is a **generator**. It contains the electromagnet and coil.

The steam cools to water which is recycled or put back in the river.

4 When the turbine spins, so does the electromagnet. So electricity is produced.

1 First they boil water to make steam. They heat the water:
◆ by burning a fuel – oil, gas, coal, wood, or even rubbish!
◆ or using the heat given out by nuclear fuel.

5 Cables carry it away to homes, schools, offices and factories.

It doesn't have to be steam!

The key to making electricity is to spin that turbine – in any way you can! So you could use a river, or the wind, or the sea …

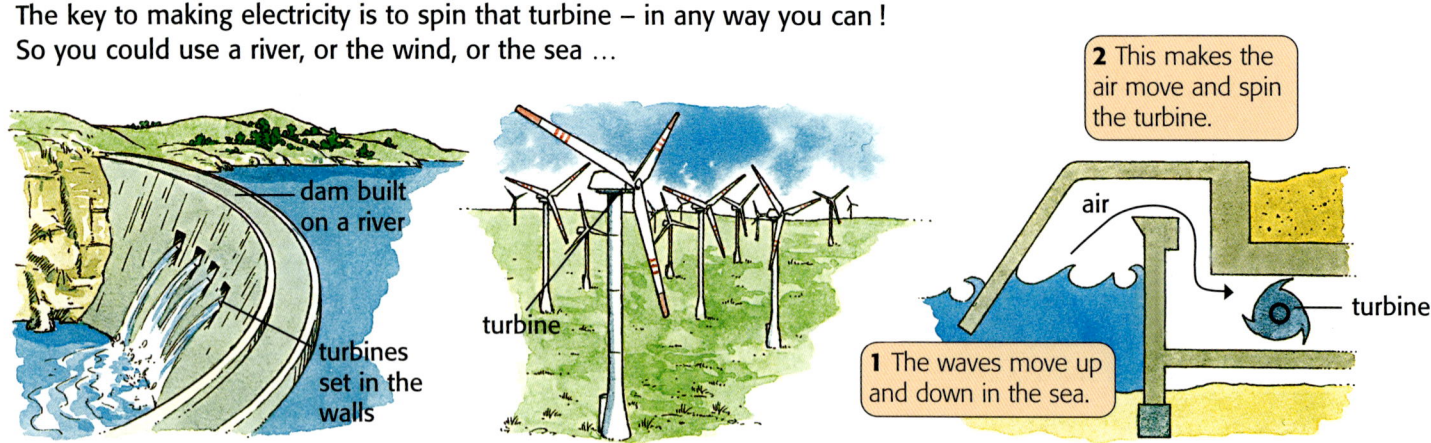

dam built on a river

turbines set in the walls

turbine

2 This makes the air move and spin the turbine.

air

turbine

1 The waves move up and down in the sea.

In a **hydroelectric** station, fast-flowing **water** spins the turbines.

On a **windfarm** the wind spins them. The more wind the better!

In the sea, **waves** and the **tide** can be used to make a turbine spin.

From power station to you

Look at this map. It shows where electricity is generated in Great Britain.

The electricity is fed into a network of cables called the **National Grid**, and carried to your home, and all around the UK.

We use more electricity at certain times of day. For example more at breakfast time than at 4 am, when most people are sleeping. But it can't be stored. So each day:

◆ The National Grid company has to estimate how much electricity we will use for each half-hour of the *next* day.

◆ Then it plans with the power stations how much to generate each half-hour.

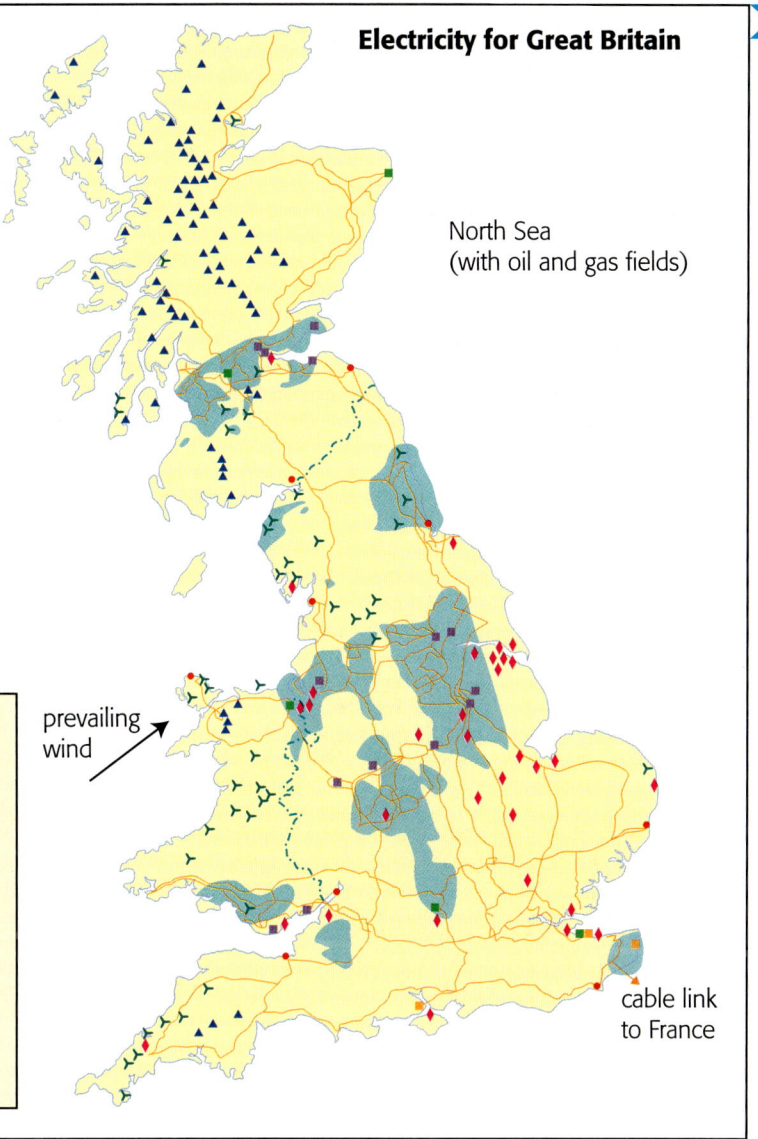

Electricity for Great Britain

North Sea
(with oil and gas fields)

prevailing wind

cable link to France

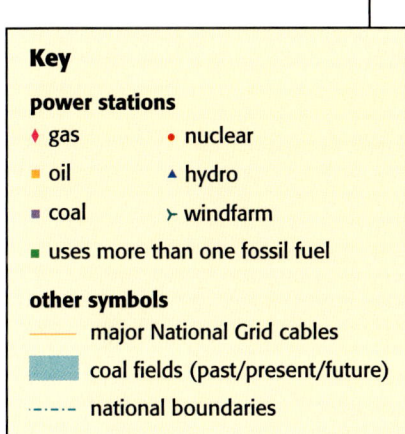

Key

power stations
◆ gas   • nuclear
■ oil   ▲ hydro
■ coal   ⊱ windfarm
■ uses more than one fossil fuel

other symbols
— major National Grid cables
▨ coal fields (past/present/future)
–·–·– national boundaries

Your turn

1 Draw a flow chart to show how electricity is generated in a power station, using gas as a fuel.

2 Most power stations are at the coast or beside rivers. Why do you think this is?

3 a List *all* the energy sources from page 74 that can be used to generate electricity.
   b Now underline the ones that are *renewable*.

4 Look at the map above. (And at page 127.)
   a Where are most of the coal-burning power stations? Suggest a reason.
   b Where are most windfarms? Why?
   c Where are most hydroelectric stations? Why?
   d Nuclear power stations are usually built in remote areas, away from towns. Why do you think that is?

5 We spend billions turning other fuels into electricity.
   a Why do we like electricity so much?
   b What advantages does it have over: **i** oil? **ii** gas?

6 Look at this pie chart for 2003.

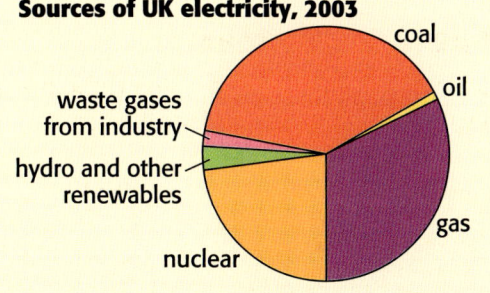

Sources of UK electricity, 2003

coal

oil

gas

nuclear

hydro and other renewables

waste gases from industry

About how much of our electricity came from:
a nuclear fuel?   **b** oil?   **c** coal?
d fossil fuels?   **e** hydro and other renewables?
Choose your answers from this list:
over two thirds   just under a quarter   one thirtieth
a bit more than one third   one sixtieth

7 The UK imports some electricity. Suggest a reason, and say where we import it from, and how. (Map!)

How the world depends on the fossil fuels

In this unit you will learn about how we depend on fossil fuels, and where they are found.

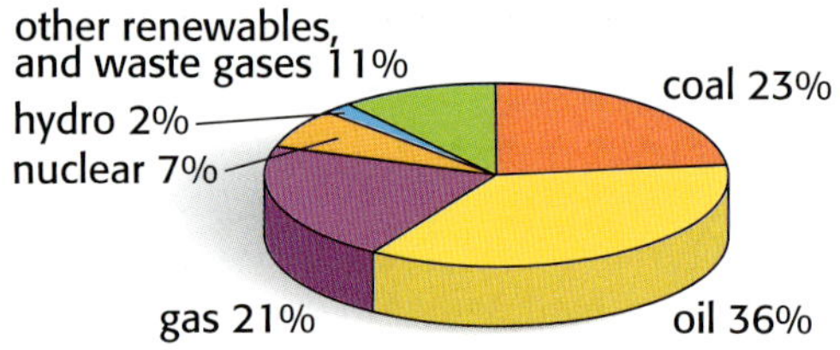

Fuelling the world

The fossil fuels – coal, oil and gas – are the world's main fuels, as this pie chart shows. Oil is number one.
And here are some reasons why they are so important …

Where the world got its energy in 2001

other renewables, and waste gases 11%
hydro 2%
nuclear 7%
coal 23%
gas 21%
oil 36%

1 Fossil fuels are used to make most of the world's electricity. Imagine life without electricity!

2 Coke (a form of coal) is used to make steel from iron ore. And we can't do without steel – for cars, buses, buildings, bridges …

3 Fossil fuels are used to heat furnaces for making cement and brick and glass. Without these – what would you live in?

4 At home, we use fossil fuels for cooking and heating.

5 Oil is turned into petrol and diesel, to run our transport. Imagine life without cars or buses or trucks.

6 Oil is also the starting point for plastics, medical drugs, shampoo, makeup, and hundreds of other things we take for granted.

Developing with fossil fuels

Some countries are more **developed** than others. That means they have better schools, hospitals, houses, roads, bridges, phone systems and so on. As you saw above, all these need fossil fuels to build or run them.

The photo above shows Los Angeles in the USA. The USA is one of the world's most developed countries – and it uses the most fossil fuels.

So who has fossil fuels?

Like most resources, fossil fuels are not shared equally around the world. The map on the next page shows the world's main deposits.

Countries without enough (or any) fossil fuels have to buy or **import** them from other countries. Or else do without.

Many poor countries can't afford to import much fossil fuel. So people in the rural areas depend on **firewood** for fuel. They may have to walk miles every day to find it.

▲ *Bringing home the fuel.*

The world's known deposits of fossil fuels

This map shows the world's main deposits of fossil fuels.

◆ The UK has oil and gas in the North Sea and plenty of coal on land. (But we also import coal and oil.)

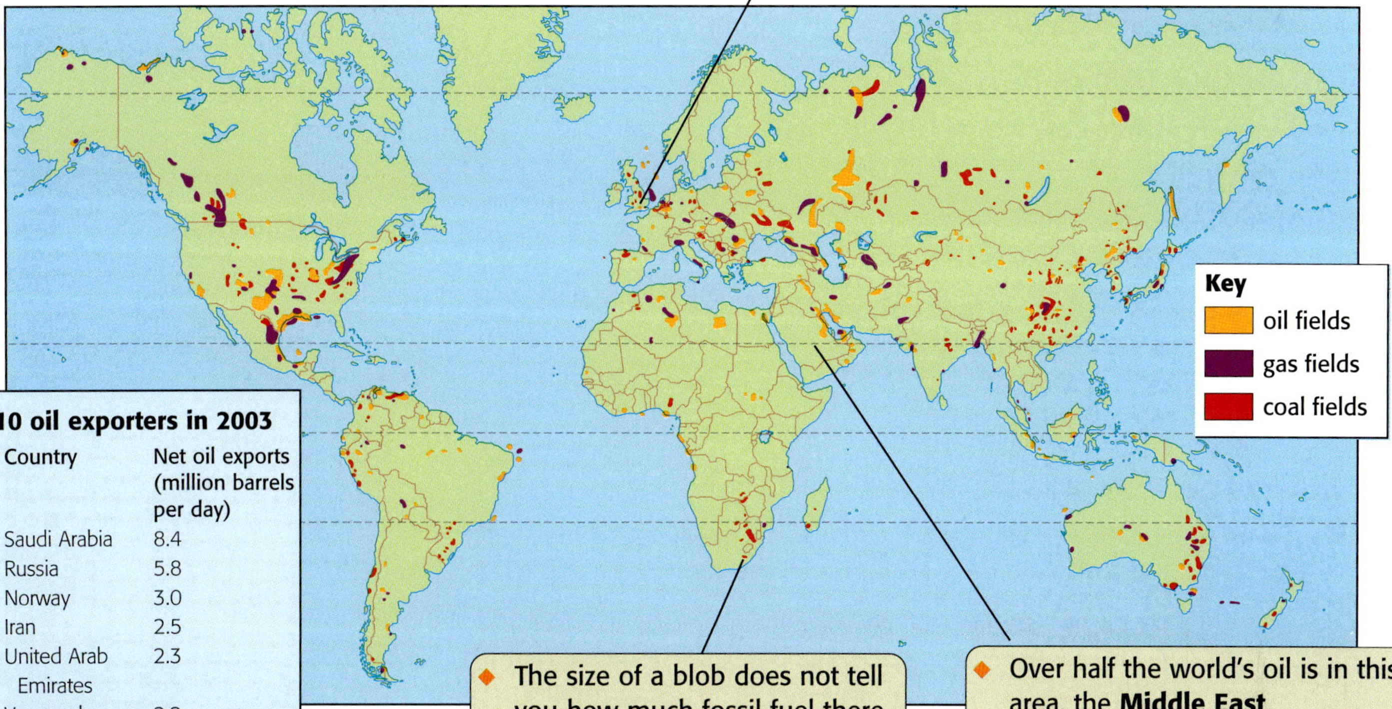

Key
- oil fields
- gas fields
- coal fields

◆ The size of a blob does not tell you how much fossil fuel there is. (A deposit could cover a small area but be very deep.)

◆ Over half the world's oil is in this area, the **Middle East**.

◆ Saudi Arabia has a quarter of the world's oil. Kuwait has a tenth.

Top 10 oil exporters in 2003

Rank	Country	Net oil exports (million barrels per day)
1	Saudi Arabia	8.4
2	Russia	5.8
3	Norway	3.0
4	Iran	2.5
5	United Arab Emirates	2.3
6	Venezuela	2.2
7	Kuwait	2.0
8	Nigeria	1.9
9	Mexico	1.7
10	Algeria	1.6

Your turn

1 From morning to night, you depend on fossil fuels. Draw a spider map to show how. Like this?

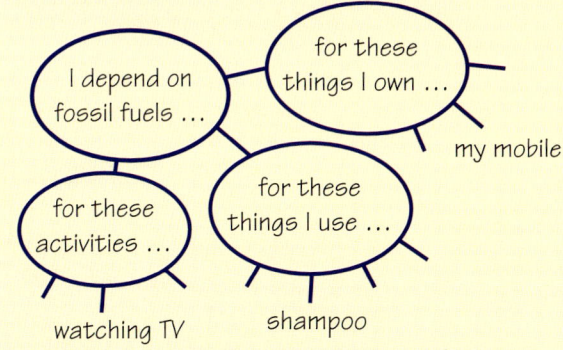

2 Why is oil the most important of the fossil fuels?

3 The world gets most of its electricity from fossil fuels. Some countries use a lot more electricity than others. Dividing the total amount a country uses in a year by its population gives the *electricity use per person*. Look at the table on the right, for the year 2000.
   a Which of the countries had the highest electricity use per person? Suggest reasons.
   b Which had the lowest? What does this tell you about that country?

4 Now draw a bar graph for the data in the table. Draw the bars horizontal, as on page 83. Turn your page sideways and use the full width.

5 Using the map on pages 128–129 to help you, name:
   a two European countries and two African countries that do not have fossil fuels
   b four countries that produce all three fuels.

6 The table above shows the top 10 oil-exporting countries, for one year.
   Find an interesting way to show this data. Then comment on it. For example you could say how many of the top 10 are in the Middle East.

7 Page 72 shows that oil and gas form under the sea. But the map above shows they are found on land too! How did they get there? See if you can explain.

Electricity use per person (kilowatt hours a year)

Australia	9000	India	350
Bangladesh	100	Kenya	150
China	800	UK	5500
France	6500	USA	12 000

What a difference oil can make!

In this unit you'll see how having a natural resource – such as oil – can make a place wealthy and help it develop.

Introducing Dubai

Dubai is in the Middle East. It is one of the seven states that make up the United Arab Emirates (UAE).

- ◆ It is not much bigger than Cornwall.
- ◆ It has a population of 1 million (mostly foreign).
- ◆ It is ruled by a Sheikh.
- ◆ It's hot and very dry. It gets up to about 24 °C in winter, and 48 °C in summer.
- ◆ Outside the city, it is mostly desert.

How Dubai was transformed

Dubai used to depend on pearl fishing, and herding sheep and goats, and growing dates. It was also a trading port for trade between India and Iran.

Then in 1966 it struck oil. And everything changed.

This shows the town of Dubai in 1966. It's on the coast, and built around this creek or inlet. It is a busy trading port. But it is not very developed.

This is the same creek in 2000, just 33 years later. Dubai is now a bustling modern city, with ten times more people than in 1967. (Most are foreigners.)

Money poured into Dubai from the sale of oil to countries which had none, or not enough, of their own. The money was used to develop Dubai. Now it has:

- ◆ modern roads, schools and hospitals
- ◆ electricity in every home
- ◆ one of the best phone systems in the world
- ◆ one of the world's most modern airports
- ◆ modern well-equipped sea ports outside the city
- ◆ a good standard of living for most people – and great luxury for some.

And thanks to the oil money, the people in Dubai don't have to pay taxes!

Shopping in the Gold Souk (market) in Dubai. ▶

Earning a living when the oil runs out …

Dubai knows its oil will run out by about 2025. So it is already planning a future without oil money. These are some of the ways it will support itself:

Tourism. It is developing as a world centre for tourism, with luxury hotels like this one, and facilities for all kinds of sports.

Information technology. It plans to be the IT centre for the Middle East. Its Internet City is home to IT companies from all over the world.

Trade. It plans to remain an important trading centre for the region, linking Europe, Asia and Africa.

Dubai's plans are succeeding. In 2004 only about 17% of the money it earned came from oil. The rest came from tourism and other services.

But there is one major issue …

The more Dubai develops, and the more tourists it gets, the more water it needs – for hotels, swimming pools, aqua parks, golf courses and so on. In fact Dubai and the UAE now consume more water per person than anywhere else in the world.

But Dubai gets very little rain. So its levels of **groundwater** (underground water) have fallen fast. Now it has to get most of its water from the sea.

It pumps in sea water, and **desalinates** it (removes the salt), and cleans it so that people can use it.

Your turn

1 Where is Dubai? Describe where it is as fully as you can, for someone who has no map to look at.

2 Dubai has changed a lot since 1966.
 a Study the two main photos on page 78 and describe the changes you see.
 b Explain what led to these changes.

3 Dubai is part of the United Arab Emirates (UAE). Some of the other UAE states also have oil. The table on the right gives some data for the UAE.
 a The table shows that people in the UAE are living longer now. Why do you think this is?
 b Literacy has also risen.
  i What does *literacy* mean? (The table will help.)
  ii Suggest reasons why it has risen.

4 **Disaster for Dubai! No more oil left to sell!**

You are Dubai's Minister of Trade. Write a letter to the newspaper in response to this newspaper heading.

5 You are Dubai's Minister for Energy. What will Dubai do for energy when the oil runs out? Write a plan. (Page 87 might help you.)

Some data for the UAE		
	In 1975	In 2003
How long people can expect to live, on average	62 years	75 years
% of people aged 15–24 who can read and write	72%	91%

The trouble with fossil fuels

Here you'll learn about the damage fossil fuels do, with oil as the example.

Oil and the environment

Fossil fuels provide energy for our homes and cars and factories.
Great! But they also do a whole lot of damage. Take oil as an example.

1 Some oil is found under the sea and some under land. To reach it, the oil companies may spoil the area. For example cut down rainforest.

2 Oil is moved around by **pipeline** (pipes) or in **tankers** (ships). If it leaks out it kills wildlife – and it may catch fire.

OIL REFINERY

4 When it burns, a cloud of stuff pours out of the power station chimneys. The key shows what's in it.

3 We burn some of the oil in power stations to make electricity.

PETE'S PETROL

5 We turn a lot of oil into petrol and diesel and burn it in engines to move ourselves around …

6 … but look what pours out of the exhausts! (Check the key.)

Key

● **carbon dioxide**. It causes **global warming**. The world is getting warmer. Bad news, as you'll see on page 82.

● **sulphur dioxide**
● **nitrogen oxides**
These gases harm our lungs. And they mix with rain to form **acid rain**. This kills trees and fish and eats into brickwork.

(Nitrogen oxides come from air, not oil. The air gets so hot in engines and furnaces that nitrogen and oxygen combine.)

● **carbon monoxide**, which is a poisonous gas

● **soot** which makes things grimy

● **water vapour**

● **other substances** (gases and tiny particles) that can damage lungs and cause cancer.

What about the other fossil fuels?

All the fossil fuels:

◆ are taken from the Earth

◆ are transported to other places

◆ are burned to release energy.

Each step affects the environment – but the last step is the worst. Most of the world's air pollution comes from burning fossil fuels.

The table on the right compares what they give out when they burn.

What the fossil fuels give out when they burn (kg of pollutant per billion BTU* of energy)			
Pollutant	**Oil**	**Gas**	**Coal**
Carbon dioxide	74 500	53 200	95 000
Nitrogen oxides	200	40	210
Sulphur dioxide	510	0.3	1180
Particulates (tiny particles of soot and other things)	38	3	1250

* BTU stands for British Thermal Unit

Did you know?

Of UK households in 2002:
◆ 73% had access to a car or van, and ...
◆ 27% had two or more cars or vans!

Your turn

1 Draw a large spider map to show all the ways we damage the environment by using so much oil. You could start like this:

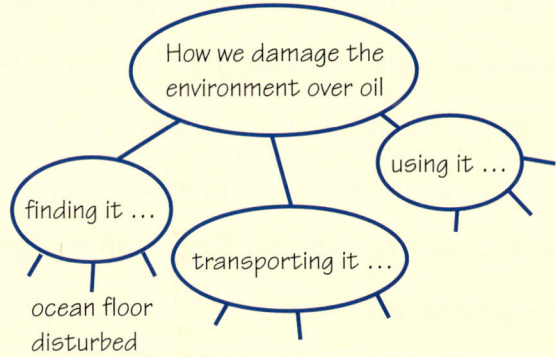

How we damage the environment over oil

finding it ...

transporting it ...

using it ...

ocean floor disturbed

2 Look at the items you wrote on your spider map. Which of them affect:

a just the place where the oil is found?
Underline these in one colour.

b other parts of the country?
Underline these in a different colour.

c other countries?
Underline these in a third colour.

Now write a colour key for your spider map.

3 Look at the table at the top of the page.

a Do all three fuels add to global warming? Explain.

b Which one may be worst for your health? Why?

c Overall, which is worst for the environment?

d Which one is 'cleanest'?

4 Photos A and B are linked to fossil fuels. For each:

a describe what you see

b say what you think caused it

c say how long you think the effects will last (weeks? months? years?)

5 If we all saved energy we would use less fossil fuel. So we would help the environment.
Write a list of steps *you* could take to save energy. (Like switch the light off when you don't need it?)

A

B

Fossil fuels and global warming

In this unit you will learn what global warming is – and how it has been linked to our use of fossil fuels.

What is global warming?

Global warming means the Earth is warming up. That's nothing new. We know it has warmed up and cooled down many times in the past. But this time it is warming up much faster than before – and it's our fault.

Why is it happening?

Ever since the Industrial Revolution, we have been burning more and more fossil fuels. Carbon dioxide is produced when they burn. And experts think this gas is the main cause of the present rapid global warming:

▲ *Pumping out carbon dioxide and steam.*

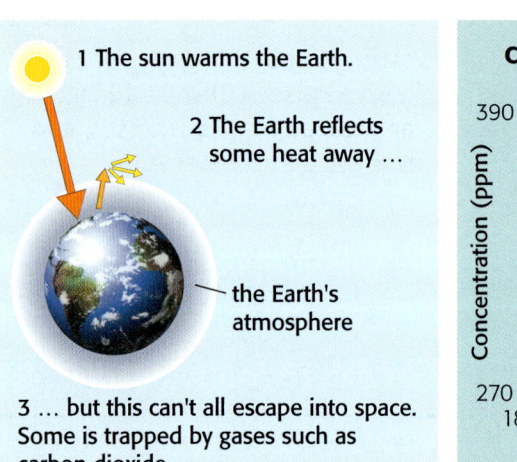

1 The sun warms the Earth.

2 The Earth reflects some heat away …

the Earth's atmosphere

3 … but this can't all escape into space. Some is trapped by gases such as carbon dioxide.

Carbon dioxide in the atmosphere

Concentration (ppm)

390

270

1860 1900 2000
Year

Average global temperature

Temperature (°C)

14

13

1860 1900 2000
Year

All air naturally contains a small % of carbon dioxide. It absorbs heat – which is lucky, because otherwise the Earth would get too cold!

But the level of carbon dioxide is rising because of all the fossil fuel we're burning. And now it's keeping in too much heat!

So the Earth is getting warmer. This shows the temperature rise. It matches the rise in carbon dioxide. And that is what's causing alarm.

Carbon dioxide is called a **greenhouse gas**, because of the way it absorbs heat. It is not the only greenhouse gas in the atmosphere. (Water vapour and methane are two others.) But it's the one that we humans pump into the air in the greatest quantities.

The result: climate change!

Global warming is already causing climate change around the world. These are some of the signs:

◆ Ice and snow on high mountains are melting (for example in the Alps).

◆ The ice around the North and South Poles is thinning fast.

◆ Melting ice sheets at the poles are causing sea levels to rise. (They have risen by up to 25 cm over the last 100 years.)

◆ Many countries are getting more storms and floods than usual (and this includes the UK).

◆ Some countries are getting more droughts than usual.

◆ Overall, the storms and floods and droughts are getting more severe.

▲ *What's happening to my ice?*

How climate change will affect us

Climate change will affect all of us. These are just some of the effects:

Low-lying coasts will get flooded by rising seas, including coasts in the UK. Low-lying islands like Tuvalu in the Pacific (above) may drown.

Storms and floods will become more frequent and do more damage in many places, including in the UK. Will you be affected?

It will get too hot and dry for crops in some places. This could lead to famines, and more refugees, and even wars about water.

What can we do?

Climate change is one of the biggest problems facing the world today. It is too late to stop it – it's happening already. But we can try to slow it down, by burning less fossil fuel. The following units will look at some options.

Your turn

1 Look at the two photos on page 82. What's the link between the two scenes? Explain.

2 Global warming will affect people everywhere. Draw a spider map to show how.

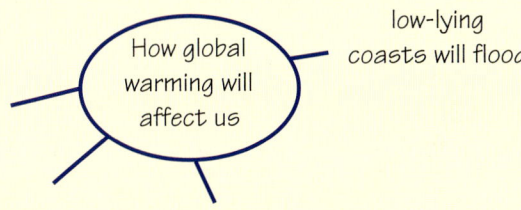

3 Some countries produce more carbon dioxide than others, because they burn more fossil fuel.
The bar graph on the right shows how much some produced *per person*, in 2000. (It is the total amount they produced that year, divided by the population.)
  a Which of them produced most carbon dioxide per person in 2000? See if you can explain why.
  b Which one produced least? Think up some reasons.
  c So will the country in b suffer least from global warming? Explain your answer.
  d Do you think a bar chart for this year would look different from the one for 2000? Explain your answer.

4 Look at the photo of Tuvalu above.
Tuvalu is a group of small islands, with a population of about 11 000. The people get heat for cooking by burning coconut shells.
You are the Prime Minister of Tuvalu. You are worried and angry about the effect of global warming on your country. Write to the President of America to complain, and to seek help.

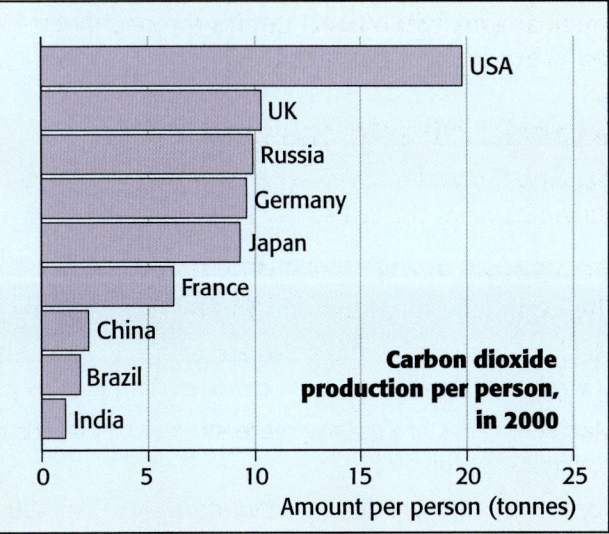

Carbon dioxide production per person, in 2000

(Bar graph showing countries from highest to lowest: USA, UK, Russia, Germany, Japan, France, China, Brazil, India)

Amount per person (tonnes): 0, 5, 10, 15, 20, 25

Saved by the wind?

In this unit you'll learn how the wind is being used to generate electricity, around the UK.

The rush to renewables

Our use of fossil fuels is not **sustainable**. They are linked with global warming – and they'll run out one day.

Now the pressure is on to get less electricity from fossil fuels, and more from **renewable** sources that won't add to global warming.

Lucky us !

In the UK, we have one free and renewable source of energy all around us: the wind ! In fact it could provide all the electricity we need. The UK is the windiest country in Europe.

Research is going on into other renewable sources – **waves**, **tides**, **solar** (using sunlight), and **biomass** (based on plants). But experts say that the wind will be the UK's main renewable source up to 2020.

Our windfarms

A **windfarm** is just a collection of tall towers with turbines at the top, and big blades to catch the wind. The diagram above shows how they work.

By the end of 2004 we had over 100 windfarms. All except one were **onshore**. The map on page 75 shows the main ones.

More offshore windfarms on the way

The UK's first offshore windfarm spun into action on 21 November 2003. Sitting in the Irish Sea, 7 km off the Welsh coast, the North Hoyle windfarm generates electricity for up to 50 000 homes.

But it is just the start. At least 30 more offshore windfarms are planned, or being built already. The map on page 85 shows just the first group, agreed in 2001.

The next group will include three very large windfarms off the east coast. Each will generate as much electricity as a large power station. One will be the largest offshore windfarm in the world.

It is hoped that wind power will provide 10% of the UK's electricity by 2010.

So next time you struggle against the wind, just think: that very same wind could be lighting your room, or powering your TV !

the wind spins the blades

the blades turn a shaft which turns a turbine - and this generates electricity

the cables run down inside the tower

tower

the cables carry the electricity away

▲ *From wind to electricity …*

Did you know?
- In 2000, the UK got 3% of its electricity from renewable resources.
- The target for 2015 is 15%.

▲ *A windfarm by a lake in North Yorkshire.*

▶ *The offshore windfarm at North Hoyle.*

Your turn

1 Answer these questions about a windfarm. For each answer give your reasons.
  a Will a windfarm contribute to global warming?
  b Will it pollute the atmosphere?
  c Does it use a renewable source of energy?
  d Will it give a steady supply of electricity?

2 Onshore windfarms tend to be:
  A on high land
  B in remote areas
  C mostly on the west side of the UK. (See page 75.)
  For each of **A** – **C**, see if you can explain why.

3 Look at the diagram on the right, for an offshore turbine.
  a How is the tower held upright?
  b How is the electricity carried to the shore?
  c You are an engineer. What difficulties might you find, in setting up an offshore windfarm?
  d Overall, which type of windfarm do you think is easier to set up, offshore or onshore? Why?

4 Look at the map on the right. It shows the most suitable areas around the UK for offshore windfarms. They were chosen after a survey of the sea floor.
  a Where is the *largest* suitable area?
  b Areas outside the blue dashed line are not suitable. Why is this?

5 Now look at the windfarms marked on the map.
  a None is within 5 km of the shore. Why do you think this is? Give as many reasons as you can.
  b Almost all are in water less than 30 m deep. Why do you think this is?

6 Plans for a windfarm may get turned down, if the windfarm is likely to:
  ◆ conflict with human activities
  ◆ harm wildlife
  ◆ spoil the environment in any other way

  a See if you can think up five examples of reasons why a plan for an onshore windfarm might get turned down. (For example, too close to people's homes.)
  b Now repeat **a** for an offshore windfarm.
  The photos on page 84 may give you ideas.

7 Windfarms have advantages and disadvantages.
  a Make a large table, like the one below, with plenty of space to write in.
  b Fill in as many advantages and disadvantages as you can.

Windfarm	Advantages	Disadvantages
onshore		
offshore		

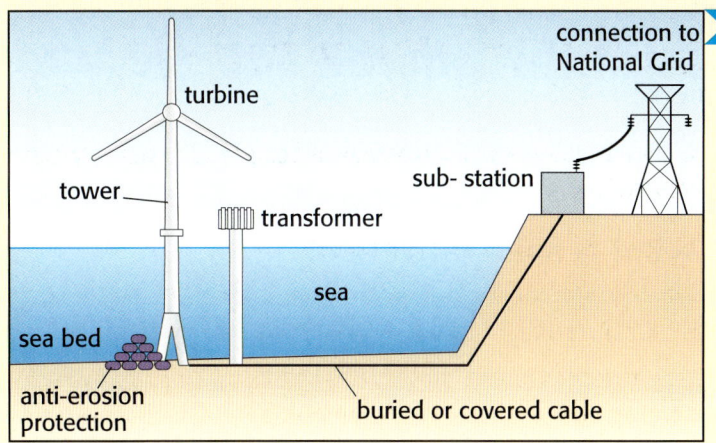
▲ Bringing the electricity onshore.

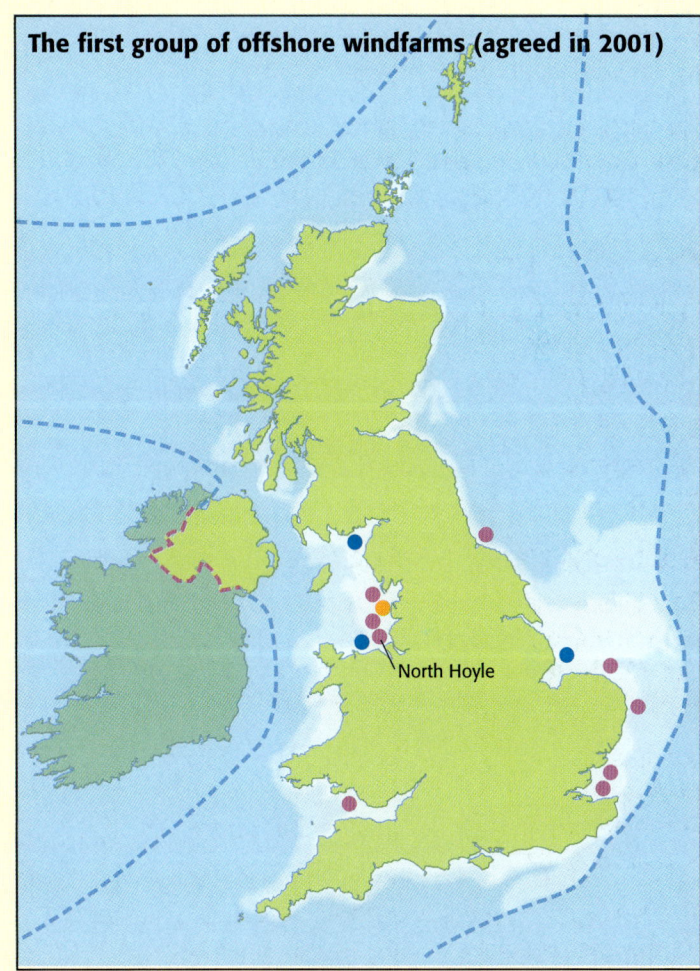

The first group of offshore windfarms (agreed in 2001)

North Hoyle

Key
Suitable areas for offshore windfarms
  water depth under 30m
  water depth 30m - 50m

Existing and proposed windfarm sites
  ● 30 turbines
  ● 60 turbines
  ● 90 turbines

Boundaries
  --- international land boundary
  --- limit of the UK continental shelf (where the UK has the right to exploit natural resources on the sea bed)

Is solar power the answer?

Here you will learn what solar power is, and see how it is being used around the world.

What is solar power?

Solar power means energy from sunlight. When the sunlight strikes a **photovoltaic cell** or **PV cell**, a current is produced.

PV cells were invented for satellites. Now they are being used everywhere.

A solar revolution?

Many poor countries have large areas with no electricity, because they can't afford the power stations or fossil fuels. But PV cells are making a world of difference.

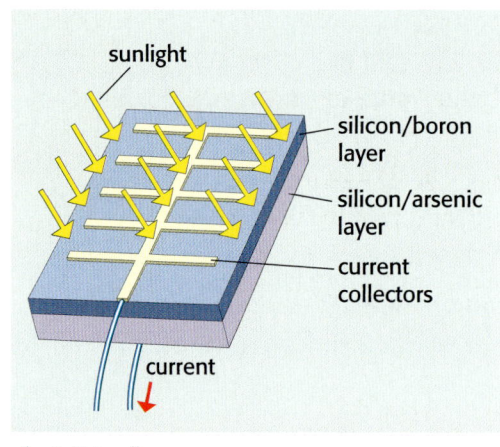

sunlight

silicon/boron layer

silicon/arsenic layer

current collectors

current

▲ A PV cell.

▲ A solar-powered lighthouse in Wales.

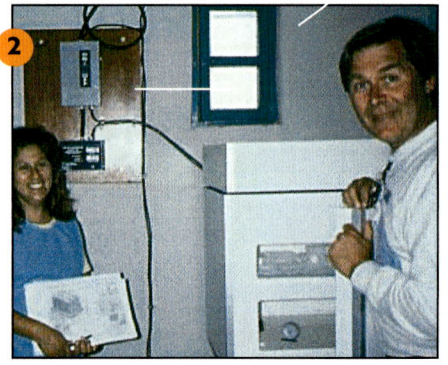

▲ A solar-powered fridge for vaccines saves lives in a clinic in Peru.

▲ Cleaning the PV cells that power his home in Sudan.

▲ PV cells on a farm in Bolivia.

▲ A solar-powered tsunami warning siren in Hawaii. These could be used anywhere, for all kinds of emergencies.

▲ Solar-powered TV in Tibet.

▲ A solar-powered phone in Australia. These could be set up anywhere.

Solar power in the UK

The UK is not the world's sunniest place. But even on a cloudy day, enough sunlight gets through to provide solar power.

Now PV cells are being made into roof tiles, and built into glass for windows – so your home could provide a lot of its own electricity.

Experts think that solar power will be providing more of the UK's electricity by 2020, and that its share will keep on growing.

A solar-powered home in the UK. ▶

Your turn

1 What is a photovoltaic cell? Describe in your own words what it does.

2 Say whether these statements about solar power are true or false. (The photos may help.)
   A Every home could make its own electricity.
   B You must live near a city to use solar power.
   C Solar power is used only in rich countries.
   D You could get a scooter to run on solar power.
   E It is not sunny enough in the UK for solar power.
   F Solar power is a renewable source of energy.
   G Solar power depends on fossil fuels.
   H Solar power makes global warming worse.

3 What are the advantages of solar power, in your opinion? List them in order of importance.

4 Look at the map below. What does it show?

5 **a** Which country gets the strongest sunshine, Greenland, Ireland or Saudi Arabia? Explain why. (Pages 128–129 will help.)
   b Which of them would be best for solar power?

6 Overall, which of the *continents* shown on the map would be best for solar power?

7 Using the map on page 77 to help you, name two *countries* with no fossil fuels, but very strong sunlight they could use for energy.

8 Now match each place in the photos on page 86 to the correct dot on this map. Start like this:
   ① =

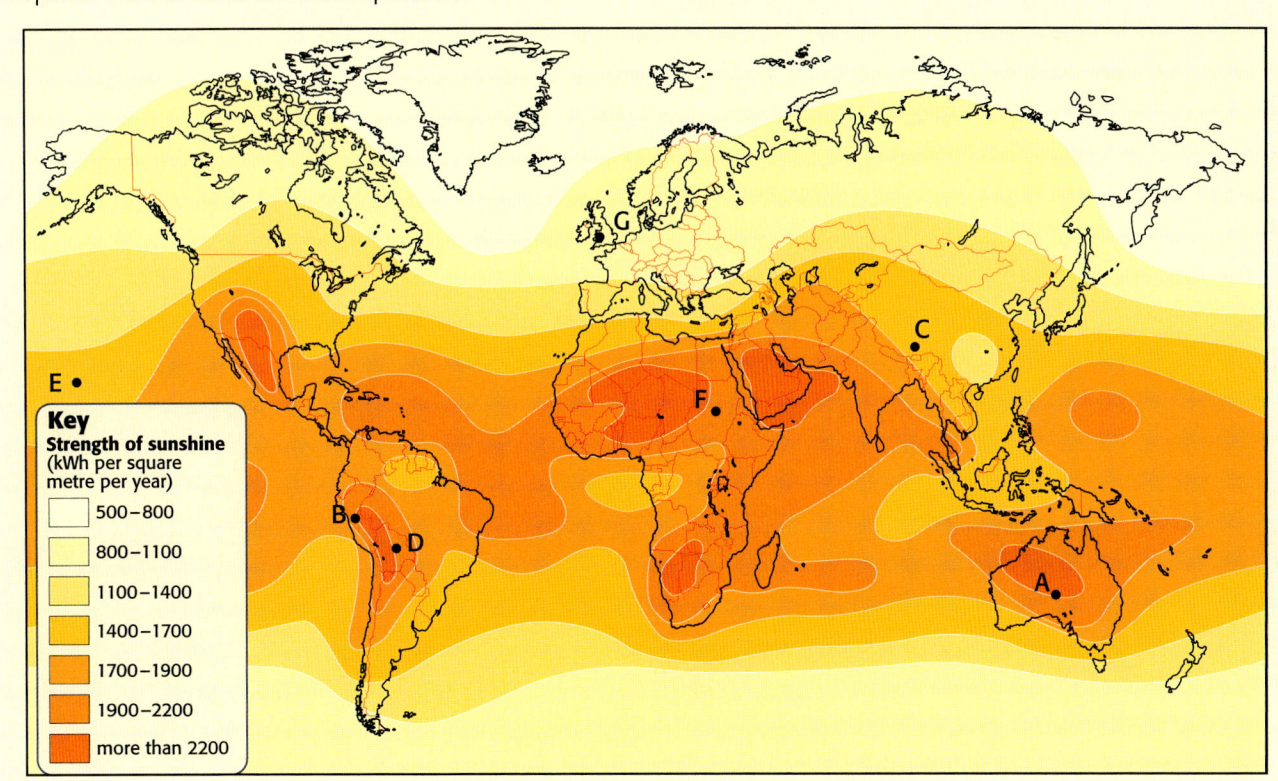

Key
Strength of sunshine
(kWh per square metre per year)

- 500–800
- 800–1100
- 1100–1400
- 1400–1700
- 1700–1900
- 1900–2200
- more than 2200

Going solar in Gosaba

Here you'll learn how solar power improved life in a rural village in India.

Where's Gosaba ?

This is Debu. He is 15. He lives in Gosaba, on a small island in an area called Sundarbans in India.

His home is the one on the far right above. It has a thatched roof and two rooms.

This sketch map shows Sundarbans, with Gosaba marked in.

CHINA
NEPAL
BHUTAN
BANGLADESH
INDIA
Bay of Bengal

1 Sundarbans is a **delta** area (like its neighbour Bangladesh). It has 102 islands. This map shows just some of them.

2 Over millions of years, water flowing out from two great rivers, the Ganges and Brahmaputra, deposited sediment in the area.

3 It built up to form the islands – and the water just ran round them.

4 Now the region is teeming with rivers, stream, and canals. Only some rivers are shown here.

5 It also has thick swampy **mangrove forests**. With Bengal tigers, turtles and crocodiles !

Kolkata (Calcutta)

I N D I A

● Gosaba

BANGLADESH

Bay of Bengal

NOT TO SCALE

9 The only way to get to most of the islands is by boat.

8 Most people live on tiny farms in small hamlets – like Debu. His father also earns some money from fishing.

7 About 200 000 people live in the area shown on this map. 15 000 live on Debu's island.

6 The climate is hot and humid. There are heavy monsoon rains from June to October.

Key
- ● city
- ● main town or village of island
- sea/river
- mangrove forest
- — · — boundary of Sundarbans
- — · — border with Bangladesh

Where Gosaba got its energy

Before 1997, the people of Gosaba used **kerosene** for lighting and cooking. Kerosene is made from oil. It gives out soot that makes walls and ceilings black, and fumes that irritate your eyes and lungs. It gives a dim light. And it can set the house on fire !

Some homes in Gosaba had TV, running on batteries. But batteries don't last long, and cost a lot. Which means less money for other things.

Solar power arrives

In 1997, some homes and other buildings in Gosaba got solar power, as a trial. Debu's home was one.

The governments of India and the USA paid for most of the project. But the users also had to pay a little – £23 a year for 5 years.

Solar power has made a big difference to Debu and his family.

In fact the whole project was so successful that the Indian government now plans to bring solar power to all of Sundarbans.

▲ Up go the PV cells on Debu's roof …

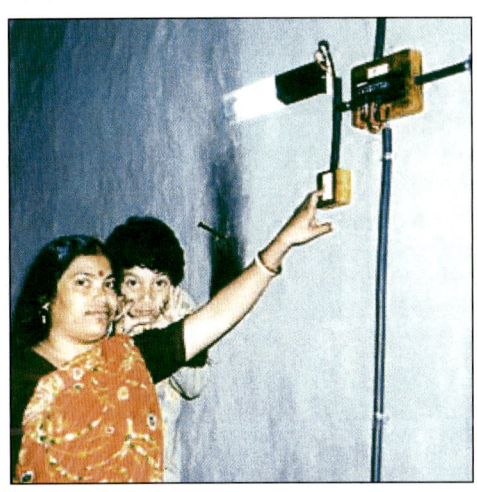
◄ … and on go the lights!

Your turn

1 a In which country is this area of Sundarbans?
  b In which continent is it?
  c Which country is it next to?

2 Explain why:
  a there are so many islands in Sundarbans
  b floods are a problem there.

3 India has a National Grid for electricity, like the UK. Cables carry electricity from power stations to different places. But India will never be able to extend its grid to Gosaba. Suggest reasons for this.

4 Before solar power, Debu's family had just two kerosene lamps like this one. They lit them every evening when it got dark, around 6. What problems can kerosene lamps cause?

5 a The table on the right shows the results of a survey in Gosaba. Which was the most common reason people gave, for liking solar power?
  b Why do you think this reason is so important to them?

6 Display the results of the survey in any way you like. For example you could draw a pictogram or bar graph. Make it look interesting!

7 Imagine you are Debu. Write to your cousin Kali in Kolkata telling her about solar power and how it has affected your family.

8 '*Solar power in Gosaba is a great example of sustainable development.*' Do you agree? Explain.

Impact of solar power on people in Gosaba	
Benefit	**% who mentioned this**
Better light	80
No fumes to irritate the eyes	85
Less coughing	10
Can earn more now since can work longer hours	25
Easier to serve food now	12
Easier to use than kerosene	64
Helps children to study	88
Can watch more TV news	44
Can watch more TV serials and films	78

The big picture

Geography is brilliant. It even covers crime! This chapter is all about crime. These are the big ideas behind the chapter:

◆ Crime affects all of us, not just the victims.

◆ It's easier to commit crimes in some places than others – so criminals have to think about geography!

◆ Maps are good for showing where crimes occur, and working out why.

◆ Today, when we build new streets and housing, we try to make them more 'crime proof'.

◆ Some crimes involve many people, in different countries. Drug trafficking is an example.

Your goals for this chapter

By the end of this chapter you should be able to answer these questions:

◆ What do these terms mean?

crime   victim   offender   sentence   secure accommodation

◆ In what ways does crime affect all of us – not just the victims?

◆ What do these terms mean?

fraud   burglary   vandalism   domestic violence
assault   environmental crime   terrorism   crime hotspot

◆ Why is some crime *not* reported to the police?

◆ In what ways can a location help to make crime easier?

◆ What kind of things can we do to cut burglaries, and street crime?

◆ Where does most of the world's heroin come from, and why, and how is heroin linked to crime?

And then …

When you finish this chapter you can come back to this page and see if you have met your goals!

Did you know?
◆ There are about 85 000 people in prison in the UK right now.
◆ That's about 1 in every 760 of the population.

Did you know?
◆ The UK has over 4 million CCTV cameras, in buildings and on streets.
◆ That's more than any other country, per person.

Did you know?
◆ There are about 300 000 known thefts from shops in England and Wales each year.

Your chapter starter

Page 90 shows policemen on patrol. They're looking out for crime.

What's a crime?

What kind of crimes could happen in that area?

Who decides what counts as a crime?

Has it got anything to do with you?

But it wasn't me.

6.1 A crime story

In this unit you will explore how crime affects more than just the victim.

The offender's story

It happened a year ago when I was 13.

I was walking through the park with my friend and we were talking about things we like. You know, clothes and all. There was a woman in front of us, quite old. My friend said 'I'm going to get her bag'. He ran and grabbed the bag. She held on and screamed. He gave a tug. So did I. She fell back on to the iron railings.

Now she's paralysed. I am sorry about her. I got an 18-month sentence. It wasn't even my idea but they said I was guilty too.

I wish it had never happened. But it did and I can't change it. Now I have a criminal record and the police will always be watching me.

At school they teach you things like cooking, and crossing the road safely, and what to do in a fire. But they never teach you not to steal – not really.

▲ *The offender.*

The victim's story

It has ruined my life. 46 years old, and in a wheelchair.

I had a good job at the hotel. My children were doing well. We were an ordinary family. And then in just a few minutes everything changed. What did I do to deserve this?

The worst part is the effect on my family. It's like a big dark cloud over all of us. We can never have a normal life again.

My husband had to leave his job and take a part-time job to look after me. My children worry all the time. My son has got really depressed. He used to do well at school but now he's getting bad reports, and he'll probably fail his exams.

I never go out now – I sit out the back in the garden. When my husband wheeled me down the street once, I got panicky. I felt everyone was staring at me.

Those two boys just got a few years between them. I got a life sentence.

So – who pays the penalty?

In this sad story, the offenders were punished for their crime. The victim was punished too. But they were not the only ones who suffered, as you'll see next.

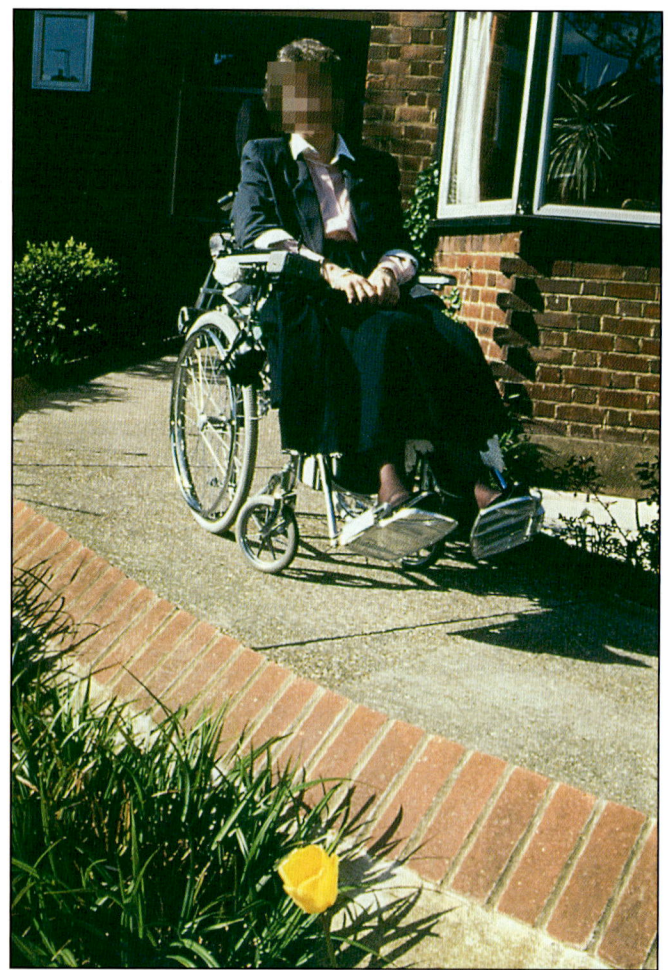

▲ *The victim.*

Paying for crime

90 km

Key

The victim and her family

- The victim and her family live here.
- This is the park where the crime took place.
- The victim had to have several serious and expensive operations in this hospital.

The offenders and their families

- The secure accommodation where the two boys are being held. They are not allowed out.
- The families of the two boys live in these houses. Their neighbours won't talk to them now.

Other people

- Five people in these houses need operations. But the hospital had to delay them in order to treat the victim. (It ran short of money.)
- Eleven people in these houses used to walk in the park. Not any more. They are too afraid.
- The owner of this house was about to sell it – but the crime put the buyers off.
- The police and prisons cost a lot to run. The money comes from taxes …
- … so everyone who pays taxes pays more because of crime.

Your turn

1 Why do you think the boy wanted the bag?

2 Who suffered because of this crime? Make a list.

3 The boy who snatched the bag was 11. He got an 18-month sentence too. Do you think it was fair that:
   a both boys got the same sentence?
   b they got 18 months?

4 Write down the meaning of each term. (Glossary?)
   victim   offender   sentence
   secure accommodation

5 We all pay for crimes other people commit. You pay every time you go shopping! Look at this:

Theft from UK shops costs £ billions every year!

To see how you pay for shop theft, write these sentences in the correct order.
   A The shop has to find money to pay for the stolen goods, and the security staff.
   B So the shop hires security staff to stop theft.
   C Shoplifters steal things from a shop.
   D So you pay more when you go shopping.
   E So it charges more for the things it sells.

6 Mugging and shoplifting are crimes. So is dumping poisonous chemicals in rivers. Which do you think is the best definition of crime?
   a An action that harms a person.
   b An action that breaks the law.
   c An action that offends people.

Different kinds of crime

In this unit you'll explore and compare different kinds of crime.

A bad bad day in the city …

1 In a back room, a man is selling new computers. Only £200 each. (His mate stole them from a truck last week.)

2 Three cars on this street are parked on double yellow lines.

3 In a shop a young woman is buying a coat using a stolen credit card.

4 A husband has just beaten his wife up again. Her face is bruised and bleeding.

5 A woman is busy writing lies on a tax form, so that she won't have to pay much tax.

6 Three people in here are watching TV. No TV licence.

7 Two boys are spraying graffiti on the railway bridge.

8 On the 2.30 train, nine people are travelling without a ticket.

9 In a café, a man of 40 waits for a young girl he contacted on the internet. (He told her he was 15.)

10 The head office of a company. Fumes from its factories around the UK are damaging people's lungs.

11 The owner is out. But a stranger is climbing in a window and will steal her jewellery.

12 A boy has just broken into a battered old car and is driving it away.

13 In the school three girls are bullying another girl. They slap her face and push her over.

14 In a secret room, three people are working very hard, printing fake £5 notes.

15 A woman drives herself home from lunch in a pub – even though she is tipsy.

16 At this corner, one young man has just stabbed another to death, because of the colour of his skin.

17 A man has just parked a car outside the embassy. It contains a bomb that will go off in 15 minutes.

18 Two men in balaclavas have just walked into a shop. One aims a gun at the staff while the other lifts cash from the tills.

19 An older boy has just caught a 12-year-old in a headlock and taken his mobile phone.

20 In the corner shop, the shopkeeper is selling cigarettes to a girl of 13.

How much crime is there in the UK?

The UK has quite a lot of crime. (Most is not very serious.) But not all of it gets reported to the police, or recorded by them.

So every year the government carries out its own survey. Households in England and Wales are asked about crimes they suffered over the past twelve months.

The survey shows many more crimes than the police records do – in fact over three times as many!

This table shows the results for one year. The numbers are all in thousands. There were nearly seven million thefts in England and Wales that year.

But the survey does not ask about crimes like fraud or drug dealing. So you need to look at police records too, to get a better picture.

British Crime Survey: one year's results

Type of crime		Number of times committed (thousands)
1 Vandalism		2465
2 Thefts	burglary	943
	of or from cars	2121
	of bicycles	370
	other household thefts	1283
	thefts from people	622
	other thefts of personal property	1321
	Total	6660
3 Violent crimes	mugging (to rob)	283
	wounding (in fights)	655
	common assault (hitting)	1654
	Total	2592
Total of all crimes		**11 717**

Your turn

1 First, pick a number from the photo to match each term below. (A different number for each.)

a murder **b** forgery
c vandalism **d** armed robbery
e burglary **f** domestic violence
g fraud **h** handling stolen goods
i a traffic offence **j** environmental crime
k terrorism **l** common assault
m car theft **n** mugging

If you get stuck the glossary may help.

2 Both young people and adults commit crime. Look at the list of crimes **a – n** above. Pick out:

a one that's more likely to be carried out by younger people (under 16) than older people
b five that are more likely to be carried out by adults
c two you think just as likely for either group.

3 Young people are often victims of crime. From the photo, pick out five crimes where young people are, or could be, victims.

4 All the crimes on the photo took place in a city. But some of them could take place in a rural area. Give the numbers for four crimes that:

a could easily take place in a tiny rural hamlet
b are unlikely to take place in a rural area.

5 Many crimes are not reported to the police. Suggest a reason why these crimes from the photo were not reported.

a 12 **b** 4 **c** 20 **d** 13

6 Look at the table above.

a How many crimes did the survey find altogether? (Check the heading of the last column!)
b Of the three main types of crime, which one was the most common?
c There were about two and a half million acts of vandalism. Give four examples of vandalism.
d Which type of theft was the most common? Suggest reasons.
e Which type of theft was the least common? Suggest reasons.

7 All crime is wrong. But some crimes are more serious than others.

a Draw a scale like the one below. Make it the width of your page, and divide it into three equal parts. Label the divisions.

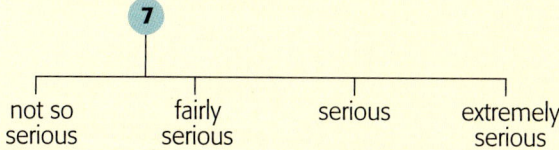

not so serious   fairly serious   serious   extremely serious

b Now mark in these six crimes (from the photo) on your scale, where you think they should go:

1   2   8   9   10   17

One number has been put in as an example.

c In **b**, how did you decide on the *most* serious and *least* serious crimes? Explain your thinking.

Did you know?

♦ Murder is quite rare compared with other crimes.
♦ There are about 13 000 times more thefts than murders!

Criminal geography!

In this unit you'll explore the links between location and crime. And find out who's most likely to get burgled!

The criminal's mental map

We all have **mental maps** (maps in our mind) of areas we know well. Look at this mental map for a criminal.

The criminal will head for areas:

♦ that he knows well
♦ that offer opportunities for crime
♦ where he can get away without being seen.

This criminal has three areas to target – near home, near work, and near where he goes for shopping and entertainment.

And now it's time to go exploring!

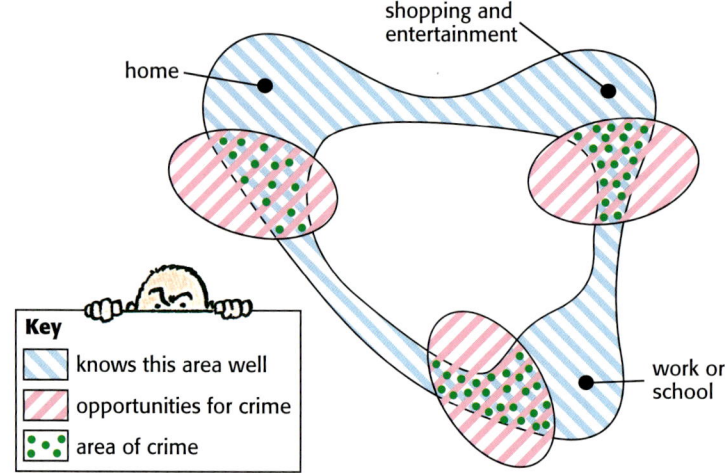

Key
▨	knows this area well
▨	opportunities for crime
⦂	area of crime

Your turn

First, put yourself in a criminal's shoes.

1 You are a house burglar. You know all the places in the photos on the opposite page.
  a Which two places would you target?
  b For each, give reasons for your choice.

2 What kinds of crimes might occur in the places shown in these photos? Give reasons for your answers.
  a 4 **b** 5 **c** 6 **d** 7 **e** 8 **f** 9

Now, back to being yourself.

3 In which place in the photos would you feel safest, walking around by yourself:
  a during the day? **b** at night?
  Give the numbers of the photos, and your reasons.

4 In which place would you feel least safe, walking around by yourself:
  a during the day? **b** at night?
  Again give the photo numbers, and your reasons.

Next, you are a crime prevention officer.

5 Choose one photo from page 97 with people in. What advice would you give those people about protecting themselves from crime, in that situation?

6 If a place shows **physical disorder** it means it looks run-down and messy.
  a Which photo do you think shows highest physical disorder?
  b Do you think there's a link between physical disorder and risk of crime? How could you check?

And finally, think about being burgled.

7 The table below shows the risk of burglary. 3.4% of households in rural areas are likely to be burgled, and 5.6% of all households.

The risk of household burglary	%
Head of household aged 16–24	15.2
Living in an area of high physical disorder	12.0
Living in rented property	9.7
Living in the inner city	8.5
Living in a council estate	8.1
Living in a flat	7.2
On a main road	6.6
Average risk of being burgled	5.6
Earning more than £30 000 a year	5.0
Living in property they own	4.2
Living in a detached house	4.1
Head of household 65 or older	3.8
Living in rural areas	3.4

Draw a bar graph to show the data in the table. It will be a wide graph so you can turn your page sideways. Start like this:

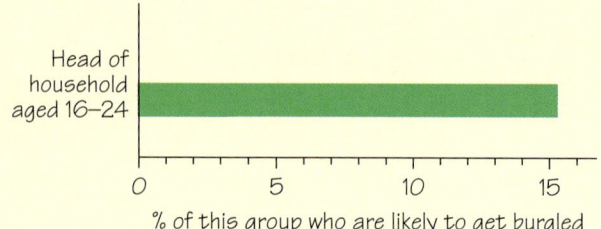

% of this group who are likely to get burgled

8 Now it's time to analyse the data in your bar graph. The text on the opposite page will help. This clue box might help too!

Suggest reasons why the risk of being burgled is:

a lowest in rural areas

b low for people over 65

c lower if you own your home than if you rent it

d above average if you live on a main road

e below average if you earn more than £30 000

f higher for flats than for detached houses

g highest where the head of the household is only 16–24.

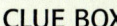

CLUE BOX

Not everyone can afford burglar alarms and good locks.

Lots of us don't know our neighbours.

In busy places nobody pays much attention to strangers.

Burglars prefer places with no-one at home.

We take more care of our own things.

If you own lots of things you might fit a burglar alarm and good door and window locks.

Mapping crime

In this unit you'll explore crime spots, using a map and an aerial photo.

Put your police hat on !

You are in charge of crime control for the area on the map below.
The matching photo on page 99 will help you answer these questions.

Evening all.

Your turn

1 There were several fights along one part of the High Street, in the last six months.
   a Suggest a reason for this. (Check building use !)
   b What could you do to prevent trouble here? Come up with some suggestions.
      Then put them in order, with the best one first.
2 Now look at square 1436.
   a What was the main crime here?
   b Suggest a reason for this. (Check the photo.)
   c What will you do to prevent this crime? Put your suggestions in order, best one first.

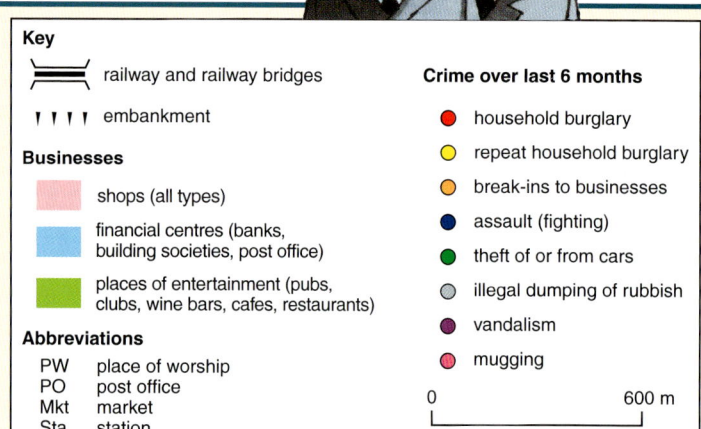

Key

railway and railway bridges

ʏ ʏ ʏ ʏ embankment

Businesses

shops (all types)

financial centres (banks, building societies, post office)

places of entertainment (pubs, clubs, wine bars, cafes, restaurants)

Abbreviations

PW   place of worship
PO   post office
Mkt market
Sta station

Crime over last 6 months

● household burglary
● repeat household burglary
● break-ins to businesses
● assault (fighting)
● theft of or from cars
● illegal dumping of rubbish
● vandalism
● mugging

0   600 m

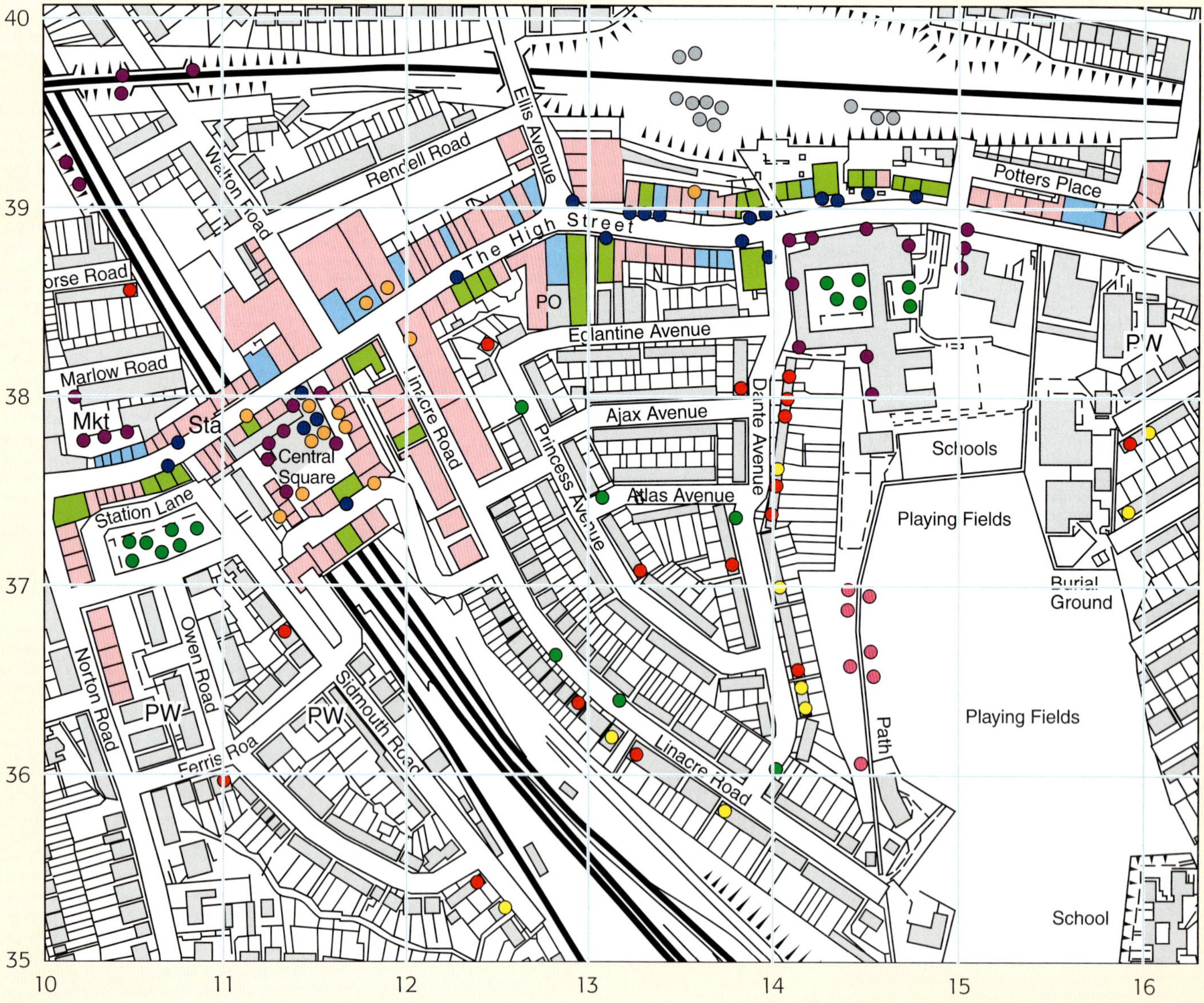

3 Yesterday two of your police team visited each house on the right of Dante Avenue (going north). They offered to write the postcode on valuable things like computers, with a special invisible ink.
  a What is a *postcode*?
  b Why did they want to write it on things?
  c Why did they choose this road?

4 Houses on the left of Dante Avenue are burgled far less often than those on the right. Suggest a reason.

5 Say which two grid squares were worst for this crime, and give reasons:
  a theft of or from cars
  b illegal dumping of rubbish

6 Vandalism is a problem too. Windows get broken, phone boxes smashed and walls sprayed with graffiti. It is a special problem in squares 1438 and 1137. Suggest reasons for this.

7 A **crime hotspot** has more crime than the other places around it. Where is the main crime hotspot in the map area? Try to give reasons for this.

8 Mr Williams rang yesterday to say he has now been burgled 6 times in 6 months. He lives at 126353. The photo below shows his house from the road.
  a Suggest reasons why his house is burgled so often. Look at the map *and* the photo.
  b Now write to Mr Williams with some advice about how he could stop his house being burgled.

In the fight against crime

In this unit you'll learn about things we can do to deter criminals.

Protecting property

Criminals like an easy target – and not to get caught. So we can make their lives more difficult. Here are two ways to protect property …

1 Make the target harder to get at. This is called **target hardening**. You could put in high fences, window bars, and strong locks.

2 Make it easier to spot that a crime is being committed. You could fit burglar alarms and bright lights, and hire security guards.

Designing out crime

The **built environment** means all the built things around us – houses, streets, shopping centres and so on. As you have seen, it can give lots of opportunities for crime.

Now people are starting to think about crime before they build something new. They try to design it so as to prevent crime.

That is called **designing out crime**. Look at this new housing estate.

Nah!

Target hardening is built in.
◆ All windows have locks, and glass that's very hard to break.
◆ The outer doors are strong, with strong locks.
◆ Every house has a burglar alarm.

BALLIOL COURT

The layout makes crime easier to spot.
◆ People can easily keep an eye on each other's homes and cars.
◆ There's only one way in and out of the estate. So burglars can't escape easily.
◆ All paths are out in the open, easy to see from the houses.

A space to watch over

In the estate above, there is a **defensible space** around the houses. That means a space people can watch over and protect.
There are no hidden alleys or corners. People can see if strangers are trying to break into houses, or steal cars.

Space like this, that people can watch over, is a good way to fight crime.

Today, the police are happy to check the plans for new developments, to make sure they are anti-crime. They will even suggest which kinds of doors, windows and locks to use.

Your turn

1 What does *target hardening* mean?

2 a First, make a larger copy of this Venn diagram.

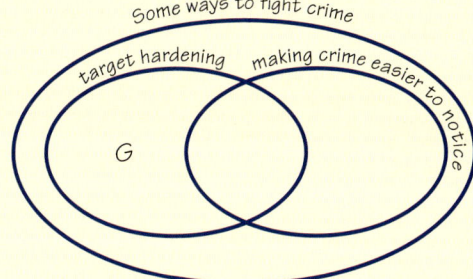

Some ways to fight crime

target hardening   making crime easier to notice

G

b Now look at the list below.
In which loop of your Venn diagram should each item go? Mark its letter in. (One is done already.)
If you think an item belongs to both loops, put the letter where they overlap.
A a lock for your bicycle
B a bullet-proof vest
C a 'krooklok' for a car steering wheel
D a CCTV camera (like the one shown on the right)
E security tags on clothes in a shop
F a guard dog
G a high wall with metal spikes on top
H a shatterproof glass screen in the post office
I a Neighbourhood Watch scheme (Glossary!)
J a bodyguard

3 CCTV (or closed circuit TV) is used in shops and on streets. Some years ago, CCTV cameras were installed in the town centre in Airdrie in Scotland. Look at this table.

Airdrie

	In the 12 months …	
	before CCTV	after CCTV
Car break-ins	480	20
Theft of cars	185	13
Serious assaults	39	22
Vandalism	207	36
Break-ins to business premises	263	15

a Overall, did CCTV reduce the number of crimes?
b Which type of crime did it reduce most?
c Which did it reduce least? Try to give a reason.

4 You are (still) in charge of crime for the area on page 98.
You have money for just two CCTV cameras.
Below is a list of grid references.
From this list, pick out the two best places for your CCTV cameras, and give your reasons.
a 145365   **b** 138375   **c** 113374
d 139389   **e** 145385   **f** 115382

5 What do these terms mean?
a designing out crime   **b** defensible space
Answer in your own words, using the photo at the bottom of page 100 to help you.

6 The methods in this unit help to reduce crime. But they don't stop it altogether! Look at these opinions:

If you want to cut crime, give young people interesting things to do.

To get rid of crime – just get rid of poverty.

To really cut crime we must teach people that it's wrong.

I think the best way to cut crime is to punish criminals very severely.

a Choose any *two* of the four opinions.
b For each, decide whether you agree or not.
Then write down what you will say to that person in reply.

a CCTV camera – it can turn, tilt and zoom

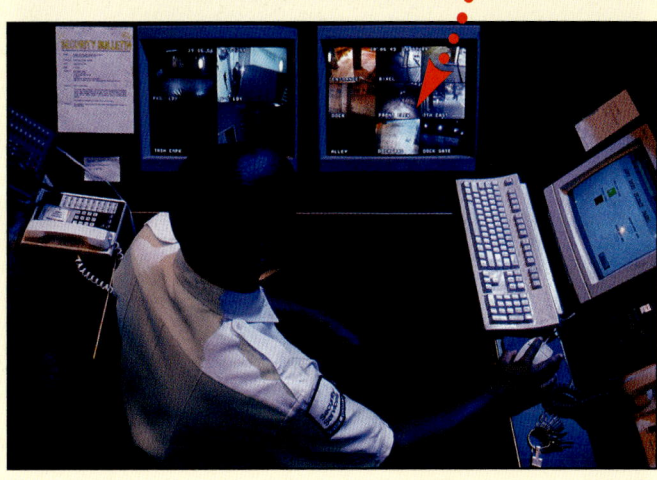

The heroin trail

Here you'll explore an example of crime that involves many people, in different countries.

The heroin story starts here

For most heroin, the story starts in Afghanistan – the world's top producer.

This is Hamid, a poor farmer. He needs money for his family. He can earn most by growing opium poppies …

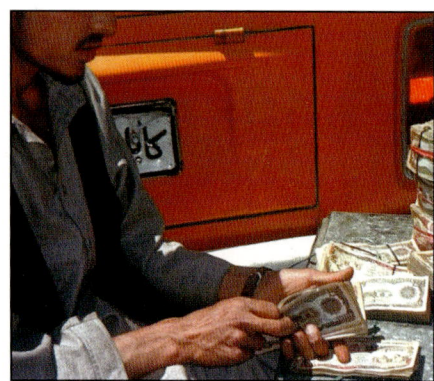

… so he goes to the local drug trader, who gives him the seeds, and enough money to last him for several months.

He plants the poppy seeds in October on land where he used to grow wheat. By the following May the poppy is ready to harvest.

He takes a white liquid from the seed heads. This is **opium gum**. He sells it to the trader for about £30 a kilo. The gum …

… is then turned into **heroin**. (1 kg of gum gives 100 g of heroin.) It is smuggled across the border to Iran, past the border patrols.

Three weeks later, in London, it is being sold for £40 000 a kilo. Emma is just about to buy a little. In time it will ruin her life.

From Afghanistan to the UK

This map shows one route used to get heroin from Afghanistan to the UK.

◆ The heroin enters Iran by camel, bike, truck.
◆ A big drug trader may send 10 or 12 trucks at a time, loaded with several tonnes of heroin – and with armed guards to protect it.
◆ From Iran, most of it goes through Turkey. From there it gets smuggled into the UK in trucks, ships, boats and planes.

A lot of heroin got sold along the way. That's why Iran has thousands of heroin addicts.

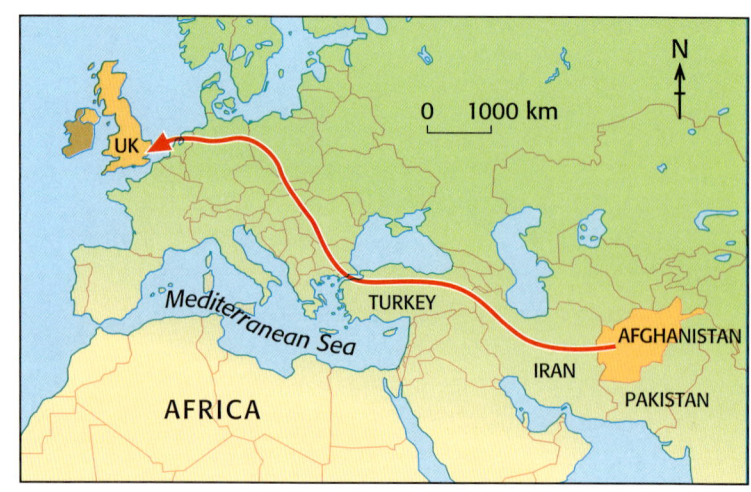

It's big business!

◆ The heroin trade is big business – worth billions of pounds a year. (The opium farmers get only a fraction of this.)
◆ It relies on people getting addicted.
◆ Some addicts then rob and steal to pay for the drug.
◆ Experts think that some of the money from the heroin trade gets used to fund terrorists.

Iran fights back

◆ Iran tries hard to stop heroin getting across the border from Afghanistan.
◆ It has spent millions putting up border fences and barriers.
◆ 42 000 soldiers and policemen patrol the border.
◆ On average, 3 per day get killed in clashes with heroin smugglers, and many more get injured.

Even if Iran wins its battle, that won't solve the heroin problem. Smugglers will just find other routes out of Afghanistan.

▲ *Iranian soldiers scan the border.*

Your turn

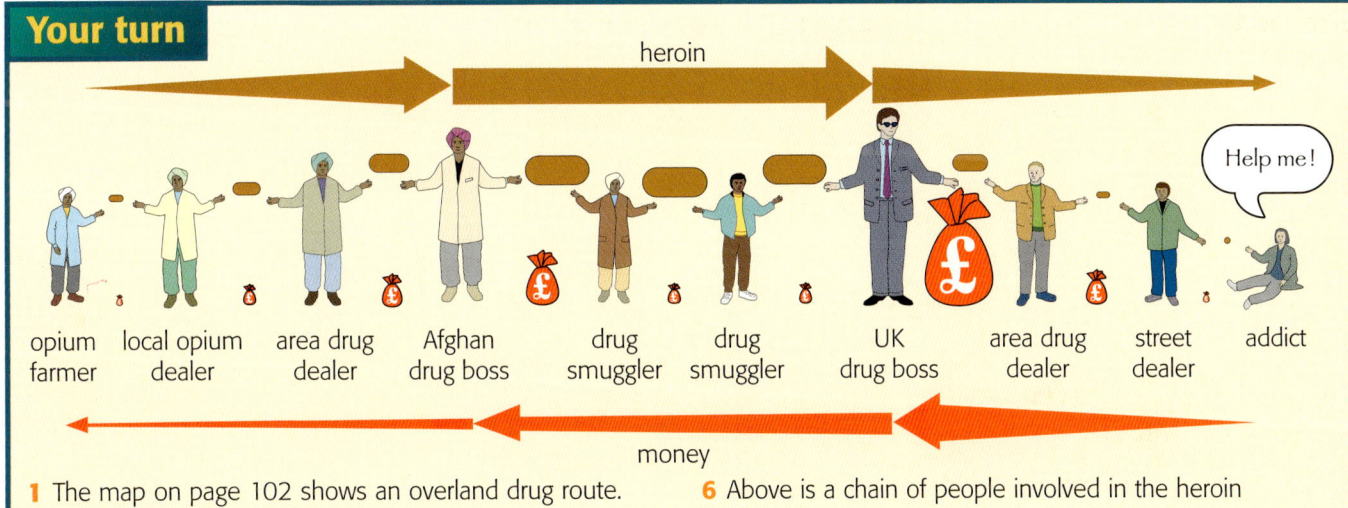

heroin

opium farmer · local opium dealer · area drug dealer · Afghan drug boss · drug smuggler · drug smuggler · UK drug boss · area drug dealer · street dealer · addict

Help me!

money

1 The map on page 102 shows an overland drug route. List the countries the heroin passes through on this route, to get to the UK. (Pages 128–129 will help.)

2 a About how long is the border between Iran and Afghanistan? (Use the map scale.)
   150 km   950 km   1800 km
   b It is hard to patrol. Why? (Clues in photos!)

3 Other countries help Iran to fight drug trafficking. (For example the UK helps with training, night-time binoculars, and bullet-proof vests for the patrols.)
   a What is *drug trafficking*? (Glossary.)
   b Why do other countries want to help Iran?

4 Many drug traffickers now avoid the Afghanistan / Iran border. They get to Iran through other countries. Which country do you think a trafficker would choose, to get to Iran from:
   a southern Afghanistan?   b northern Afghanistan?

5 Drug trafficking is an example of *organized crime*. Explain the term in italics. (Glossary?)

6 Above is a chain of people involved in the heroin business.
   a Most got involved for one reason. What was it?
   b Is each person in the chain a criminal? Explain your answer.
   c Why did the user start taking heroin? Suggest some possible reasons.

7 You're a world leader. You want to persuade Hamid and other farmers never to grow opium poppies again. What will you do? Write an action plan.

8 Look at this opinion.
   a Do you agree that drug dealing has no victims?
   b Write a response to this person. Answer as fully as you can, giving reasons for what you think.

Drug dealing is a crime with no victims – people buy drugs because they want to!

7 Oi Brazil !

Welcome to Brazil! The fifth largest country in the world, with the fifth largest population. Where you'll find …

▲ … the world's largest rainforest, full of exotic plants and animals …

▲ … huge cities …

▲ … glorious sandy beaches …

▲ … great food …

▲ … great poverty …

▲ … great wealth …

▲ … people of every race and colour …

▲ …and spectacular scenery.

Equator

60°

SOUTH AMERICA

Tropic of Capricorn

BRAZIL

The big picture

This chapter is all about Brazil. These are the big ideas behind the chapter:

◆ Brazil is a large country, rich in natural resources.

◆ It is a land of contrasts (in climate, population density and so on).

◆ It is at a medium level of development. (It has a lively economy – but a great deal of poverty and inequality.)

◆ Like every country, Brazil depends on other countries for many things.

◆ The rainforest is at risk as Brazil develops.

Brazil at a glance

Area: 8.5 million sq km
(5th largest country in the world)
Population: 178 million people
(5th largest population)
How wealthy is it?
9th largest economy in the world
How developed is it?
Ranks about 70th in the world

Your goals for this chapter

By the end of this chapter you should be able to answer these questions:

◆ Where in the world is Brazil?

◆ What can I say about these, and where are they on the map?

   Brazil's main physical features   its climate zones   its ecosystems

◆ What kinds of natural resources does Brazil have?

◆ Why does Brazil have such a big mixture of races?

◆ Which parts of Brazil are most crowded? And most empty? And why?

◆ Which are Brazil's top 10 cities, and where are they on the map?

◆ What is Brazil's employment structure like? And how has it changed?

◆ What clues can I look for, to see how developed a country is?

◆ What do these terms mean?

   GDP   GDP per capita   life expectancy   infant mortality
   adult literacy rate   undernourished

◆ How developed is Brazil, compared to countries like the UK and India?

◆ Brazil is said to have an unequal society. Why is this?

◆ In what ways are Brazil's North East and South East regions different?

◆ In what ways are Brazil and the rest of the world interdependent?

◆ Why is the rainforest at risk, as Brazil develops?

Did you know?

◆ Brazil is about 35 times larger than the UK...
◆ ... but has only about 3 times as many people.

Did you know?

◆ Brazil is named after a tree that grows there: the brazil tree, which produces brazil nuts.

Did you know?

◆ The official language of Brazil is Portuguese.

And then ...

When you finish this chapter you can come back to this page and see if you have met your goals!

Your chapter starter

The photos on page 104 were taken in Brazil.

Where's Brazil?

From the photos, do you think it would be a good place to live?

What else do you know about Brazil, that's not mentioned here?

Terra do futebal!

What's Brazil like?

In this unit you'll learn about Brazil's main physical features, and its climate zones.

Brazil's physical features

The Amazon basin and the Brazilian Highlands are Brazil's two main physical features. (Look at the map below.)

The Brazilian Highlands

◆ A mix of ancient hills, plateaux (high flat areas) and mountains.
◆ They rise sharply from the coast, forming a steep slope called the Great Escarpment.
◆ There's just a narrow strip of land between the escarpment and the Atlantic Ocean.

The River Amazon

◆ Rises in Peru and flows through Brazil to the Atlantic Ocean.
◆ The world's second longest river – 6580 km. (The Nile is first.)
◆ Drains over a third of Brazil, including the rainforest (above).
◆ Has hundreds of tributaries.
◆ Is over 80 km wide at its mouth!

Did you know?

◆ There is not even one bridge over the Amazon, in its 6580 km journey to the ocean.

Guyana Highland

River Amazon

Amazon Basin

River Sao Francisco

Brazilian Highlands

Pantanal

River Paraná

0   500 km

N

Rio de Janeiro

Key
height (m)

1200 and over
800–1200
200–800
0–200
- - - edge of drainage basin

The coast has many miles of beautiful sandy beaches.

The Sugar Loaf mountain above Rio de Janeiro is made of granite. You can go up it by cable car.

Other rivers

◆ Brazil has a great many rivers. The map above shows just the main ones. Note those names!
◆ The Paraná is the second longest river in South America (4200 km).

Did you know?

◆ Some native Indians believe the Amazon is the moon's tears.
◆ She weeps because she loves the sun but can't get closer to him.

Brazil's climate

Brazil is huge – over four-fifths the size of Europe. So it is not surprising that it has a range of climates.

Most of Brazil lies in the tropics so is hot all year, with an average temperature of around 25 °C. But rainfall varies, due to factors such as:

◆ the height of the land

◆ the distance from the coast

◆ the prevailing wind direction.

Now look at its climate zones.

hot with very dry season
◆ hot all year and gets a bit hotter in the dry season
◆ not that much rain in the wet season, and if it fails there is drought.

hot and wet
◆ hot all year – the temperature does not vary much
◆ very wet, with most rain falling in the first half of the year.

a bit cooler, and wet
◆ a bit cooler since it's further from the equator
◆ wet all year but a bit drier towards the middle of the year.

hot and wet, with dry season
◆ quite hot all year (like a hot summer's day in the UK)
◆ has a wet and dry season
◆ most rain falls in December to March when the sun is more directly overhead.

milder and wet
◆ has different seasons, like us
◆ some rain all year round
◆ you may even get snow in winter (around July).

Equator

prevailing wind

Tropic of Capricorn

N

0   500 km

Your turn

1 Which are the two main physical features of Brazil?

2 Write down three facts about the Amazon.

3 This is about the climate map above. (Unit 2.7 and the map on page 106 will help you answer it.)
  a It is always cooler at D than at A. Why?
  b It is always cooler at E than at F. Why?
  c Give a reason why it's wetter at F than at B.
  d C is very close to the equator, and to the Amazon. Try to explain why it's always hot and wet there.

4 On the right are four climate graphs. Match them to the four places A–D on the map above.

5 Copy and complete, using words from the list below:
  The _____ _____ of Brazil is _____ and _____ .
  The large central area is _____ with a _____ _____.
  The _____ is _____ with four seasons like the UK.
  The driest part of all is in the _____ _____.
  south   hot   north east   wet
  milder   dry season   north west

6 A challenge! When it's winter in London it is summer at D. Explain why. Draw diagrams if that helps.

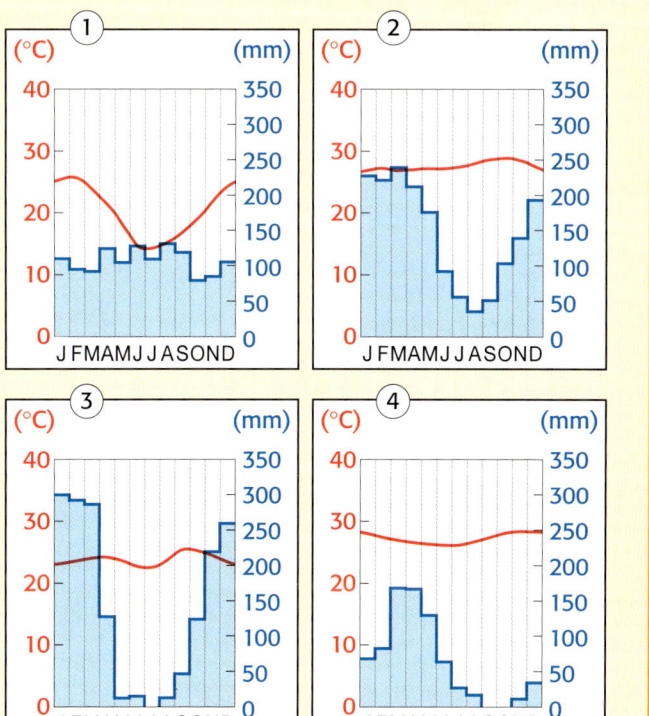

Brazil's natural riches

In this unit you'll learn about Brazil's ecosystems and natural resources.

Brazil's ecosystems

Brazil has some very different ecosystems. Look at them:

Equator

Tropic of Capricorn

0   500 km

N

The caatinga

◆ Semi-arid (like a desert).
◆ The plants are mainly shrubs and cacti, with very few trees.
◆ Lots of scorpions, spiders, snakes, and colourful birds live here.
There's a photo of it on page 121.

Did you know?
◆ Brazil has over 1600 species of birds.

The tropical rainforest

◆ The largest area of rainforest in the world. It covers about 40% of Brazil!
◆ It grows thick and lush.
◆ It teems with plants, animals and insects. (Parrots, monkeys, sloths and orchids just for a start.)

The Mata Atlantica

◆ 500 years ago the coast was covered in thick forest. (*Mata* means forest.)
◆ This had a vast range of trees and plants, including the brazil trees that gave Brazil its name.
◆ But most of it has been cut down. Only about one tenth is left.

The Pantanal

◆ The world's largest swampland.
◆ It's full of water loving plants and animals, including giant anaconda – snakes that can swim.

The cerrado

◆ This is savanna (as in Unit 3.7).
◆ In the dry season the grass gets so dry that lightning sets it on fire.
◆ There are not many trees – and they have thick bark to protect them against fire.
◆ The animals here include deer, rhea (like ostriches) and wolves.
◆ You'll see lots of termite mounds like this one.

The pampas

◆ These are grassy plains.
◆ Now they are heavily farmed, with many cattle ranches.

Brazil's natural resources

For centuries the wood in Brazil's forests has been used as a resource. But Brazil is rich in other natural resources too.

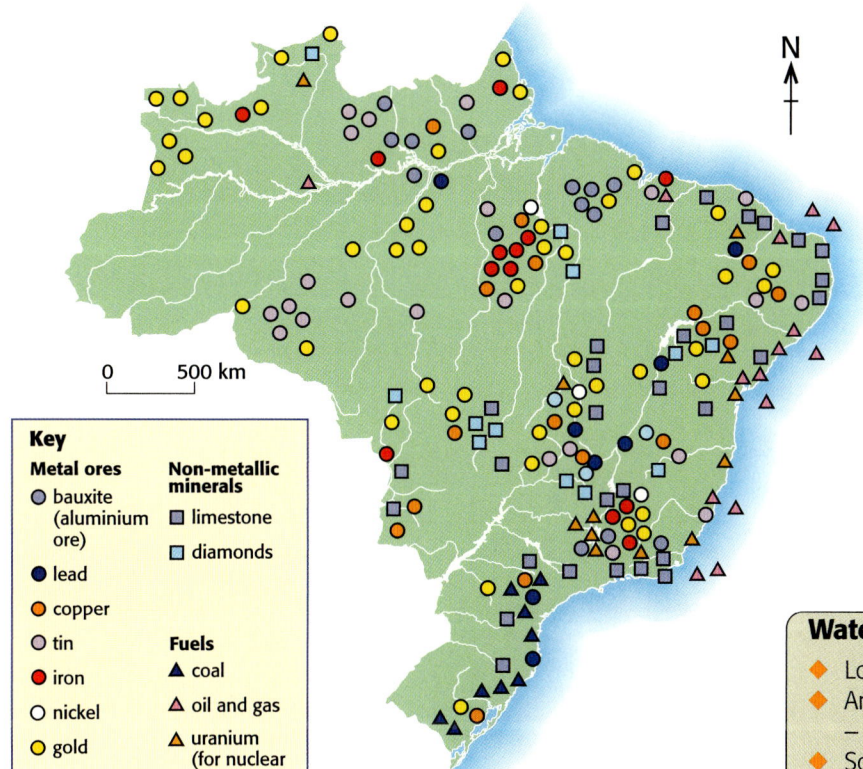

Key

Metal ores
- bauxite (aluminium ore)
- lead
- copper
- tin
- iron
- nickel
- gold
- zinc

Non-metallic minerals
- limestone
- diamonds

Fuels
- coal
- oil and gas
- uranium (for nuclear fuel)

Fuels
- Brazil has some oil and gas. (But not nearly enough for its needs.)
- It also grows sugar cane to make **ethanol**, which is used as a fuel for cars and power stations.

Minerals
- Brazil is one of the world's top producers of iron, aluminium, tin and several other metals …
- … and of diamonds and other precious stones …

Soil and climate
- Brazil has a wide range of soils – and climates.
- So it can grow a wide range of crops: coffee, sugar cane, soya beans, rice, bananas, oranges, cotton and more.

Water
- Lots of rivers for supplying water.
- And many of them are fast and powerful – great for hydroelectricity (page 74).
- So Brazil gets 90% of its electricity from hydro. (It has some very large dams!)

Brazil is lucky. Its natural resources are helping to make it wealthy. For example it is the world's top exporter of coffee, sugar, soya beans, beef, oranges and orange juice, and the second largest exporter of iron ore.

But the map above does not tell the full story. So far, only about one-third of Brazil has been fully explored for minerals. There's much more to find!

Your turn

1 a What is an ecosystem? (Unit 3.1 will help.)
  b Name six ecosystems in Brazil and write two sentences about each.

2 Look at the map on page 108.
  a Plants grow really well at X on the map. Why?
  b A cactus can store water in its stem. Explain why cacti have evolved at Y, but are not found at Z. Pages 47 and 107 may help.

3 Why has most of the Mata Atlantica gone? (Clues on pages 110 and 112.)

4 Look at Brazil's other natural resources, above. Which are found in the rainforest? List them.

5 We can destroy ecosytems in our search for resources.
  a Make a grid like the one started on the right, for Brazil's rainforest. Show logging (cutting down trees for timber), farming, mining, dams, oil exploration.
  b On your grid, mark X where you think two things are in conflict, ✓ where they benefit each other, and O if you think they don't affect each other.
  c From your grid, would you say that exploiting resources puts the rainforest under threat? Explain.

6 You are the President of Brazil. Write a speech for TV, explaining why Brazil has a great future, free from poverty.

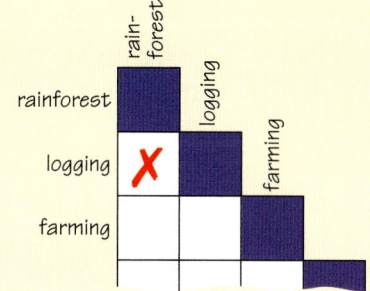

The peopling of Brazil

In this unit you will learn why Brazil has such a great mix of races.

The Indios

50 000 years ago, the plants and animals had Brazil to themselves. But then at some point – we don't know when – the first humans arrived. They had spread out slowly from East Africa:

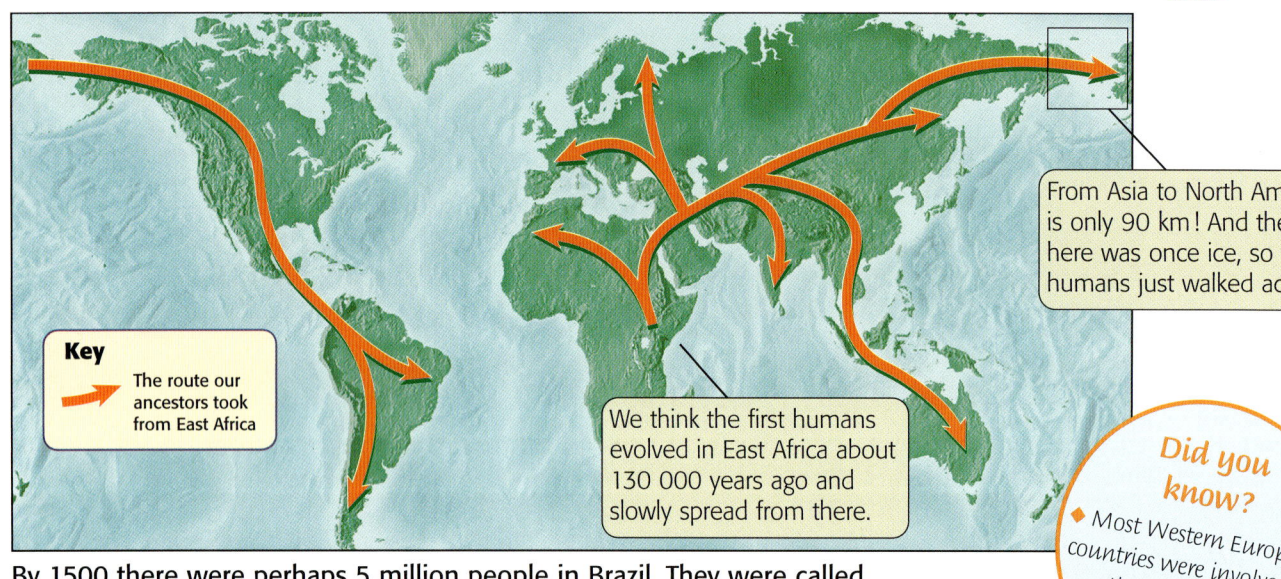

Key
The route our ancestors took from East Africa

From Asia to North America is only 90 km! And the sea here was once ice, so humans just walked across.

We think the first humans evolved in East Africa about 130 000 years ago and slowly spread from there.

By 1500 there were perhaps 5 million people in Brazil. They were called Indians or Indios – by mistake. Because when Christopher Columbus first reached South America, he thought it was India.

The arrival of the Portuguese

On 22 April 1500, a fleet of Portuguese sailing ships arrived at the coast of Brazil. They were led by a nobleman named Pedro Alvarez Cabral. He claimed the land for Portugal.

At first, the Portuguese exported brazilwood from their new colony. Then they switched to sugar cane. Europe was mad about sugar and it grew well in the warm moist climate along the coast.

The slave trade begins

Cutting sugar cane is hard work. At first, Indios were forced to work on the sugar plantations. But they rebelled. Then the Portuguese had another idea. They would 'buy' people in Africa in exchange for cheap goods, and ship them to Brazil to work. It was the start of Europe's **slave trade**.

In 1538 the first slaves arrived. Over the next 300 years at least 4 million African slaves were taken to Brazil. They were forced to work without pay and treated like animals. Many more died at sea in the filthy crowded ships. But at last, in 1888, slavery was abolished in Brazil.

The fortune hunters

By 1700, Brazil's sugar cane industry had begun to decline. And then – gold and diamonds were found. Half a million more Portuguese arrived, hoping to make their fortune. The slaves were put to work in the mines.

▲ *The sugar cane harvest.*

Workers from Europe

When slavery ended, Brazil took in workers from Europe. This table shows just the largest groups who came. Most worked on the land. But as towns and cities grew and spread, more workers of all kinds were needed. Like builders, doctors, teachers, engineers, cooks …

Today, you'll find people in Brazil from every race on the Earth.

Immigrants to Brazil, 1876–1976	
Italians	1 600 000
Portuguese	1 500 000
Spanish	600 000
German	300 000
Japanese	250 000

▲ *At a football match in multiracial Brazil.*

Did you know?
- Brazil once had an emperor (in Portugal).
- Now it's a republic. (No royal family.)

Your turn

1 Explain each of these facts.
  a Humans did not reach South America until long after they'd reached North America.
  b About 40% of Brazilians are of African descent.
  c Brazil is a multicultural society. (Glossary?)

2 Look how Brazil's population has grown:

Year	Brazil's population (millions)
1872	9.9
1900	17.3
1940	41.2
1950	51.9
1960	70.1
1970	93.2
1980	121.3
1991	146.9
2002	176.3
2020	?

  a Show this data as a line graph. (Use a full page.)
  b In 1960 the population was 70.1 million.
   i By about which year had this figure doubled?
   ii How many years did it take to double?
   iii At this rate, what might it reach in 2020?

3 Its fast population rise means Brazil needs more and more schools. What else does it have to think about? Give your answer as a spider map.

Brazil's population rise means it needs …

more schools   more teachers   more homes

4 A **population pyramid** is a special bar chart that shows ages. Look at this population pyramid for Brazil, for the year 2000. It shows that males aged 10–14 formed nearly 5% of the population.

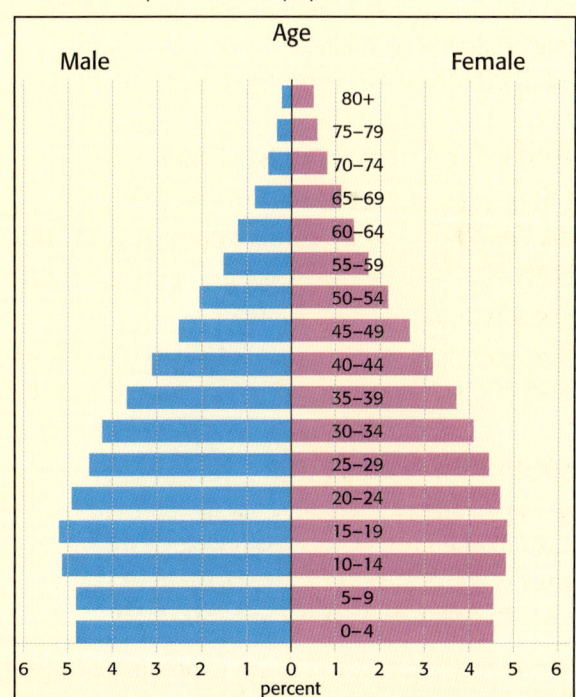

  a About what % of the population consisted of:
   i girls aged 10–14?   **ii** men aged 35–39?
   iii women aged 50–54?   **iv** children up to age 4?
  b Overall, which was the largest age group?

5 '*Brazil is a country of young people.*' Do you agree? Give evidence to back up your answer.

So where is everyone?

In this unit you'll see how Brazil's population is spread around the country, and learn about favelas.

Population distribution

This map shows how people are spread around Brazil. Some areas are highly populated and some are almost empty.

Look at the main cities. Rio de Janeiro (*River of January*) is famous. But São Paolo (*Saint Paul*) is larger. Brasilia is the capital of Brazil. It was built as a new city and 'opened' in 1960.

The table shows the populations of the ten largest cities. In fact most of these cities have spread out to join other towns and cities, giving huge **agglomerations**.

The São Paolo agglomeration has over 19 million people!

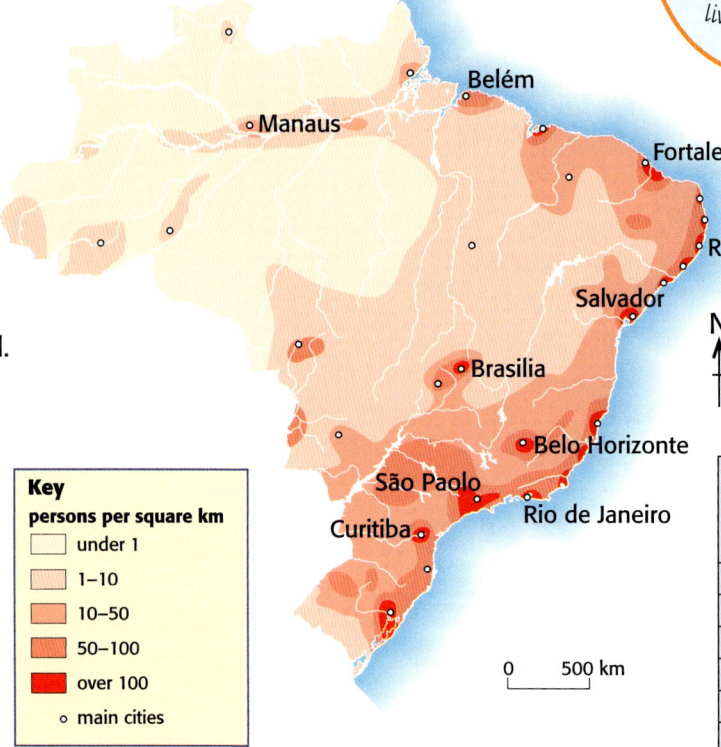

Key
persons per square km
☐	under 1
☐	1–10
☐	10–50
☐	50–100
☐	over 100
○	main cities

0   500 km

The top 10 cities	
Name	Population (millions)
São Paolo	10.3
Rio de Janeiro	6.2
Salvador	2.6
Belo Horizonte	2.4
Fortaleza	2.3
Brasilia	2.2
Curitiba	1.7
Manaus	1.6
Recife	1.5
Belém	1.4

Why the cities are growing

Brazil's cities are growing fast. Because people are living longer. Because many Brazilians have large families. And because lots of people from rural areas are moving to the cities, for reasons like these …

There are lots of good jobs here. Not like in my village.

And you can earn more in the city.

It's good to be near hospitals and dentists. Not like in rural areas!

Schools are better in the city – and I want my children to have a good education.

It's nice to have all those shops close by.

Life was boring in my village. It's much more exciting here.

Life in the favelas

Many poor people from rural areas have crowded into Brazil's cities, hoping to find work.

This is a photo of São Paolo. In front is a favela – a collection of shacks built on waste ground, without permission. The poorest people in the city live here.

◆ The shacks are built from anything – bricks, old sheets of metal, bits of wood and plastic.

◆ Most have no running water, or electricity. But many are hooked up illegally to cables and water mains.

◆ There are open drains everywhere, and rain turns the paths to muddy sewers.

◆ People get work wherever they can in the city – in factories, or on building sites, or as servants in rich people's homes.

◆ Not many favela children finish school. They work or beg instead.

◆ There is a lot of disease, because of all the germs.

◆ There is a lot of crime, and violence, and drug use.

All of Brazil's cities have favelas. Rio de Janeiro and São Paolo have most. In fact about 20% of Rio's population lives in favelas.

The government is trying to improve favelas, and provide them with water and other services. But progress is slow.

▲ A favela in São Paolo.

Did you know?
◆ In Rio there are special trips around the favelas for tourists.

Your turn

1 Copy and complete these sentences using words or phrases from the list below. (Check the map!)
   a The ____ _____ of Brazil is the most crowded part.
   b Most Brazilians live on or near the ____.
   c Overall, the rainforest area has ____ ____ people.
   d The centre of Brazil is quite _____ populated.
   e The area around São Paolo is ____ populated.
   f São Paolo is Brazil's _____ city and Rio de Janeiro is _____.

   sparsely   lots of   smallest   very few
   second   north west   south east   densely
   coast   largest

2 Suggest reasons why most Brazilians live on or near the coast. (Think about Brazil's history, given on page 110. The map on page 106 may help too.)

3 **a** Look at this table. Compared with the UK:
   i about many times larger is Brazil in area?
   ii about how many times larger is its population?
   b Work out the population density for each country.

4 Today São Paolo is nearly three times larger than it was 30 years ago. Give some reasons for this.

5 You have just moved to São Paolo from a small village, to find work. You have rented a room at **X** in the favela above. Write a letter to your sister telling her about your new home and its surroundings.

6 Now think about this person's opinion. What would you say in reply?

They should bring the bulldozers in and clear that favela away.

	Brazil	UK
Area (sq km)	8.5 million	0.24 million
Population	178 million	60 million
Population density (number of people per sq km)	?	?

What does everyone do?

In this unit you will learn how people in Brazil earn a living.

At work in Brazil

About 70 million adults in Brazil are out at work, earning a living.
So what kind of work do they do?

Around 16 million work in the **primary sector** – taking materials from the Earth or sea. Most are in farming, like this orange farmer …

… but mining is also important, since Brazil has great mineral wealth. And the long coastline means fishing is important too.

Around 17 million work in the **secondary sector**, or **manufacturing**. For example in factories that make clothing …

… or furniture, or TVs, or mobile phones, or more expensive things like steel, cars, planes, and even satellites !

Over 36 million are in the **tertiary sector** – they provide **services**. For example teach, or work in offices, or sell things, or drive taxis.

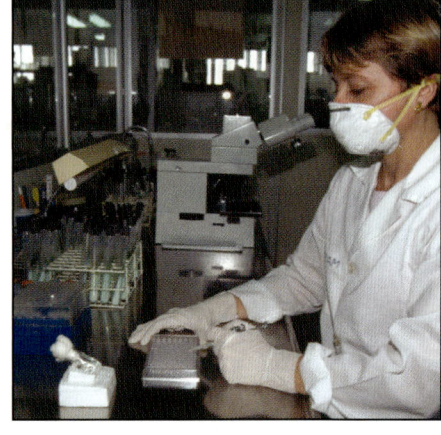

And a small number work in the **quaternary sector**, doing advanced research. For example in solar power, or new medicines.

Brazil's employment structure

This pie chart shows Brazil's **employment structure**: the % who work in each sector. (The % in the quaternary sector is too small to show up.)

At the same time, Brazil has quite a lot of **unemployment**. There are many adults who want to work but can't get a job. In some years up to 8 million are jobless. The government gives money to help some of them.

Also, many young people work to help their families. Among children aged 10–14, three out of every twenty go to work, often after school.
(These are not included in the pie chart.)

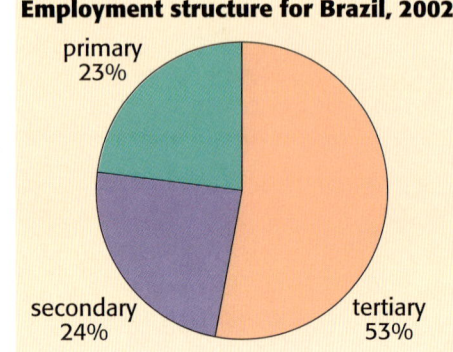

Employment structure for Brazil, 2002

primary 23%

secondary 24%

tertiary 53%

How employment has changed over the years

Employment in Brazil wasn't always like it is today.

1880

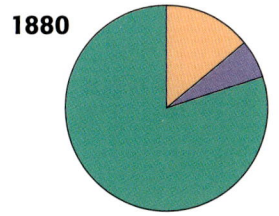

1980

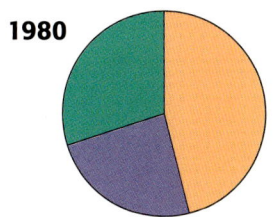

Today

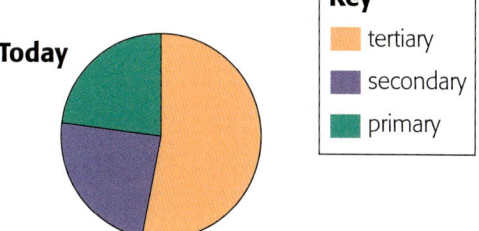

Key
- tertiary
- secondary
- primary

For hundreds of years after the Portuguese arrived, most people worked in the primary sector – producing things like sugar cane, rubber, and metal ores for export.

Meanwhile Brazil had to import machinery and other goods. But around 1950 it began to build factories to make its own goods – so the secondary sector grew fast.

As Brazil got better off, the demand for services grew. More teachers were needed, and doctors, nurses, shop staff, secretaries … So the tertiary sector took over.

Your turn

1 In which sector of Brazil's economy do these work?
   a Isadora, a soap star
   b Felipe, a farmer who grows oranges
   c Lula, elected President of Brazil in 2002
   d Paulo, a miner in the iron ore mine at Carajas
   e Julia, who weaves rugs for tourists
   f Felipe, who assembles mobile phones in the Nokia factory in Manaus

2 See if you can explain these facts about employment structure in Brazil.
   A 5 years after the Portuguese arrived, almost all of the workers were in the primary sector.
   B As farms and mines get more machinery, employment in the primary sector falls.
   C As factories get more computers and robots, the secondary sector shrinks.
   D As people get wealthier, the tertiary sector grows.
   E A boom in tourism brings a rise in the tertiary sector.

3 **Employment structure**

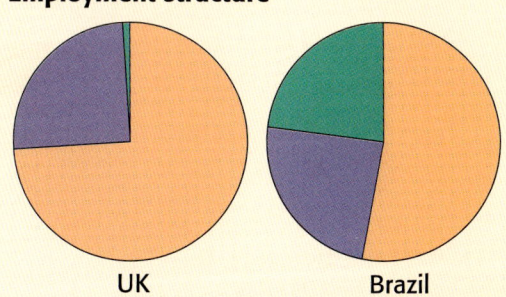

UK   Brazil

Compare these pie charts for Brazil and the UK.
   a Which country has a higher % of workers:
     i in farming?   ii providing services?
   b Which country has *most workers*? Explain.
   c Usually, as a country develops, the % of workers in the primary sector falls. Which country appears to be more developed?

4 The pie charts above give the *overall* employment structure for Brazil. But in every country, employment structure changes from region to region.

This map shows Brazil's five regions. The largest one, the North, is about sixteen times the size of the UK!

Brazil's regions and their populations

14 million
NORTH
48 million
NORTH EAST
WEST CENTRAL
15 million
SOUTH EAST
75 million
26 million
SOUTH
0 500 km

Use the maps you've met so far in this chapter to help you answer these questions. Give your reasons.
   a In which region is the % of workers in the primary sector likely to be: i highest? ii lowest?
   b In which region is the % of workers in the tertiary sector likely to be highest?
   c Which region has most workers?

5 It's time to predict the future.
   a Do you think employment in the primary sector for Brazil (or the UK) is ever likely to fall to 0%? Explain.
   b Draw a pie chart to show what you think Brazil's employment structure might be, in 2050.

Here you will learn what 'developed' means, and how we measure development. And then explore some data to see how developed Brazil is.

What does development mean?

Some countries are more **developed** than others. That means their people have a higher standard of living. Look at this list:

> **A highly developed country is likely to have** …
> ◆ good roads, railways, airports, phone systems
> ◆ electricity and piped water in all homes
> ◆ good hospitals and schools for everyone
> ◆ lots of other services (shops, cinemas, gyms and so on)
> ◆ modern factories
> ◆ enough food for everyone
> ◆ opportunity for everyone to work, and earn a living
> ◆ little or no poverty

A *less developed* country may have some of those things. For example it may have some good roads – and a lot of dirt tracks.

Every country in the world is at a different stage of development. Some are *more developed* than others. Some have a long way to go.

How can we measure development?

If you go to a country and look around, you can get a good idea of how developed it is. But to really find out, you need to *measure* development, using an **indicator**.

One indicator is the country's **gross domestic product** or **GDP**. It is the total value of the goods and services the country produces in a year:

▲ *This area is a lot more developed …*

▲ *… than this one.*

GDP per capita for 2002: US$ 2600

It's what we'd each get if the GDP were shared out equally.

Some chance!

Some PPP values for you.

GDP per capita for 2002 ($US PPP)	
USA	35 800
UK	26 400
Portugal	11 900
Brazil	7800
China	4580
India	2700
Kenya	1000

That's purchas[ing] power parity.

Think of GDP as the total wealth the country produces in a year. (It is given in US dollars to make it easy to compare countries.)

GDP per capita is the GDP divided by the population. It gives you an idea of how well off people are, on average.

But a dollar buys more in some places than others. So figures can be adjusted to **PPP** values to let you compare countries more fairly.

Usually, **the higher the GDP per capita, the more developed a country is**. But GDP per capita does not tell the full story. It does not say what the country produces. It might produce lots of guns, but not enough food! And it does not tell you whether the wealth is divided fairly.

Other indicators to look at

GDP per capita gives you an idea of how developed a country is. But for a true picture you need to look at other signs or **indicators** too. Like these:

That's it?

Life expectancy
How long a person in that country can expect to live.

Infant mortality
How many babies per thousand born alive who die before they reach 1.

Adult literacy rate
% of people aged 15 and over who can read and write a simple sentence.

Undernourished people
% of the population who don't get enough to eat, and live in hunger.

Your turn

It's time to explore, to see how developed Brazil is.

1 First, make a list like the one on page 116 to show what you'd expect to find in a *less developed* country. (For example *not enough good hospitals*.)

2 a What does *GDP per capita* mean?
 b Why is GDP per capita given:
   i in US dollars? ii often in US dollars PPP?
 c Draw a bar graph for the data for GDP per capita (US$ PPP) from the bottom of page 116.
 d Now, using your graph to help you, write a paragraph comparing Brazil with the other countries.

3 a What does *life expectancy* mean?
 b As a country develops, life expectancy rises. Why? Suggest as many reasons as you can. Give your answer as a spider map, like this:

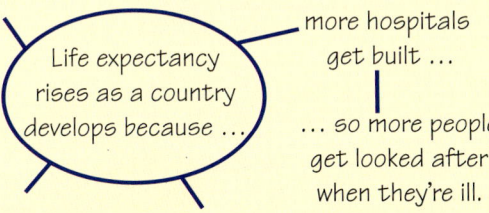

Life expectancy rises as a country develops because …

more hospitals get built …

… so more people get looked after when they're ill.

4 Now look at the other three indicators at the top of this page. For each, say whether it will *rise* or *fall* as the country develops, and give one reason.

5 **Changes in Brazil**

Indicator	1970	2002
GDP per capita ($ US PPP)	5600	7800
Life expectancy (years)	60	68
Infant mortality (per 1000 babies)	95	30
Adult literacy rate, %	66	87
% undernourished	not known	10

Look at the table above. Is Brazil growing more developed, less developed or staying the same? Give evidence to support your answer.

6 Now look at the table at the bottom of the page.
 a Using this data, see if you can put the 7 countries in order, with the most developed one first. (Perhaps you could rank each country from 1 to 7 for each indicator, then add up its rank numbers?)
 b Compare your list with the list for *GDP per capita* on page 116. Is Brazil in the same place in each?

7 So far you have met five indicators of development. There are many others! Decide if this could be used as an indicator, and say why:
 a the amount of electricity used per person
 b the number of cars per thousand people
 c the % of the population with access to the internet
 d how happy the people feel.

Country	Life expectancy (years)	Infant mortality per 1000 babies	Adult literacy rate (%)	% of population undernourished
Brazil	68	30	87	10
China	71	31	91	9
India	64	67	61	24
Kenya	45	78	84	44
Portugal	76	5	93	low
UK	78	5	99	low
USA	77	7	97	low

Inequality in Brazil

In this unit you will learn about one big challenge Brazil has to tackle: the inequality in its society.

Barbra's day

My mum woke me as usual at 6 am – groan. Coconut pancakes and orange juice for breakfast. Then dad's driver drove me to school for 7. We had Miss Cardoso today – boring! When school finished at 12 we had dance class for an hour. We do all kinds of modern dance.

Magaretta's mother drove us home, and we got my mum and my two brothers and went to the beach. We do that two or three times a week. We joined in a game of volleyball for a while, and swam. Magaretta and I read magazines.

After the beach, homework for an hour. Then dad came home from the office and we had dinner. Lucia is our cook and she cooked feijoada today. It's a bean and pork stew. Now I'm going to watch TV. Then I'll have a bath and go to bed. But first I want mum to promise to take me shopping for clothes tomorrow. It's Saturday, and I need something for Anita's party.

▲ Barbra, aged 14.

Did you know?
◆ Over 25 million people in Brazil live in abject (severe) poverty.

▲ Pedro, aged 14.

Pedro's day

I always wake at 5 am. You can't sleep late in our house – not with all seven of us in one room and the baby crying! I grabbed my bucket and sponge and ran. It's about 3 km to our junction.

Francesco was already there and traffic was busy. So I filled my bucket at the petrol station tap and got started. You have to be fast washing windscreens at the traffic lights – they don't stay on red that long.

Most of the drivers are okay. But some are really nasty – they wait till you finish and then grin and drive off without giving you any money.

At 11 we took a break. We went to the market and bought bread and soup. We ate on the corner as usual. Francesco went on as usual about getting a proper job. He says there are classes to teach poor people like us about computers, and we should try to get into one. But we can't even read!

We'll stay at the junction until it's dark and most people have gone home from work. Then I'll run home really fast. I'm afraid a gang in the favela will attack me and take my money. Or else I'll fall into a drain and ruin my jeans!

I make about 8 reals a day. (*About £1.60.*) When I get home I'll give most of it to my mother – she has to pay the rent on Friday. Then we'll have bean stew, as usual. And then I'll crash out. Tomorrow is another busy day.

An unequal society

Brazil is rich in natural resources. It is developing fast. But it has one big problem: **inequality**. Some people are very wealthy. Millions are very poor.

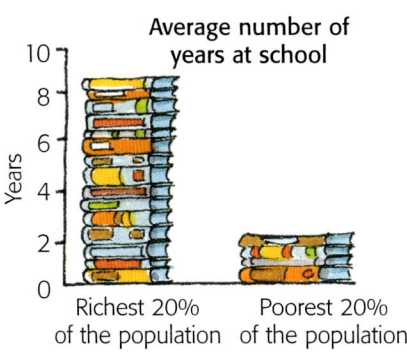

Average number of years at school

Each person here represents 10% of Brazil's population. You can see that 47% of Brazil's wealth is owned by just 10% of the people!

1% of the population owns almost half of Brazil's land. And millions of rural families have no land, and are forced to work for big landowners.

On top of that, Brazil's poorest people don't have much education. So they have even less chance of improving their lives.

The roots of this inequality lie deep in the past. Portuguese kings gave out huge tracts of land in Brazil as gifts and rewards to people. The new landowners got slaves to work on the land at first, for no pay. When slavery was abolished they hired workers, but paid them very little.

Today the landowners' families still own the land, and have got richer and richer. Their workers have not.

Did you know?
- *In Brazil, by law, all young people aged 7–14 should be at school …*
- *… but around one-fifth are not.*

Making things fairer

Brazil's government is trying to make life fairer. It is buying land from big landowners and sharing it out to poor people, with money to help them start farming. But the process is slow, and there's a long way to go.

Your turn

1 Make a large table to compare Barbra and Pedro's day. You could do it like this:

	Barbra	Pedro
morning	breakfast of …	

2 *Why* has Barbra ended up with a more comfortable life than Pedro? Try to suggest some reasons.

3 Compare these pie charts for Brazil and the UK.

How wealth is distributed

Goes to:
- 🟥 the richest 20%
- 🟩 the poorest 20%
- 🟨 the other 60% of the population

Brazil   UK

a Is there inequality in the UK? Explain.
b Which has a more unequal society, Brazil or the UK?

4 The government wants to make Brazil a more equal society. Here are two of the things it is doing.

We are helping poor people to get started as farmers.

We are providing better schools in poor areas.

Draw a flow chart to show how each will help to reduce inequality.
You could start the first one as shown on the right.
(Then think about how the farmers could use the money they earn.)

Poor people get land, and help, to start farming.
↓
Now they can grow food to feed their families.
↓
They can grow extra food to sell.

Compare two regions

Here you will see how Brazil is divided up – and then compare two regions, to see how different they are.

How Brazil is divided up

Brazil is big: over four-fifths the size of Europe! To make it easier to manage, it is divided into five main regions, and the regions are divided into states. Look at the map on the right.

RORAIMA
AMAPÁ
Manaus
Belém
AMAZONAS
NORTH
PARÁ
MARANHÃO
CEARÁ
RIO G DO N
NORTH EAST
PARAÍBA
ACRE
TOCANTINS
PIAUÍ
PERNAMBUCO
ALAGOA
RONDÔNIA
MATTO GROSSO
SERGIPE
BAHIA
WEST CENTRAL
Salvador
FEDERAL DISTRICT
Brasilia
GOIÁS
MINAS GERAIS
MATTO GROSSO DO SUL
SOUTH EAST
ESPÍRITO SANTO
SÃO PAOLO
São Paolo
RIO DE JANEIRO
Rio de Janeiro
PARANÁ
SANTA CATERINA
SOUTH
RIO GRANDE DO SUL
N
Key
boundary of region
state boundary
state capital (not all shown)
0
500 km

North East versus South East

The regions are big too. The smallest one, the South, is nearly three times the size of the UK. So it's not surprising that there are some big differences between regions.

Now you have to become a geography detective, and compare two regions – the North East and South East – to see what the differences are.

There are clues below, and in the earlier maps in this chapter. So, when you're ready, go to *Your turn*.

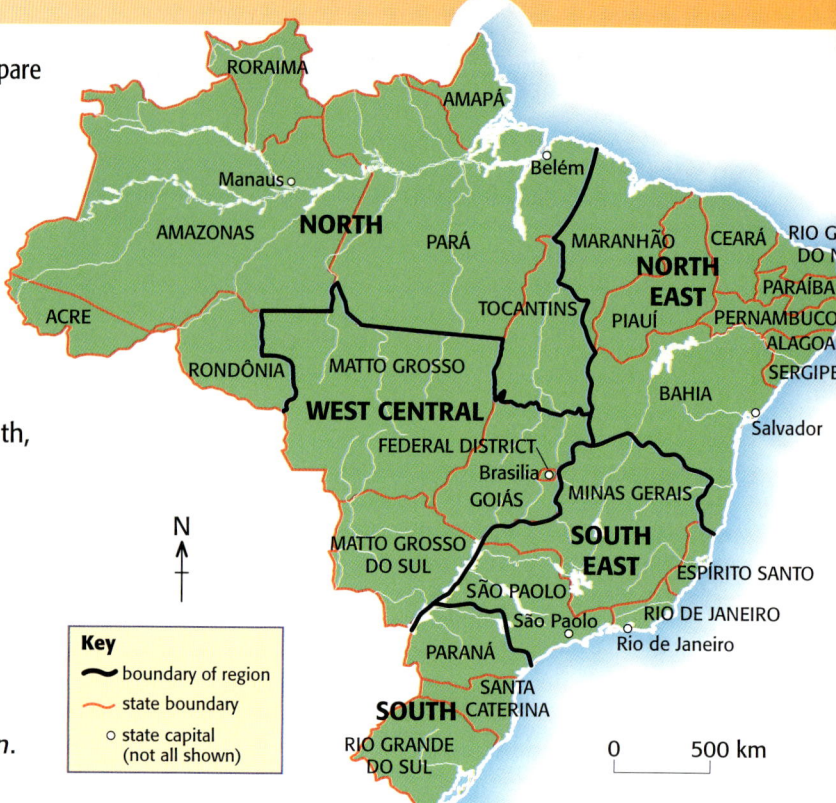

The clue box

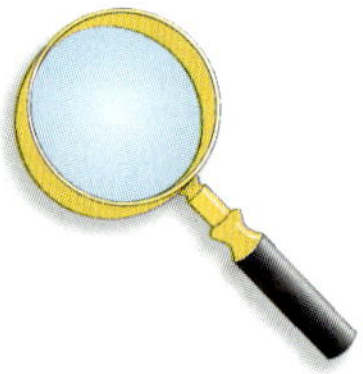

Contribution to GDP

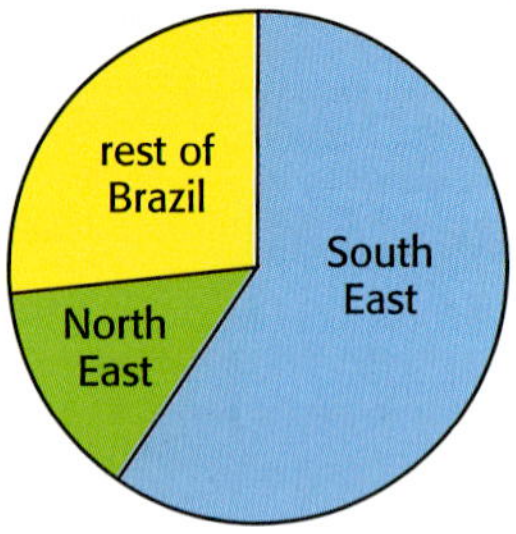

rest of Brazil
South East
North East

Some social indicators

	South East	North East
Life expectancy	69.6	65.8
Adult literacy	92.3	75.1
% of households with electricity	98	78
% of urban households with public water supply	99.5	86.1
% of children in urban areas not attending school	4.7	9.5

Resources for the two regions

Key
gold
bauxite (aluminium ore)
copper
iron
other metals
diamonds
coal
oil and gas
uranium (for nuclear fuels)

N
0
500 km

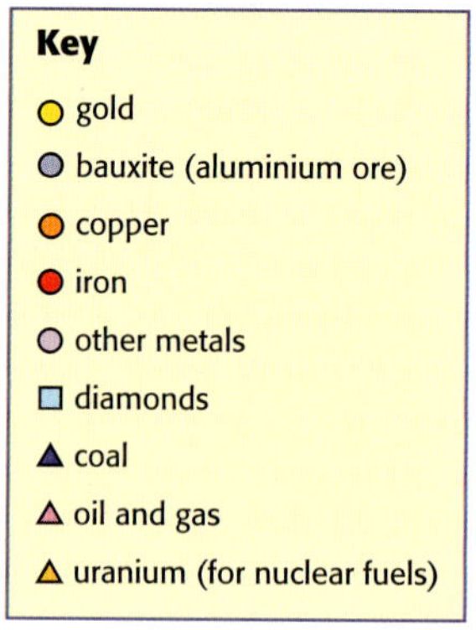

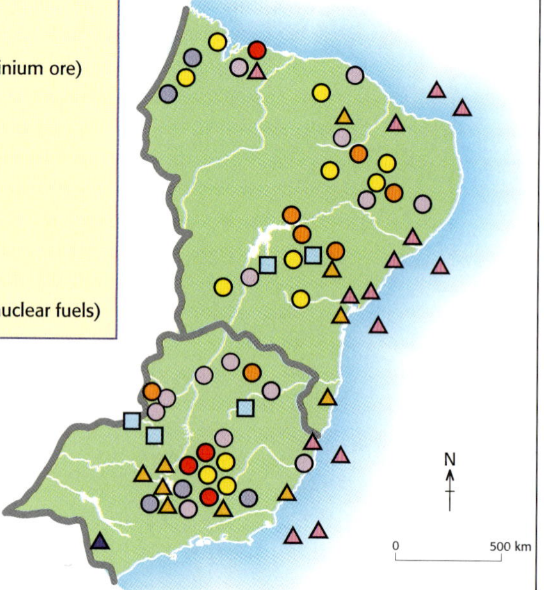

Economic activity for the two regions

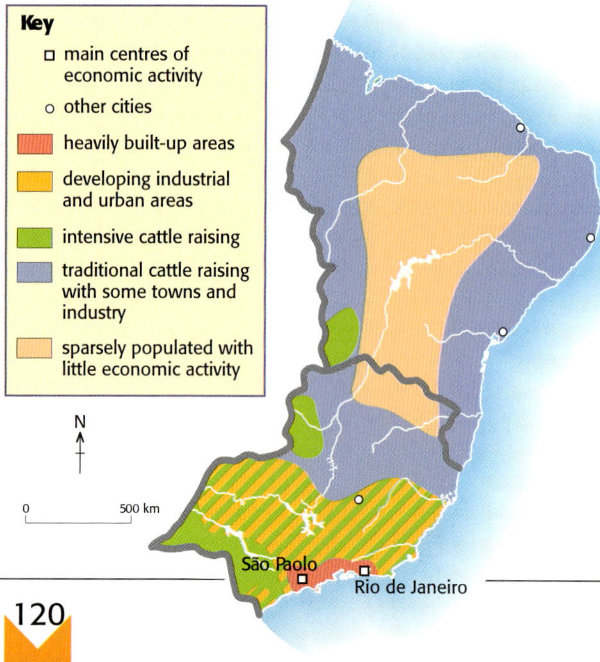

Key
main centres of economic activity
other cities
heavily built-up areas
developing industrial and urban areas
intensive cattle raising
traditional cattle raising with some towns and industry
sparsely populated with little economic activity
N
0
500 km
São Paolo
Rio de Janeiro

Population (millions)	
North East	48
South East	75

▲ Farmland in the South East region.

▲ A small farm in the caatinga in the North East region.

Your turn

Don't forget to look back at the earlier maps.

1 First, a question about Brazil's regions. Which one:
 a is largest?
 b is smallest?
 c does the Amazon river flow through?
 d is almost all rainforest?
 e probably has the most beaches?
 f has an area that suffers drought?
 g gets most rainfall?
 h is home to the Pantanal?
 i does the equator run through?
 j lies outside the tropics?
 k has Brazil's capital city?

2 a Make a copy of the table on the right.
 b Then put ticks in the correct columns. (For some items you might need to tick both columns!)

3 Photos X and Y above show farming areas.
 a X shows *intensive* farming. What do you think that means?
 b Which area appears to have a better climate for farming? How could you tell?
 c Could differences in farming make one area wealthier than the other? Explain. Which one might be wealthier?

4 A and B on the right describe the NE and SE regions. But which is which? Match each to the correct region.

5 A good detective tries to think up explanations. So now you have to try to explain why the South East of Brazil is so much more developed than the North East. You can give your answer in any form you choose. For example as a strip cartoon, or a written report, or a flow chart, or a spider map, or an interview with a politician.

Description	NE	SE
Has more high land		✔
Has Brazil's largest cities		
Has a larger area		
Is more crowded, overall		
Gets more rain, overall		
Often suffers drought		
Has a better climate for farming		
Has deposits of metal ores		
Has oil, gas and diamonds		
Has more industry		
Produces most of Brazil's goods and services		
Has a higher % of homes with electricity		
Is more developed		

A

This is the economic core of Brazil. It covers only 11% of the area of Brazil, but has 44% of the workforce. It has lots of factories. It provides more jobs in manufacturing than any other region. Overall, the workers here are better paid than in other regions.

B

This covers 18% of Brazil's area, but has only 4% of its workforce. To help it, the government has given big grants to industries to set up factories here. Some have done very well. But they use machines rather than people so have not created many new jobs.

Brazil's place in the world

In this unit you'll learn how Brazil and other countries depend on each other.

We're interdependent !

Every country depends to some extent on other countries. Countries are **interdependent**. Look at Brazil …

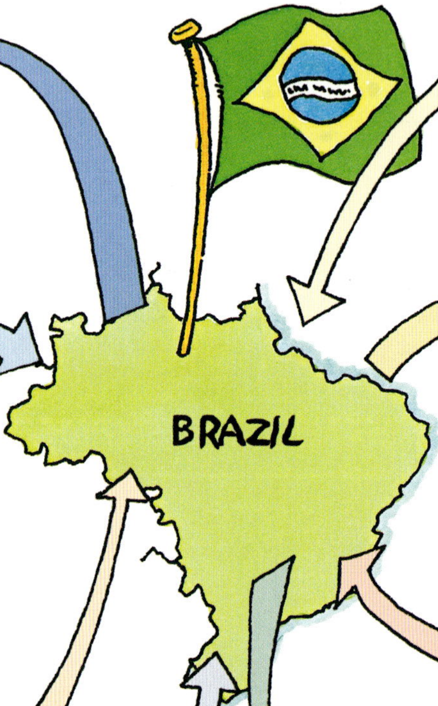

> **Did you know?**
> - Brazil's currency is called the real or R$.
> - R$1 = 100 centavos.

BRAZIL

TRADE

Sugar
Coffee

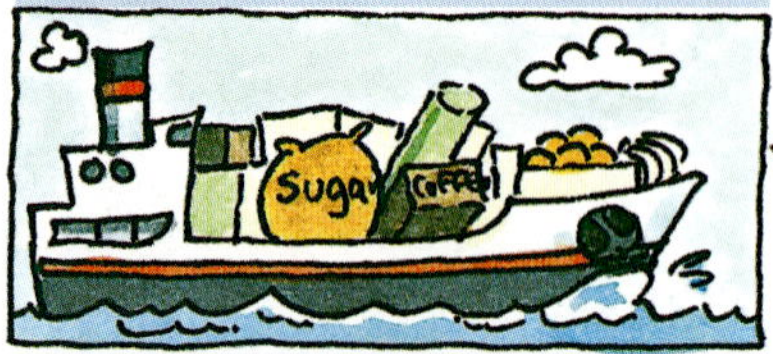

Exports
Brazil sells goods and services to other countries every year. (It earned $73 billion in 2003.)

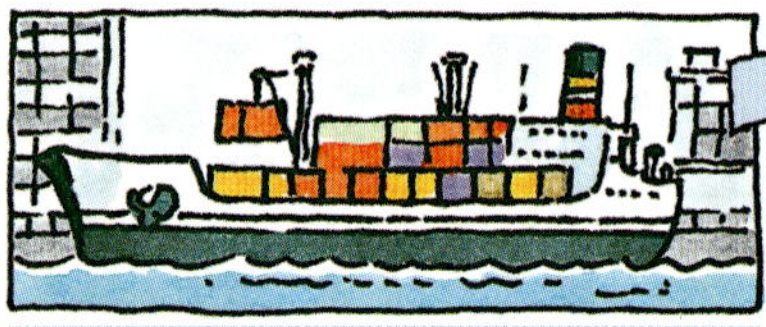

Imports
Brazil buys goods and services from other countries every year. (It spent $48 billion in 2003.)

TOURISM

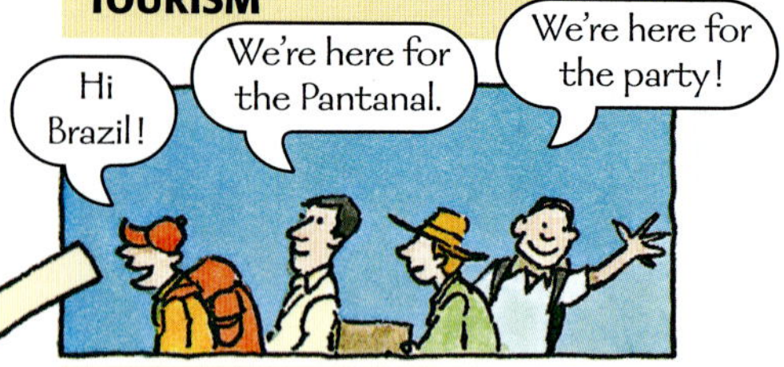

Hi Brazil!
We're here for the Pantanal.
We're here for the party!

Several million tourists visit Brazil each year, for its carnivals, culture, scenery, food, wildlife …

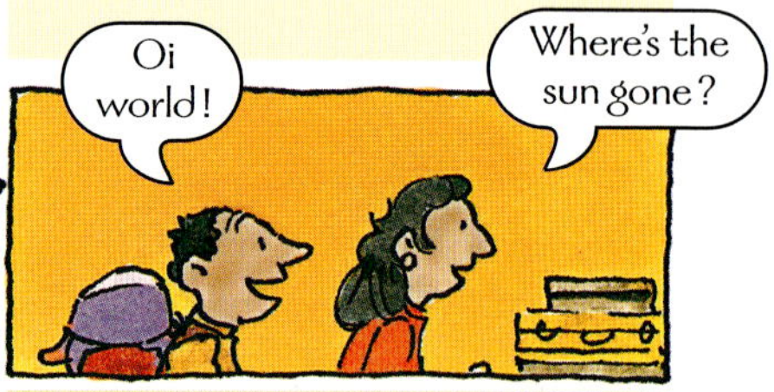

Oi world!
Where's the sun gone?

… and millions of Brazilians go off to visit other countries.

LOANS

Another 500 million …
… for 50 years.
At 5% interest.
Okay.

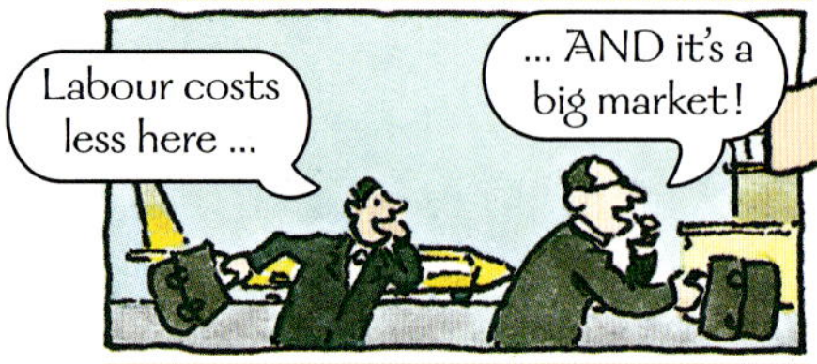

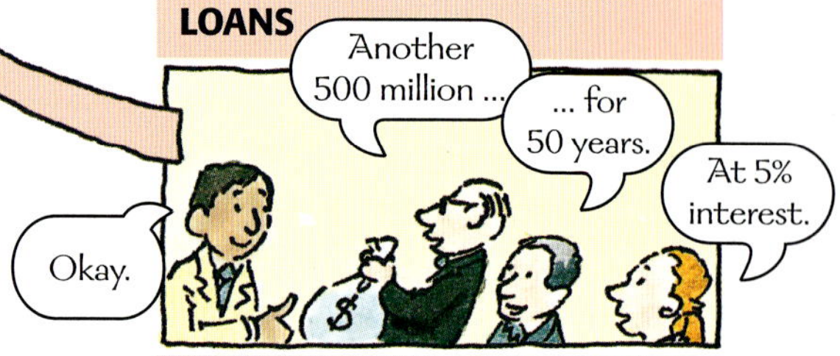

Brazil's government borrowed a lot of money from other countries (around $150 billion). It has to repay it – with interest!

FOREIGN INVESTMENT

Labour costs less here …
… AND it's a big market!

Hundreds of foreign companies have set up branches in Brazil. Including big companies like Ford, Shell and McDonald's.

AID

We'll help you …
… if you promise to buy things from us.
Okay.

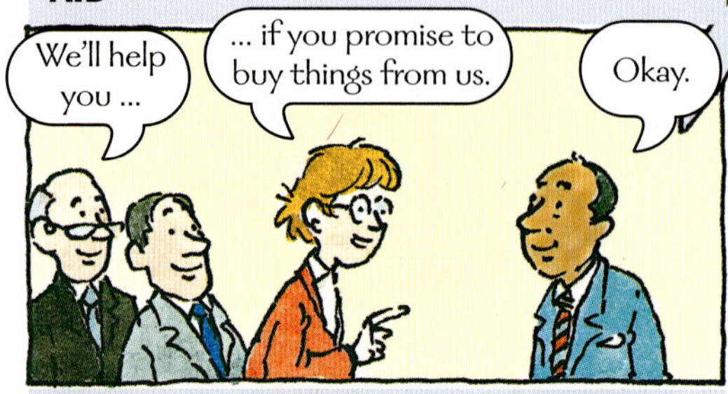

Other countries give aid to Brazil to help it develop. ($376 million in 2002.) It usually has to promise something in return!

> **Did you know?**
> In 2003 the UK …
> - bought $1.9 billion of goods from Brazil, and
> - sold $1.2 billion of goods to Brazil.

TREATIES

YES TO FIGHT GLOBAL WARMING
NO NUCLEAR TESTING
NO DUMPING AT SEA
YES TO SAVING THE WHALE
What a lot of treaties!

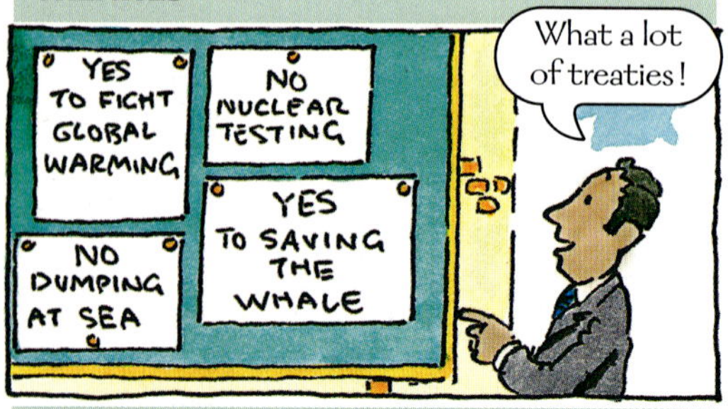

Brazil has signed many **treaties** or agreements with other countries to help make the world more peaceful and safe.

The importance of trade to Brazil

Ever since the Portuguese arrived in 1500, trade has been important to Brazil. For hundreds of years it depended on different 'star' exports for a living. Look at this graph:

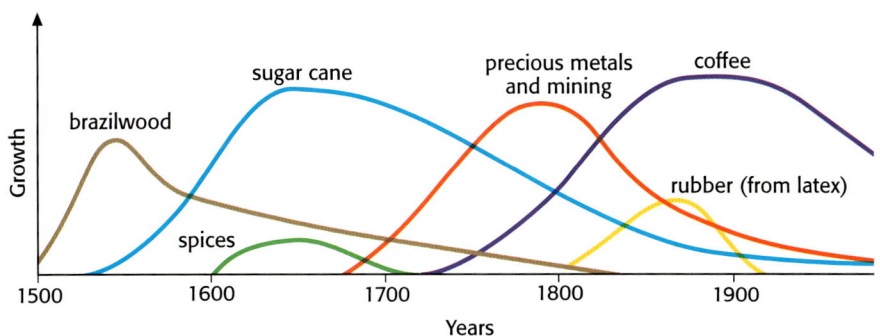

But it's dangerous to depend too much on just a few exports. As the graph shows, all exports decline in the end! A product may go out of fashion. Or another country may start to sell it more cheaply. (Both of these happened with rubber made from latex.)

Meanwhile, for hundreds of years, Brazil imported machinery and other goods it needed. They cost a fortune. So it decided to *make* them instead of importing them. This is called **import substitution**.

The plan worked well. As you'll see below, Brazil now exports more **manufactured products** than **primary products**, by value.

▲ *Brazil makes millions of cars for export.*

Brazil's top five exports in 2003
cars
nuclear reactors and boilers
iron and steel
fruit, nuts, seeds
fuels and oils made from crude oil

Did you know?
◆ Brazil is the world's top exporter of coffee ... and orange juice!

Your turn

1 Countries are *interdependent*. What does that mean?
2 List six ways Brazil depends on other countries. ('To buy its goods' is one.)
3 Look at the pie chart below.
   a What do you think *primary products* are? Give two other examples (not already given below).
   b What does *manufactured products* mean?
   c Some of the goods Brazil exports are called *semi-manufactured*. Leather is an example. Why are they called this?

Brazil's exports, by value, 2002

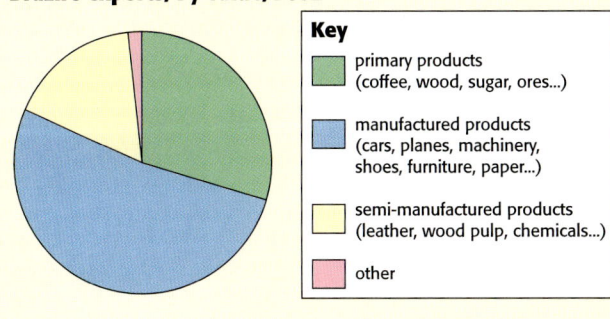

Key
■ primary products (coffee, wood, sugar, ores...)
■ manufactured products (cars, planes, machinery, shoes, furniture, paper...)
■ semi-manufactured products (leather, wood pulp, chemicals...)
■ other

4 In 2003, Brazil exported goods worth US$ 73 billion. It imported goods worth US$ 48 billion.
   a So it earned more than it spent. How much more?
   b i If it keeps earning more than it spends, in foreign trade, is that a good thing or a bad thing?
     ii Draw a spider map like this to show why.

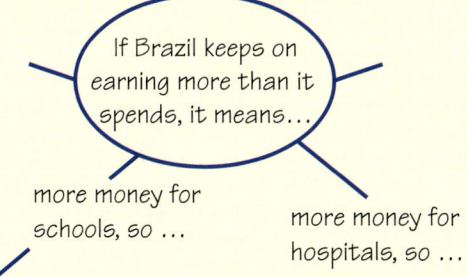

If Brazil keeps on earning more than it spends, it means...

more money for schools, so ...

more money for hospitals, so ...

   c Which is wiser to import: clothes or machinery? Why?
5 Brazil does not attract as many tourists as it could. You are the Minister of Tourism. Write a report for the President of Brazil, saying:
   a why Brazil has a lot to offer tourists
   b why it's important to attract more tourists
   c what steps you will take to attract more tourists.

The challenges facing Brazil

In this unit you'll learn about Brazil's plans for its future – and how they threaten the rainforest.

Brazil's plans for the future

Brazil is rich in resources. But as you saw earlier, it has problems too.

These give us headaches ...

Our problems
- Millions living in poverty
- Great inequality
- Millions with little or no education
- $ billions owed to other countries (for loans)

... but we can make life better ...

Our dreams
- No more poverty
- A good education for all
- A fair society
- Our debts paid off

All this will cost a lot !

... if we put our minds to it.

Our plan
Earn lots of money to make our dreams come true, by ...
- producing more crops, beef, metals, cars, gems, planes ...
- and selling them to other countries.

But to produce more, and export more, Brazil needs:
- more dams, to give more electricity
- more roads, railways and waterways, to transport crops and goods.

In 1999, the government set out its plans to meet these needs. It called them *Avanca Brasil*, or *Forward Brazil*. 338 new projects are planned, all over Brazil, at a cost of around 40 billion dollars ! They will take years to complete – and Brazil will have to borrow lots more money.

Rainforest, here we come !

This map shows some of the plans for the Amazon region of Brazil. They upset a lot of people, because they threaten the rainforest.

▲ A dam in Brazil. When they build a dam, a large area behind it gets flooded.

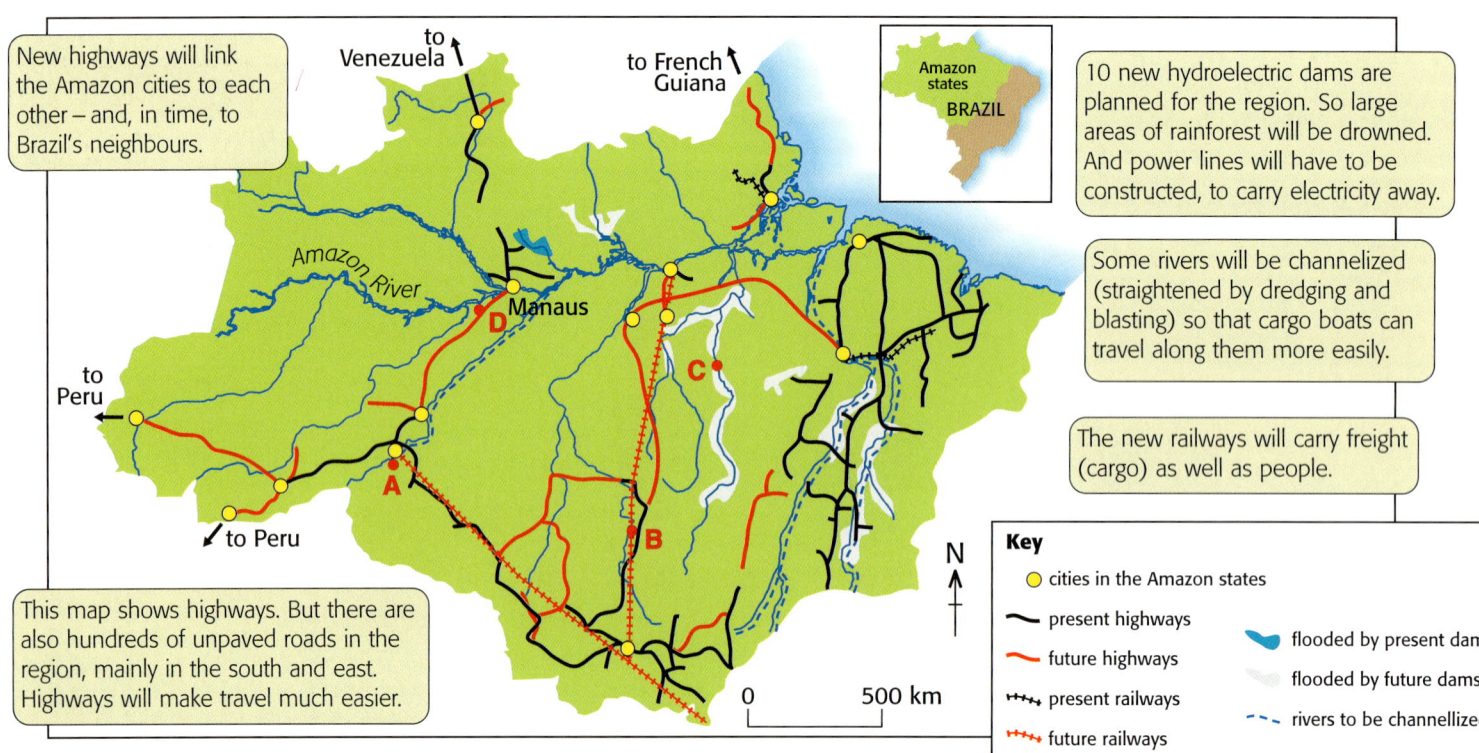

New highways will link the Amazon cities to each other – and, in time, to Brazil's neighbours.

10 new hydroelectric dams are planned for the region. So large areas of rainforest will be drowned. And power lines will have to be constructed, to carry electricity away.

Some rivers will be channelized (straightened by dredging and blasting) so that cargo boats can travel along them more easily.

The new railways will carry freight (cargo) as well as people.

This map shows highways. But there are also hundreds of unpaved roads in the region, mainly in the south and east. Highways will make travel much easier.

to Venezuela

to French Guiana

Amazon states BRAZIL

Amazon River

Manaus

to Peru

to Peru

N

Key
- ○ cities in the Amazon states
- — present highways
- — future highways
- ⊢⊢⊢ present railways
- ⊢⊢⊢ future railways
- flooded by present dam
- flooded by future dams
- - - rivers to be channellized

0   500 km

How will the rainforest be affected?

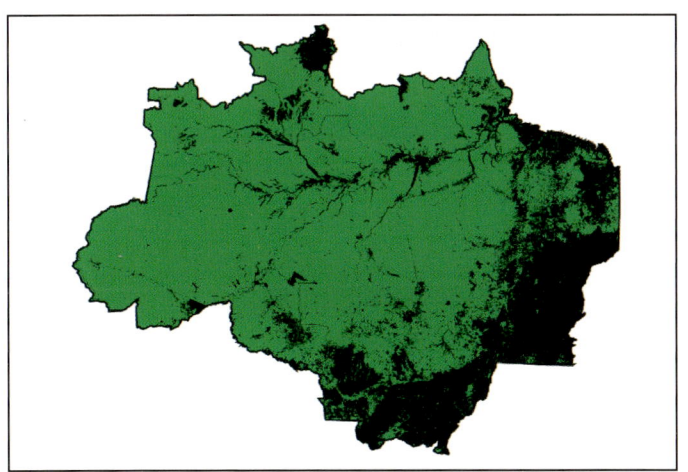

This is the Amazon rainforest in 2000. Much of it has already been **degraded** (ruined) by logging, ranching, and slash-and-burn farming. (See page 52 for photos!)

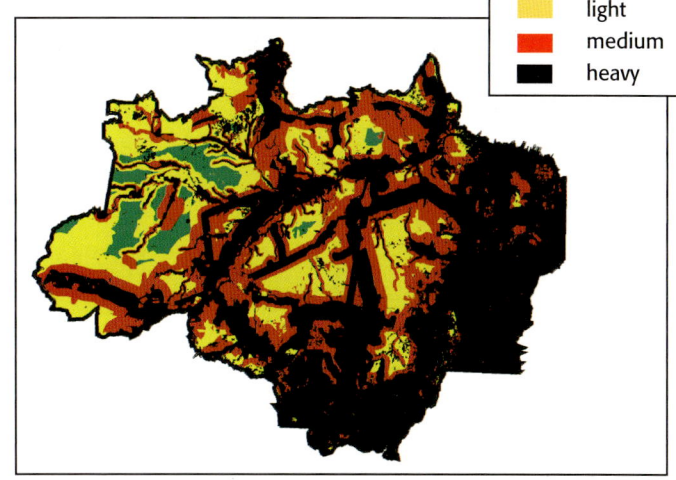

Some scientists have warned that it could look like this by 2020, as a result of the planned projects. Only the areas in green may be unspoiled.

Roads are the big problem. When roads are built, people follow – loggers, and ranchers, and poor farmers who just want a patch of soil to farm. They clear the trees near the road first, then work their way into the forest.

Now there's pressure on Brazil's government to rethink its plans, and make sure they are **sustainable**. It has promised to do this.

Did you know?
- In 1960 about 2 million people lived in Brazil's rainforest.
- By 2000 there were over 20 million.

Your turn

1 How does the government think its plans will help Brazil? Is it right to want these things for its people?

2 Big projects bring benefits – and can do harm. Look at the list on the right below. The people and animals in it *might* be affected by the plans shown on the map. This is what you have to do:

a Make a *large* table with headings like this:

(1) Affected	(2) Will gain because …	(3) Will lose because …	(4) Overall impact

b Look at the first entry on the list: soyabean farmers.
 i Will they be affected by the projects? If you think *yes*, name them in column (1) in your table.
 ii Will they gain? If *yes*, explain why in column (2).
 iii Will they lose in any way? If you think so, explain why in column (3).

c Repeat b for all the other entries in the list.

d And now the hardest part. For each entry in your table, decide whether the *overall* impact is positive or negative. If positive write a ✓ in column (4). If negative write a ✗.

3 Look at your table for **2**. Do you think everyone would end up with the same table as you? For example a soyabean farmer? Or Pedro? Explain.

4 Many people have protested about the plans on the map. Look at this protestor. Do you agree with her? Write down what you will say in reply.

> Ban all new projects in the Amazon region now!

5 The Brazilian government has promised that the projects will do as little harm to the rainforest as possible. How could it ensure this? Answer in bullet points. (Unit 3.6 may give you some ideas.)

Will these be affected by the rainforest plans?
farmers at **A** on the map, growing soya beans for export
ranchers at **B**, producing beef to export for hamburgers
poor Brazilians looking for a patch of land to farm
the residents of Manaus
an Indio tribe living at **C** on the banks of the Xingu river
macaws (rainforest parrots)
people living in the UK
peacock bass (fish) breeding at **D** in the Madeira river
Barbra (page 118)
Pedro (page 118)
the owner of a shoe factory in Peru

Ordnance Survey symbols

ROADS AND PATHS

M 1 or A 6(M)	Motorway
A 35	Dual carriageway
A 31(T) or A 35	Trunk or main road
B 3074	Secondary road
	Narrow road with passing places
	Road under construction
	Road generally more than 4 m wide
	Road generally less than 4 m wide
	Other road, drive or track, fenced and unfenced
	Gradient: steeper than 1 in 5; 1 in 7 to 1 in 5
Ferry	Ferry; Ferry P – passenger only
	Path

PUBLIC RIGHTS OF WAY

(Not applicable to Scotland)

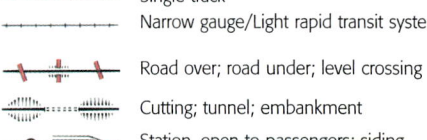

1:25 000	1:50 000	
		Footpath
		Road used as a public footpath
		Bridleway
		Byway open to all traffic

RAILWAYS

	Multiple track
	Single track
	Narrow gauge/Light rapid transit system
	Road over; road under; level crossing
	Cutting; tunnel; embankment
	Station, open to passengers; siding

BOUNDARIES

	National
	District
	County, Unitary Authority, Metropolitan District or London Borough
	National Park

HEIGHTS/ROCK FEATURES

Contour lines

· 144 Spot height to the nearest metre above sea level

outcrop cliff scree

ABBREVIATIONS

P	Post office	PC	Public convenience (rural areas)
PH	Public house	TH	Town Hall, Guildhall or equivalent
MS	Milestone	Sch	School
MP	Milepost	Coll	College
CH	Clubhouse	Mus	Museum
CG	Coastguard	Cemy	Cemetery
Fm	Farm		

ANTIQUITIES

VILLA	Roman	⚔	Battlefield (with date)
Castle	Non-Roman	☆	Tumulus

LAND FEATURES

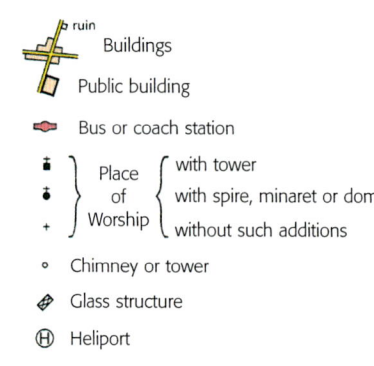

ruin	Buildings
	Public building
	Bus or coach station
	Place of Worship with tower
	with spire, minaret or dome
	without such additions
○	Chimney or tower
	Glass structure
Ⓗ	Heliport
△	Triangulation pillar
	Mast
	Wind pump / wind generator
	Windmill
+	Graticule intersection
	Cutting, embankment
	Quarry
	Spoil heap, refuse tip or dump
	Coniferous wood
	Non-coniferous wood
	Mixed wood
	Orchard
	Park or ornamental ground
	Forestry Commission access land
	National Trust – always open
	National Trust, limited access, observe local signs
	National Trust for Scotland

TOURIST INFORMATION

P	Parking
V	Visitor centre
i	Information centre
✆	Telephone
	Camp site/ Caravan site
	Golf course or links
	Viewpoint
PC	Public convenience
	Picnic site
	Pub/s
✝	Cathedral/Abbey
🏛	Museum
	Castle/fort
	Building of historic interest
	English Heritage
	Garden
	Nature reserve
	Water activities
	Fishing
☆	Other tourist feature

WATER FEATURES

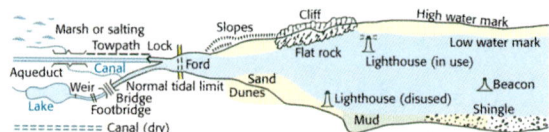

Marsh or salting Slopes Cliff High water mark
Towpath Lock Flat rock Low water mark
Aqueduct Canal Ford Lighthouse (in use)
  Normal tidal limit Sand Low water mark
Lake Weir Dunes
  Bridge Footbridge Mud Lighthouse (disused) Shingle Beacon
Canal (dry)

Map of the British Isles

● red labels show places you study in this book

Key

- – – – – international boundary
- ———— national boundary
- ～～ river
- lake
- ▲ highest point in the UK

towns
- ■ largest cities
- ● large cities and towns

Land height
measured in metres above sea level

	more than 1000 m
	500 - 1000 m
	200 - 500 m
	100 - 200 m
	less than 100 m
	land below sea level

Scale
1: 4 500 000

One centimetre on the map represents 45 kilometres on the ground.

0   45   90   135   180 km

Transverse Mercator Projection

Shetland Islands

Orkney Islands

Cape Wrath

Outer Hebrides

Lewis

Skye

NORTHWEST HIGHLANDS

Great Glen
Loch Ness
River Spey
CAIRNGORMS
River Dee
● Aberdeen

1344m ▲
Ben Nevis

GRAMPIAN MOUNTAINS

R. Tay

SCOTLAND

Mull

Loch Lomond

● Dundee

Islay

Firth of Forth

● Glasgow   ● Edinburgh

River Clyde

SOUTHERN UPLANDS

R. Tweed

UNITED KINGDOM

NORTHERN IRELAND

ANTRIM MOUNTAINS

R. Bann

Lough Neagh

River Erne

● Belfast

North Channel

Firth of Clyde

CHEVIOT HILLS

Newcastle upon Tyne
River Tyne
● Sunderland

North Sea

Stockton-on-Tees
● Middlesbrough
NORTH YORK MOORS

LAKE DISTRICT

River Eden

River Tees

P E N N I N E S

Isle of Man

River Ouse

REPUBLIC OF IRELAND

Lough Corrib

R. Boyne

R. Liffey

● Dublin

WICKLOW MOUNTAINS

River Shannon

Barrow

River Suir

River Blackwater

● Cork

Irish Sea

North Hoyle windfarm

Anglesey

CAMBRIAN MOUNTAINS

Cardigan Bay

WALES

River Teifi

River Tywi

BRECON BEACONS

River Usk

● Swansea   ● Cardiff   ● Newport

St George's Channel

NORTH ATLANTIC OCEAN

● Blackpool   ● Preston   ● Bradford   ● Leeds
● Huddersfield   River Aire
● Liverpool   ● Bolton   ● Manchester
    ● Stockport
● Warrington   ● Sheffield
R. Dee   R. Mersey

Kingston-upon-Hull
River Humber

ENGLAND
● Stoke-on-Trent
● Derby   ● Nottingham   The Wash   R. Wensum
● Telford   R. Trent   ● Happisburgh

● Walsall   ● Leicester   THE FENS   ● Norwich
● Wolverhampton   Peterborough
● Dudley   ■ Birmingham   ● Coventry   R. Great Ouse
● Solihull   Northampton   R. Stour   ● Ipswich
R. Wye   R. Severn   River Avon   ● Milton Keynes
COTSWOLD HILLS   CHILTERN HILLS   ● Luton
R. Thames   ● Reading   London ■   ● Basildon
● Bristol   ● Southend-on-Sea

Bristol Channel   SALISBURY PLAIN   NORTH DOWNS

EXMOOR   SOUTH DOWNS   Strait of Dover

R. Exe   ● Southampton   ● Brighton
● Bournemouth   ● Portsmouth
Poole   Isle of Wight

DARTMOOR

● Plymouth   ● Torbay   Dorset coast

Land's End

Isles of Scilly

English Channel

NORTH ATLANTIC OCEAN

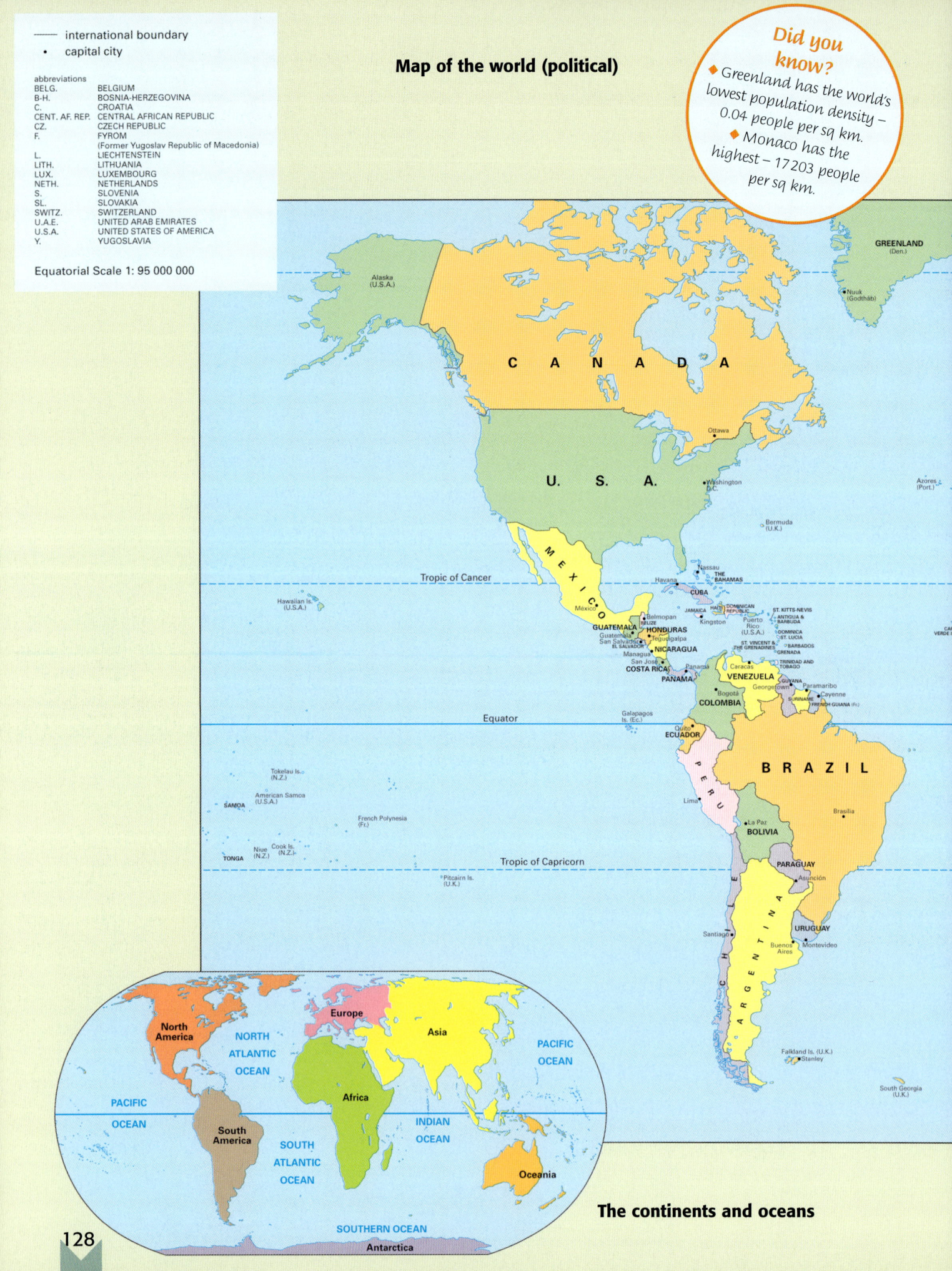

Map of the world (political)

international boundary
• capital city

abbreviations
BELG.   BELGIUM
B-H.   BOSNIA-HERZEGOVINA
C.   CROATIA
CENT. AF. REP. CENTRAL AFRICAN REPUBLIC
CZ.   CZECH REPUBLIC
F.   FYROM
                (Former Yugoslav Republic of Macedonia)
L.   LIECHTENSTEIN
LITH.   LITHUANIA
LUX.   LUXEMBOURG
NETH.   NETHERLANDS
S.   SLOVENIA
SL.   SLOVAKIA
SWITZ.   SWITZERLAND
U.A.E.   UNITED ARAB EMIRATES
U.S.A.   UNITED STATES OF AMERICA
Y.   YUGOSLAVIA

Equatorial Scale 1: 95 000 000

Did you know?
◆ Greenland has the world's lowest population density – 0.04 people per sq km.
◆ Monaco has the highest – 17 203 people per sq km.

GREENLAND
(Den.)

Alaska
(U.S.A.)

Nuuk
(Godthåb)

C A N A D A

Ottawa

U. S. A.

Washington D.C.

Azores
(Port.)

Bermuda
(U.K.)

Tropic of Cancer

Hawaiian Is.
(U.S.A.)

M E X I C O

México

Havana
CUBA
Nassau
THE BAHAMAS

HAITI DOMINICAN REPUBLIC
JAMAICA
Kingston
Puerto Rico
(U.S.A.)

ST. KITTS-NEVIS
ANTIGUA & BARBUDA
DOMINICA
ST. LUCIA
ST. VINCENT &
THE GRENADINES
BARBADOS
GRENADA

CAPE VERDE IS.

GUATEMALA
Belmopan
BELIZE
Guatemala
San Salvador
EL SALVADOR
Tegucigalpa
HONDURAS
Managua
NICARAGUA
San José
COSTA RICA
Panama
PANAMA

Caracas
VENEZUELA
TRINIDAD AND TOBAGO
GUYANA
Georgetown
Paramaribo
SURINAME
Cayenne
FRENCH GUIANA (Fr.)

Bogotá
COLOMBIA

Equator

Galapagos
Is. (Ec.)

Quito
ECUADOR

P E R U

Lima

B R A Z I L

Brasília

Tokelau Is.
(N.Z.)

American Samoa
(U.S.A.)
SAMOA

French Polynesia
(Fr.)

La Paz
BOLIVIA

Tropic of Capricorn

Niue
(N.Z.)
Cook Is.
(N.Z.)
TONGA

Pitcairn Is.
(U.K.)

PARAGUAY
Asunción

A R G E N T I N A

C H I L E

Santiago
Buenos Aires
Montevideo
URUGUAY

Falkland Is. (U.K.)
Stanley

South Georgia
(U.K.)

The continents and oceans

North
America
NORTH
ATLANTIC
OCEAN
Europe
Asia
PACIFIC
OCEAN

PACIFIC
OCEAN
Africa
INDIAN
OCEAN
South
America
SOUTH
ATLANTIC
OCEAN
Oceania

SOUTHERN OCEAN
Antarctica

128

Population of the world's continents

- ◆ Asia   3.92 billion
- ◆ Africa   0.90 billion
- ◆ Europe   0.72 billion
- ◆ N America   0.48 billion
- ◆ S America   0.35 billion
- ◆ Oceania   0.03 billion

The world's top five languages
(native speakers)

- ◆ Chinese (Mandarin)   over 1 billion
- ◆ Hindi   498 million
- ◆ Spanish   391 million
- ◆ English   512 milion
- ◆ Arabic   245 milion

Did you know?
The world has:
- ◆ over 200 countries
- ◆ over 6 billion people
- ◆ over 6000 different languages.

Did you know?
- ◆ The world's largest gathering took place on 24 January 2001 ...
- ◆ ... when 30 million pilgrims gathered at Allahabad in India for a Hindu festival.

Glossary

A

abrasion – scraping something away

acid rain – rain with acidic gases dissolved in it; it can kill fish and plants

adapted – changed to suit the conditions; plants have adapted to suit the climate

adult literacy rate – the % of people aged 15 and over who can read and write a simple sentence

air mass – a huge block of air moving over the Earth; it can be warm or cold, damp or dry, depending on where it came from

air pressure – the weight of air pressing down on the Earth's surface

altitude – height of a place above sea level

anemometer – an instrument for measuring wind speed

arch – the curved outline left when the sea erodes the inside of a cave away

attrition – how rocks and stones get worn away by banging against each other

B

backwash – the water that rolls back down a beach after a wave has broken

barometer – an instrument for measuring air pressure

bay – a smooth curve of coast between two headlands

beach – an area made of sand or small stones deposited by waves

beach replenishment – adding sand to a beach to replace the sand the waves have carried away

biome – a very large ecosystem

birth rate – the number of births in a country in a year, per thousand people

burglary – breaking into a building to steal

buttress roots – large roots that grow above the ground to support tall trees

C

carnivore – eats animals

cash crop – a crop grown for sale abroad

CCTV – closed circuit television, used in shops and on streets to fight crime

cliff – a very steep slope of rock

climate – the 'average' weather in a place

cloud cover – how much of the sky is hidden by cloud; given in eighths (oktas)

coast – where the land meets the sea

coastal defences – barriers to protect the coast from erosion or flooding by the sea; for example groynes and sea walls

common assault – hitting or threatening to hit someone

consumers – they feed on other living things in an ecosystem

convectional rainfall – rain caused by the sun heating the ground; the ground then heats the air, which rises to form clouds

crime – an action that breaks the law

criminal – someone who commits a serious crime, or lives a life of crime

D

death rate – the number of deaths in a country in a year, per thousand people

decomposers – they break down dead and waste material in an ecosystem; bacteria and fungi are examples

defensible space – a space that people can watch over and protect from criminals

delta – flat area of deposited material at the mouth of a river, where it enters the sea

densely populated area – lots of people live there

deposit – to drop material; waves deposit sand and small stones in sheltered parts of the coast, forming beaches

depression – a weather system made up of two fronts, a warm front chased by a cold one; it brings wet windy weather

desertification – when a place starts to turn into a desert

developed country – enjoys good public services and a high standard of living

domestic violence – violence in the home; for example a man punching his wife

drought – when lack of rain leads to a water shortage

drug trafficking – smuggling and selling illegal drugs such as heroin

E

economic – to do with money and finance

ecosystem – a unit made up of living things and their non-living environment; for example a pond, a forest, a desert

environment – everything around you; the air, soil, rivers and climate are part of our natural environment

environmental crime – an action that breaks an environmental law, such as dumping harmful waste in rivers

erosion – wearing away of rock, stones and soil by rivers, waves, the wind or glaciers

escarpment – a tall steep slope at the edge of high land

ethanol – an alcohol made from plant material (such as sugar cane); it burns well so can be used as fuel

exports – things a country sells to other countries

F

favela – a slum in a South American city

fetch – the length of water the wind blows over, before it meets the coast

food chain – a chain of names and arrows, showing what species feed on

food web – a network of food chains, showing how they link together

forgery – faking a document or signature

fossil fuels – coal, oil and natural gas; called fossil fuels because they are the remains of plants and animals that lived millions of years ago

fraud – making false claims, usually in order to make money

front – the leading edge of an air mass; a warm front means a warm air mass is arriving

frontal rainfall – rain caused when a warm front meets a cold one

fuel – something we use to provide energy; we usually burn fuels to release their energy (except for nuclear fuel)

G

geology – the study of rocks

global warming – the way temperatures around the world are rising

greenhouse gases – gases like carbon dioxide and methane that trap heat around the Earth, giving global warming

gross domestic product (GDP) – the total value of all the goods and services produced in a country, in a year

groynes – barriers of wood or stone down a beach, to stop sand being washed away

H

headland – land that juts out into the sea

herbivore – an animal that eats only plants

hydraulic action – the action of water pressure in breaking up rock

hydroelectricity – electricity generated when a river spins a turbine

I

import subsitution – when a country makes something it used to import

imports – things a country buys from other countries

Indios – the native 'Indians' whose ancestors were the first settlers in Brazil

inequality – the unequal sharing of wealth in a society

infant mortality – how many babies out of every 1000 born alive, who die before their first birthday

intensive farming – aims to produce as much of a crop, or as many animals, as possible, on a given piece of land

interdependent – depend on each other

isolated settlement – a farm or small hamlet quite far from others

L

laterite – a highly weathered soil that bakes in the sun to form a hard layer

latitude – how far a place is north or south of the equator, measured in degrees

life expectancy – how many years a new baby can expect to live, on average

logging – cutting down trees for timber

longshore drift – how sand and other material is carried parallel to the shore, by the waves

M

mental map – a map that you carry in your mind; it might not be very accurate !

meteorologist – a person who studies weather and climate

mugging – a physical attack on a person in the street in order to steal something

multicultural – has many ethnic groups

N

National Grid – the network of power stations and cables that supply our electricity

natural increase – the birth rate minus the death rate, given as a %

Neighbourhood Watch – a scheme where neighbours keep an eye on each others' homes to help prevent crime

North Atlantic Drift – a warm current in the Atlantic Ocean; it keeps our west coast warmer in winter

nuclear fuel – a substance with unstable atoms that break down, giving out a large amount of energy

O

offender – a person who commits a crime (often used for people under 18)

omnivore – eats both plants and animals; most humans are omnivores

organized crime – crime that's planned and carried out by a group of people; usually on a large scale and over a long period

P

pastoralists – people who rear grass-eating animals for a living; they move with them to find pasture (grass to eat)

physical map – shows mountains, rivers and other physical features

plain – a large area of flat land

political map – shows how the world is divided into different countries; it has borders marked in

pollution – anything that spoils the environment; for example traffic fumes, factory waste, sewage, litter, noise

population – the number of people living in a place

population density – the average number of people per square kilometre

population pyramid – a bar graph showing the population, divided into males and females in different age groups

precipitation – water falling from the sky; it could fall as rain, hail, sleet or snow

prevailing wind – the wind that blows most often; in the UK it is a south west wind (it blows *from* the south west)

primary products – things collected from the ground and sea; for example crops, metal ores, timber

producers – they make their own food from carbon dioxide and water; plants are producers

public enquiry – an enquiry set up to let people give their point of view (for example about plans for a new road)

PV (photovoltaic) cell – a cell that converts sunlight into electricity

R

relief rainfall – rain caused when air is forced to rise over a hill or mountain

renewable resource – a resource that we can grow or make more of; for example wood

resources – things we need to live, or use to earn a living; for example food, fuel

rural area – an area of countryside, where people live on farms and in villages

S

salt marsh – a low-lying marshy area by the sea, with salty water from the tides

satellite image – a picture taken by a camera carried on a satellite

savanna – an ecosystem that is usually hot but with wet and dry seasons

secure accomodation – a type of prison for young offenders

semi-manufactured goods – goods such as leather that will then be made into other things (for example shoes and bags)

sentence – the punishment for a crime

shingle – small pebbles

slave trade – buying and selling people to work as slaves

social – about people and society (while *economic* is about money and finance)

solar power – power we get by using sunlight as a fuel, for example in PV cells

solution – the dissolving of minerals from rock by water

sparsely populated area – very few people live there

species – type of plant or animal

spit – a strip of sand or shingle in the sea

stack – a pillar of rock left standing in the sea when the top of an arch collapses

stump – the remains of a stack which the sea has eroded away

sustainable – can be carried on into the future without harming people, or wildlife, or the environment

swash – the water that rushes up the beach when a wave breaks

T

target hardening – installing things to make it harder for criminals to get at their targets (for example steel shutters)

temperature – how hot or cold something is, measured in degrees Centigrade

terrorism – violent acts (such as bombings) carried out for political reasons

thermometer – an instrument for measuring temperature

tides – the rise and fall in sea level, due mainly to the pull of the moon

traffic offences – offences to do with driving and parking vehicles

transport – the carrying away of material by rivers, waves, the wind or glaciers

treaty – an agreement between countries

tropics – the part of the Earth that lies between the Tropic of Cancer (23.5 °N) and the Tropic of Capricorn (23.5 °S)

U

urban area – a built-up area, such as part of a city; it's the opposite of rural

V

vandalism – wilful damage to property; for example smashing up phone boxes

vegetation – all the trees and other plants growing in a place

victim – a person against whom a crime is committed

visibility – how far you can see; on a foggy day in could be just 1 or 2 metres

W

wave-cut notch – a notch cut in a cliff face by the action of waves

wave-cut platform – the flat rocky area left behind when waves erode a cliff away

weather – the state of the atmosphere

weathering – the breaking down of rock; it is caused mainly by the weather

wind – air in motion

wind direction – the direction the wind blows *from*

windfarm – a group of wind turbines set up to generate electricity from the wind

wind speed – how fast the wind blows

wind vane – an instrument for showing the wind direction

Index